Melchior Wańkowicz

Melchior Wańkowicz

Poland's Master of the Written Word

By Aleksandra Ziolkowska-Boehm

Foreword by Charles S. Kraszewski

Translated by Agnieszka Maria Gernand

LEXINGTON BOOKS
Lanham • Boulder • New York • Toronto • Plymouth, UK

Published by Lexington Books
A wholly owned subsidiary of The Rowman & Littlefield Publishing Group, Inc.
4501 Forbes Boulevard, Suite 200, Lanham, Maryland 20706
www.rowman.com

10 Thornbury Road, Plymouth PL6 7PP, United Kingdom

Copyright © 2013 by Lexington Books

Court documents reprinted by permission of the Instytut Pamieci Narodowej (IPN).

British Library Cataloguing in Publication Information Available

Library of Congress Cataloging-in-Publication Data

Ziółkowska-Boehm, Aleksandra, 1949–
[Na tropach Wańkowicza. English]
Melchior Wańkowicz : Poland's master of the written word / Aleksandra Ziółkowska-Boehm ; foreword by Charles S. Kraszewski ; translated by Agnieszka Maria Gernand.
pages cm
Includes bibliographical references and index.
ISBN 978-0-7391-7590-3 (cloth : alk. paper)—ISBN 978-0-7391-7591-0 (electronic)
1. Wańkowicz, Melchior, 1891–1974. 2. Authors, Polish—20th century—Biography. I. Gernand, Agnieszka Maria. II. Title.
PG7182.A5Z9213 2013
891.8'537—dc23
2013010596

∞™ The paper used in this publication meets the minimum requirements of American National Standard for Information Sciences Permanence of Paper for Printed Library Materials, ANSI/NISO Z39.48-1992.

Printed in the United States of America

Contents

Acknowledgments

I would like to thank the translators: Agnieszka Maria Gernand and Charles S. Kraszewski. I am grateful for permission of the Warsaw Instytut Pamięci Narodowej (IPN) to quote their archives and *The Polish Review* for use of published articles.

Special appreciation is extended to Dawid Walendowski for granting permission to use the excerpt of *The Battle of Monte Cassino*.

My thanks for giving permission to use their quotations is extended to: Jan Olszewski, Janusz Brochwicz Lewiński "Gryf," Krzysztof Masłoń, Anna Bernat, and Stanisław M. Jankowski. I also thank Barbara Romanowicz and Lucjan Sniadower.

The photos presented in the book are from Wańkowicz and my archives and from the archives of Janusz Brochwicz Lewinski "Gryf."

Many thanks to Professors Anna Cienciala and Piotr Wandycz for their remarks on Polish history.

I wish to express my appreciation to: Lindsey R. Porambo, Stephanie Brooks, Justin Race, and Erin E. Walpole for their advice, professionalism, and patience during the book's publication phases.

As always, for encouragement and constant help, I am grateful to my husband Norman Boehm, who told me that after reading the book several times he matured in admiration for Wańkowicz as a writer, as a human being, and as a very fine and honorable man. After reading the fragment of *The Battle of Monte Cassino* Norman expressed a desire to read the entire book since he enjoyed the excerpt very much.

Foreword

Charles S. Kraszewski

Reportage is one of the more interesting genres for an author to work in. On the boundary between journalism and history, it requires of the practitioner the reporter's eye for matters of public interest, and the historian's sense of the gravity of the events he or she is reporting on—which in turn is something between a sixth-sense receptivity to the hidden wheels of history and a gambler's faith in his system as he places down his chips before the roulette wheel spins. It is a genre that, while immersed in historical (and ephemeral) reality, requires a poetic talent for engaging prose: something that will bring the experienced *in flagranti* again to vivid life on the cold pages of the book in the reader's hands. It is no surprise, then, that so great a poet as Zbigniew Herbert took up the reporter's pen in *The Barbarian in the Garden*. However, the greatest of the practitioners of reportage, like Egon Kisch and Ryszard Kapuściński, didn't just dabble in it—they made their living from it, as did perhaps the greatest of the lot in Poland, the hero of this book, Melchior Wańkowicz.

Melchior Wańkowicz: Poland's Master of the Written Word is from the able pen of Wańkowicz's secretary and propagator of his works, Aleksandra Ziółkowska-Boehm. Whether the receptor of this book is himself a Wańkowicz scholar, or just beginning to become acquainted with his works; whether he or she reads it at the beginning of the adventure, after it, or while following the writer on his journeys across two continents, in war, in peace, and during the subtle war waged between Polish society and the PRL (Polish Republic) regime. Ziółkowska's book is an engaging, informative, and indeed encyclopedic consideration of Wańkowicz and his writings. It provides a necessary historical and biographical context, which is so full of interest in its own right, that most readers will be pulled on to not put the book down.

Melchior Wańkowicz: Poland's Master of the Written Word is a collection of fifteen chapters written by Ziółkowska-Boehm, a practitioner of reportage herself, whose interests range from Polish literature and history to the plight of Native Americans. An intimate literary collaborator of Wańkowicz, her splendid obsession with his published works makes her not only the perfect, but really the only person who could contextualize the gigantic career of the writer in an accessible, yet meticulously documented, fashion.

The fifteen essays are arranged in loose chronological order. They range from the pre-war account of Wańkowicz's role in the creation of Rój Publishers ("Roy," during its wartime hiatus in New York), which published, among other works, the poems of Kazimierz Wierzyński, and the first edition of Witold Gombrowicz's *Ferdydurke*, through a moving account of Wańkowicz's 1974 funeral. While all of the essays are intriguing—and readers of *Monte Cassino* and other of Wańkowicz's works will be quite pleased with those dealing with the genesis and surrounding realia of his famous books—it is those which reveal the *man* Wańkowicz, who he was, and especially who he was in regard to the Communist authorities who at times tolerated and at other times persecuted him, that are most noteworthy and valuable.

Ziółkowska-Boehm constructs her complex and many-sided portrait of Wańkowicz from four main sources. First, there are the eyewitness accounts, such as her description of the funeral—how different a picture one gets from the relation of a person who was actually there, than from the relation of the official, Communist Party reporters covering the event:

> From the gate, the casket was borne by, among others, Krzysztof Kąkolewski and Jan Józef Lipski. At the head of the funeral procession walked Bishop Kraszewski, priests, and a Dominican father representing the parish church on Dominikanska Street. PRL television, which transmitted the funeral, took great pains to avoid showing the priests. [. . .] Before the grave was covered, a new voice was heard. A man, standing near the grave, read a few sentences written down on a sheet of paper. He said that we should all remember Katyń and observe its anniversary. Later on, Marta [Erdman, Wańkowicz's daughter] and I learned that this man was Wojciech Ziembinski, who later was to be a member of KOR.

But these are not simply the memoirs of a person who knew the protagonist (as are, for example, the *Discretions* of Mary de Rachewiltz, Ezra Pound's daughter). Ziółkowska-Boehm draws expertly and generously from the published works of others, building a model corpus of secondary sources that help in the fleshing out of the character of Wańkowicz from perspectives other than her own. In her description of the manner in which the PRL regime sought to hijack the funeral of the writer so often at odds with them, she cites Aleksander Małachowski's introduction to the 1993 PWN publisher's edition of Wańkowicz's *Ziela na kraterze* (*Herbs at the Crater*):

> A soon as she got off the plane from the U.S., Marta Erdman, Melchior's daughter, was offered a splendid funeral for her father, paid for by the state. I had to object to this, as just a few days earlier, Melchior kept me and my wife by his side until three o'clock in the morning, and made us swear that we would not allow the state to organize an official, government-sponsored funeral, for "they'd certainly like to be photographed over my coffin." [. . .] Melchior's funeral, according to his will, was a religious affair, the costs of which were borne by his family.

Thirdly, there are, of course, citations from Wańkowicz's own writings. Although *Melchior Wańkowicz: Poland's Master of the Written Word* is not a biography, in fragments such as "On the Tip of the Tongue" glimpses of Wańkowicz the man, before he became Wańkowicz the writer, abound. There we meet him, in his reminiscences, as a child in the eastern marshes of Poland, long lost to her eastern neighbor; there we are treated to Wańkowicz's own prose, such as this vignette from *Karafka La Fontaine'a* (*La Fontaine's Carafe*):

> I think that a language is like a powerful stream. A rotting tree limb, withered leaves, manure, mud from cows bathing upstream, the sweat of horses through a ford, the effluvia of emptied sewage header, all fall into it—but just gaze at it a few kilometers downstream: it is completely clear, it sparkles like crystal. A language has a great power of self-cleansing.

What is this but something that falls just barely short of a Baudelairean prose poem? Ziółkowska-Boehm's talent for centering the reader's focus on such examples of Wańkowicz's writings brilliantly showcases her critical sense for using them, not merely as illustrations of a biographical thesis, but as a thrilling advertisement for Wańkowicz's books encouraging the reader of her book to pass beyond it, into the writer's works.

As we noted before, Ziółkowska-Boehm is herself an accomplished writer of reportages. A fourth of her sources—sometimes the most insightful—are those that arise from her reporter's legwork. Much of the information upon which the chapters dealing with Wańkowicz's arrest and political trials are based comes from her accessing newly available state documents from the IPN archives, and interviews with some of the participants of his persecution (which began with his signing of the Writers' Union open letter of protest in 1964). Fascinating, both for its content and the effective reportorial strategy it portrays, is her 1990 interview with the prosecutor who conducted the Wańkowicz case on behalf of the Communist régime. In reply to her

question "What did your contacts with Wańkowicz look like during the interrogation," he replies ingenuously:

> I don't know if this is found in your archives, but, at the end of the case, Mr.
> Wańkowicz paid me a compliment. "Sir," he said "I don't like this People's
> Poland, but as a Pole I'll tell you that I'm happy that Poland has fostered such
> officials as yourself."
>
> The atmosphere of our conversation was always good; he understood that I
> had to carry out my duties, and I treated his with extra attention, not like a
> criminal. . . . After all, his services to literature were so great. . . . I myself had
> a humanistic, liberal education, and literature always interested me.

This from a person who, at the beginning of the interview, but one page
previously, protested, "I'm no literary critic, but I was aware of the caliber of
Wańkowicz's writing and his position as a writer. And so I realized that this
case would arouse much interest, which could turn against the country."

From this it seems apparent that the prosecutor entered the interview with
a certain mistrust; he starts flinging about asterisks and reveals his motiva-
tion as that of a representative of the system currently ruling "the country,"
who, in effect, *did* approach Wańkowicz as a threat, in short, a "criminal,"
albeit only in a political sense. Then, when set at ease by his interlocutor that
this interview will not be an "interrogation" itself, he loosens his tie and
begins revealing his "humanistic education," his "interest in literature," and
starts shining the apple for the artist, whose services to letters he is now able
to critically appraise and applaud. Ziółkowska-Boehm's handling of the
interview is a masterful, classroom example of the work of a skilled reporter,
who subtly unmasks her source and warns the reader, trust him (and other
old, official sources) at your own risk.

Doublethink and Newspeak, as Orwell explains to us, are art forms in
their own right. The métier of the author of reportages—and in this, the genre
may indeed be as old as Herodotus—also partakes of the artistic, insofar as
the real information presented us by the reporter is "packaged" in the attrac-
tive, poetic style described above. Sometimes, it is not so much the sources
as the reporter that we must approach with careful tread. The subjective often
gets the upperhand in reportage—witness Herbert's spiteful and simplistic
characterization of Ezra Pound, met by chance on his Italian travels in *Barbarian* and formed from hearsay and published information from only one
perspective, and dealing with only one aspect of the great poet's life. Witness
too Melchior Wańkowicz himself, who suggests to the Polish readers of *W
pępku Ameryki* that the state of Utah is ruled according to the theocratic
principles of the Church of Latter Day Saints, or, in *Atlantyk-Pacyfik* that the
"American police" possess a full set of the fingerprints of just about every
citizen of the United States in which, as a matter of fact, the individual's right
to privacy is so jealously guarded, that to date the federal government has not

been able to introduce a system of national ID cards, even in this day of the global war on terror.

I mention this, not in disparagement of Wańkowicz, whose writings I myself value greatly, but in support and praise of the many-faceted reportage which is Aleksandra Ziółkowska-Boehm's *Melchior Wańkowicz: Poland's Master of the Written Word*. Meticulously researched, innovative, and challenging, as well as written in a pleasant style, it is a trustworthy, really indispensable, guide to the great writer, and his writings. In her objective scholarly base of sources, and in her unique subjective perspective on the writer she knew and admired, Ziółkowska-Boehm gets it right.

Prof. Charles S. Kraszewski
King's College, Pennsylvania

Melchior Wańkowicz

Battle of Monte Cassino *(Fragment)*

Translation by Charles S. Kraszewski

Entering the ring, we greet those who came before us.

The Americans were the first to storm the cloister. On 2 January, the Fifth Army was ordered to "undertake as strong a thrust as possible on Cassino and Forsinone, shortly before the landing, so as to break through the German front, after which link up with the sea operation will be effected."

Thus attacked the Americans, and the thrust was bloodier than anything the Fifth Army had encountered.

First of all, I went to see them and familiarize myself with their deeds.

IN THE AMERICAN PRESS QUARTERS

The staff of the Fifth Army is a city unto itself. The neat brown squares of the American tents, with flaps pinned back, stand in a pine wood. The air is fresh with ozone. Water trucks drive over the wooded trails moistening the dust.

Six thousand people live here, discreetly spread about the endless forest glades. The telephone system might easily serve a city of twenty thousand. Their cables could connect New York with Los Angeles, and return as far as Chicago—stretched many times the entire length of Poland.

There are twenty-five restaurants and cafés here. Two hundred military police keep the peace. This movable town consumes twenty-five thousand gallons of water daily. It has everything—even a bank, the daily transactions of which reach one million dollars.

And every few weeks all of this is transported to another outpost, after which no one can know just when this giant conglomerate of tents disappeared, and where it will reappear again for a few days.

In the staff quarters itself there is, *lege artis*, a hotel for stars and generals. But I make my way to the press quarters. I am met with a minimum of nicety and a maximum of help.

"Do you have a place to sleep?"

"Yes."

"A means of transportation?"

"Yes."

"What is it you wish to work on?"

"First of all, I'd like to familiarize myself with the Fifth Army's battles for Monte Cassino, and then I'd like to speak with the participants."

"Would you like to go and see the chief of the historical section at fourteen hundred hours? Well. In the meantime, have a seat."

The chief of the historical section, a colonel, has his office ten miles away. Without a word, he hands me a gigantic dossier. I have a look therein, and find reports from divisions, regiments, battalions, with aerial photos, both perpendicular and oblique, as well as situational sketches, attached to each.

"Naturally! Please take it with you."

After dinner (for which I pay myself, but well worth it: tomato juice, toast, and a splendid turkey), I make my way to the correspondents' tent. A long table, well lighted by electric lamps, the length of which clatter a row of typewriters. If we add to that clamor the incessant radio, and the constant chatter or whistling of each correspondent, one can gather something of the constant hum of sound there that still does not hamper work.

Every now and then new information is hung up on the board. For example, Colonel Whitmore, the morale officer of the Fifth Army, informs us:

> Perhaps the correspondents will be interested to learn that, when General Sosnkowski arrived, no one in the entire quarters of the Fifth Army knew what the Polish national anthem was. Then Mary Kozierowska, a WAC from Hudson, Pennsylvania, was connected with an officer of the Polish Signal Corps, who sung it to her over the telephone. Warrant Officer Wilmont Trumbull of 15 Franconia St., Worcester, Massachusetts, immediately transcribed the melody.

From time to time all of the typewriters grow silent as everyone listens closely to something important coming over the intercom. Sometimes it's a joke, and these busy people explode with laughter. An original synchronization of radio and work—it doesn't disturb them at all, yet some helpful little brain cell is always directed toward it.

THE THIRTY-SIXTH DIVISION BOGS DOWN AT THE RAPIDO

Slowly, from the piles of documents, there began to take shape the history of those who went before us.

The goal of the Allied offensive was the liberation of Rome. The plan of this offensive was based on an assault from the sea at Anzio, coupled with a frontal attack along both banks of the river Liri.

First to move was the Thirty-Sixth American Division. They headed straight for the monastery. On 20 January, the 141st Regiment attacked the Trocchio La Pieta S. Angelo in Te dice line.

The landscape was—so to speak—Novemberish. Before the regiment lay soggy ground, covered with ditches and divided with fences.

They came from the land of robots, from the cult of the machine. They trained upon the German positions a thirty-minute barrage, shooting off thirty-one thousand shells.

After this, they set off. Dusk was falling, as it was 7 p.m. The darkening, bush-covered bank of the river Rapido, across which they were to force their way, became invisible. They slogged through the muddy meadow, tossed into the air by the force of the German mines defending the riverbank.

The First Battalion crumpled beneath German fire. One of its companies lost its way and helplessly floundered, like a fish beating against a boat's side, beneath a concentrated artillery barrage, while another was misled by a sapper into the minefield. Only the remnants of Company C made their way to the crossing point on schedule, but had to take cover under fire, as it turned out that the artillery fire made futile the construction of a bridge to carry an eight-ton load.

The Second Battalion was dragging a full four footbridges. But one was lost to the mines, a second was destroyed by artillery fire, the third floundered hopelessly in the mud, so that only the fourth was thrown across at four in the morning.

The swift current of this mountain river capsized the rubber boats, and the steep bank made their manipulation difficult. The boats were a complete failure.

Finally, two companies pushed their way across that one bridge.

The Third Battalion never made it to the river.

And just then, that is at 5:15 a.m., General Wilbur, second in command of the division, ordered the troops on the near side of the river to retreat, and the two companies on the far side to dig in. Bitter advice!

Throughout the entire next day, the German artillery cut off all communication with these companies. They were enveloped by furious smoke screens, which also had the effect of making action against the enemy so much more difficult. The commander of the 131st Field Artillery, which was supporting the 141st Regiment, reported with despair: "Our observers can see nothing through that smoke; under its cover the enemy snipers make their way almost to our very lines and shoot our soldiers; we can give them no artillery cover whatsoever."

At the same time as the 141st, the 143rd tried to cross the river farther north. At this point, which lay toward the bottom of its course, the river was broader and the current less strong.

At 8 p.m. the Third Platoon of Company C, led by Lieutenant Nunex, was the first to make its way across the river. The next platoon was also able to get across in rubber boats, after which they were destroyed by artillery fire.

At 10:55 p.m. (reads the report of the commander of the 143rd):

> I made my own way to the river accompanied by Brigadier Kendall and Captain Steffen. We found there Major Frasior, the commander of First Battalion, who was attempting to gather transport. But there were no sappers. We created a group of bearers and, making our way to the place with them, where we were to take the boats, we found an officer and twenty-eight soldiers dug in foxholes. Five boats were grouped together and the First Battalion made their way across. They took on such fire that their commander requested permission to retreat. The commanding general refused this permission, but before the refusal was received, the battalion had retreated.

And thus the battalion of the Third Regiment never crossed the river.

On the evening of 21 January, when the entire day was spent on the smoke-screening of the few platoons dug in on the other side of the river, both regiments launched a new attack. Again the boats capsized, the footbridges were destroyed, and still the 141st Regiment made its way six hundred yards toward the river before having to take cover under fire. The American boys didn't learn how to fight from the very start, but they did know how to die.

At 6:30 p.m. the 143rd Infantry crossed the river under the cover of smoke. They moved forward. They came upon barbed-wired positions under a crossfire of machine gun nests, firing in a low fan, so that those who ran were hit in the legs, and those who were crawling were hit in the rump.

The First Battalion pushed through in two companies. Still, at 11:17 p.m. there was no sight of the third.

At 11:40 p.m. the Second Battalion reached the river, but the sappers couldn't direct them to the bridges. Captain Volheim finally located them, and the battalion got across in two companies.

Only then did hell break loose on the far bank. The Germans occupied lines in the very vicinity, and hand grenades came into play. Then, the *Nebelwerfer*, a weapon previously unknown to the Americans, began to boom out. These are mortars first intended as smoke agents, which were subsequently ingeniously adapted to the hurling of crushing charges. They are made of six barrels joined together, in which the shells are fired simultaneously by electricity from the safety of a bunker. The shells themselves are of a gigantic caliber: 150 mm, even 240 mm. It was the Russians who first thought of using this sort of weapon, the "Maria Ivanovna," which filled the Germans with terror at Sevastopol.[1] The salvoes scream uncannily. You might say that they giggle. The shells don't scatter widely, but pack a mighty punch. It should also be added that the Germans fired three batteries of three *Nebel-werfers* each at a time.

Crushed and decimated, the remains of the Second and Third Battalions withdrew to the left bank just after midnight.

Major Frasior, in command of the First Battalion, reported at 1:35 a.m. that he was wounded, but remaining at his post, although Company C of the battalion never reached them.

Major Meath, sent to take over command of the battalion and free Major Frasior, made his way quickly to the post along with Captain Westbrook; however, the fire was so intense that they only reached the battalion at 5 a.m. Completely shattered, the battalion's few remnants had already fled across the river.

Thus, the second attack at dawn of 22 January also was broken.

The greatly heartened Germans made a strong counter-attack that very day. It was beaten back, but with the loss of the few remaining on the opposite bank.

In the evening, it turned out that 1,002 NCOs (non-commissioned officers) and soldiers were wounded or killed, as well as 48 officers, among whom were the commanding officers of the Second and Third Battalions as well as their replacements.

It turned out that a breakthrough of the line in the Liri river valley and a march on Rome through that route was impossible—as long as the Monte Cassino massif was there to flank it.

SUCCESSES OF THE FRENCH AND THE AMERICAN THIRTY-FOURTH DIVISION

This truth was not understood in the first attempt, and so they attempted to pass the monastery by from the right as well.

Consequently, right after the American Thirty-Sixth Division, the Thirty-Fourth attacked right at the position where our Carpathian Division now encamps.

However, before we move on to speak of this assault, we must note that, simultaneously with the Thirty-Sixth Division, to their north, the French attacked, their left wing catching against the position currently occupied by our Kresy Division.

Let us tear ourselves away for a moment from the American reports, so as to insert what I heard at another time from the French.

The terrrain over which the French were striving to move was soaked with Germans. All observation points, all mortar pits were in their hands. The Germans held the terrain in a system of bunkers, rest shelters, and covered places, through which their reserves moved freely along a net of perfectly concealed communications.

The French had to descend down the steep sides of valleys, completely exposed to the enemy's vision, in order to ascend again heights of 700, 800, 900 meters, again under fire.

These alpine exercises had to be carried out while dragging the majority of their materiel on their own backs, as not every unit had mules assigned to it.

The Fourth Tunesian Rifles Regiment began the attack under the command of Lieutenant Roux. The entire regiment was aware of the fact that they were being offered as a holocaust.

The maneuver itself was a simple one, too simple: they were to make their way to the foothills of Belvedere, at night, cross the icy Rapido (it was January), which, in places, reached to their breast, all the while carrying their entire armory and three day's rations on their backs, without overcoat or blanket, so that they might attack, with their heart in their throat, at dawn of the next day.

They would have to rush across two kilometers to the bunkers before they would be able to toss their grenades.

Then they were to descend from 500 to 200 meters, climb anew to 470, descend 60 and ascend to 700, descend once more to 500 in order to finally occupy the mountain, after a further climb to its summit at 862 meters.

The attack began on 25 January. Thanks to the self-sacrifice of the Ninth Company, which advanced with fixed bayonets, an opening was effected for two battalions. From that company there returned but two French NCOs, one native NCO, and fifteen troops.

It rained hard that night. At dawn everything began again.

They made their way deep into the thicket of bunkers, and then the hidden, rear bunkers opened fire, cutting them off. The Tunesian Rifles felt like mortally cornered beasts, falling into a fury. They picked up the body of the fallen Lieutenant Boukkas and, carrying him like a standard, rushed at the bunkers.

Nothing helped—the night of the 26–27 January found them in a fatal trap: without water, without food, almost without ammunition, and without hope of receiving more.

Fire poured in upon the surrounded men from all sides; 300 meters to the front, 300 from behind, small-caliber arms, mortars, cannons, *Nebelwerfers* pounded at them.

Two days without water, 5 without food, 30 bayonet charges, their regimental commander killed, 2 battalion commanders wounded, 11 captains killed, every single company commander killed or wounded, 23 out of about 40 officers killed, 162 NCOs killed, 1,300 troops fallen along the way: thus the balance of that attack.

The determined fighting of other divisions too paid glorious tribute to the best ancient traditions of French soldiery.

I will mention but one example from all of which I was told.

Captain Tixier was an officer who acquitted himself nobly during the French campaign. Thirty-one years old. Three children. Wounded on 29 January, he declined evacuation to the rear.

On 30 January, a shell tore away his brow (*sic: l'éclat d'obus lui fait sauter le front*—I consulted doctors and was told that this was possible), depriving him of both eyes and his nose. He was taken to a medic's post with this horrible wound. He was not in shock, but conversed intelligently. He understood that he had been blinded, but he did not agree to be evacuated out of turn. At last, he was evacuated to Naples along with fourteen riflemen. Along the way he tore off his epaulettes so as not to be distinguished in any way from the regular soldiers and entered himself in the hospital registry as his own orderly. He died twelve days later.

In general, the French were beaten back. However, thanks to their assault, Castellone found itself in Allied hands.

Besides this, along with the numerous Germans killed, twelve hundred POWs were taken.

In this partial French success, on the left wing of their attack, the Thirty-Fourth American Division, which made its assault between the French and the Thirty-Sixth American, played its role. It is their history that I have just finished searching through.

It is now late, that I come to the end of this first phase. One can narrate it briefly, but study it long—from the reports of individual units, the photos of muddy fields covered with rocky craters, filled with water, fields, divided by fences and ditches, from artillery plans, deciphered and interpreted aerial photos translated into maps with a thousand conventional symbols.

I lifted my head. The garrulous group of correspondents has thinned. I took in hand a second file of reports. This—the Thirty-Fourth Division. . . . Surely we're there . . .

"Do you perhaps have a map of this section of the terrain?" I asked the correspondent sitting alongside me, whose fingers, in the American manner, clambered incessantly over the typewriter keyboard like insects.

"Of course." He doubled the speed of his jaws, chewing his gum. Leaning back in his chair toward the wall with the distribution list, he drew back the tent flap and called: "Hello, boys. Number seventeen and eighteen."

After a while an NCO from the tent next door, servicing the press corps, entered with the requested clippings.

My interested neighbor took a look at what I was studying.

"You see," I explained, "we're there. . . . And perhaps . . ."

"I see." He nodded his head. "Jimmy," he called to someone. "You were there. Come here and tell us."

Little black Jimmy, certainly someone of Spanish extraction, leaned over the table.

"Here's where we were standing," he pointed below a blocked rectangle. "That rectangle is Villa, a huge POW barracks still from the last war. There were Germans there."

I cast my eye at a large map of Italy hanging on the wall. I saw the rising massif, the narrow Liri valley to the west, above which dominated the huge monastery. Nearby ran the ancient road to Rome, beside which there was no other.

But Jimmy, quick as a spark, brushing the map spread on the table with this crow-black mop of hair, said passionately: "There were Jerries in Villa, and we were over here. . . . Oh, do you see, sir? Here, the Thirty-Fourth. About 2,000 yards from the Rapido river. An evil river!"—he shivered—"a muddy approach, a swift current, 80 feet wide, 12 feet deep, and above it and Villa, above all of us, 2,000 yards directly hangs the monastery of Monte Cassino, looking right down in all of our mess kits. On the northwest an amphitheater bristling with weapons. Each and every terrace higher than the other and shooting out above the other: Maiola, Castellone, Cairo, 400 meters elevation above every 1,000."

He glanced at his watch. The time when the speed-mad motorcyclist would drive up in his helmet, behind his celluloid windscreen, with the red bag for special deliveries, was approaching. Jimmy waved his hand.

"But what can I tell you, sir. The boys from the Thirty-Fourth are close at hand, because the division is standing in reserve."

And he resumed moving his quick insect-fingers over the typewriter keyboard.

NOTE

1. Actually, this weapon was used first on 14 July 1941 at Orsza (editor's note).

Figure F.1. Wańkowicz at Monte Cassino.

Figure F.2. Wańkowicz writing at Monte Cassino.

Melchior Wańkowicz's Main Books

(In chronological order with date of first editions)

- *Strzępy epopei* (*Rags of an Epic*) (1923), Warsaw
- *O małej Małgosi* (*About Maggie*) (1924), Warsaw, story for children
- *Jak Kulusia żabki poznała* (*How Did Frogs Meet Kulusia*) (1925), Warsaw, story for children
- *O Małgosi, świneczce, króliczku, muszce i o niegrzecznym piesku* (*About Maggie, Piggy, Bunny, Fly, and a Naughty Doggy*) (1925), Warsaw, story for children
- *Szpital w Cichiniczach* (*The Hospital in Cichinicze*) (1926), Warsaw
- *W kościołach Meksyku* (*In the Churches of Mexico*) (1927), Warsaw
- *Szczenięce lata* (*The Puppy Years*) (1934), Warsaw
- *Opierzona rewolucja* (*The Fledgling Revolution*) (1934), Warsaw
- *Na tropach Smętka* (*On the Trail of Smętek*) (1936), Warsaw
- *COP* (1937), Warsaw
- *Sztafeta* (*Courier*) (1939), Warsaw
- *Te pierwsze walki* (*These First Battles*) (1940), Bucharest
- *Z generałem Sosnkowskim* (*Alongside General Sosnkowski*) (1940), using a pseudonym Jerzy Łużyc, Bucharest
- *De profundis* (1943), Tel Aviv
- *Wrześniowym szlakiem* (*On the Roads of September*) (1943), using a pseudonym Jerzy Łużyc, Jerusalem
- *Dzieje rodziny Korzeniewskich* (*The Korzeniewski Family Saga*) (1944), New York and Rome
- *Bitwa o Monte Cassino* (*The Battle of Monte Cassino*) (1945–1947), 3 volumes, Milan
- *Monte Cassino* (1945), Edinburgh

- *Wrzesień żagwiący (September Aflame)* (1947), London
- *Kundlizm (Mongrelism)* (1947), Rome and London
- *Klub trzeciego miejsca (Third Place Club)* (1949), Paris
- *Ziele na kraterze (Herbs at the Crater)* (1950), New York
- *Polacy i Ameryka (Poles and America)* (1952), London
- *Tworzywo (Matter)* (1954), New York; Transl. (by Krystyna Cękalska) as Three Generations, Canadian Polish Research Institute, (1973) Toronto
- *Było to pod Monte Cassino (It Was at Monte Cassino)* (1954), London
- *Drogą do Urzędowa (The Road to Urzędów)* (1955), New York
- *Monte Cassino* (1959), Warsaw
- *Westerplatte* (1959), Warsaw
- *Hubalczycy (The Partisans of Major Hubal)* (1959), Warsaw
- *Tędy i owędy (This Way and That)* (1961), Warsaw
- *Walczący Gryf (Fighting Gryf)* (1964), Warsaw
- *Prosto od krowy (Straight from the Cow* [i.e., *The Horse's Mouth*]) (1965), Warsaw
- *Jak mądry puchacz tańczył trojaka (The Dancing Owl)* (1967), Warsaw, story for children
- *W ślady Kolumba (In Columbus's Footsteps)*, 3 volumes: *Atlantyk–Pacyfik (Atlantic–Pacific)* (1967), Warsaw
- *W pępku Ameryki (In the Midst of America)* (1969), Warsaw
- *Królik i oceany (Bunny and Oceans)* (1968), Warsaw
- *Zupa na gwoździu (Nail Soup)* (1967), Warsaw
- *Szkice spod Monte Cassino (Sketches from Monte Cassino)* (1969), Warsaw
- *Od Stołpców po Kair (From Stolpce to Cairo)* (1969), Warsaw
- *Przez cztery klimaty (Through Four Climates)* (1972), Warsaw
- *Karafka La Fontaine'a (La Fontaine's Carafe)*, 2 volumes (1972, 1981), Warsaw
- *Wojna i pióro (War and Pen)* (1974), Warsaw
- *Anoda i katoda (The Anode and Cathode)*, 2 volumes (1980–1981), Warsaw

Aleksandra Ziółkowska-Boehm has written introductions, footnotes, epilogues, and so forth, to

- *Melchior Wańkowicz, Reportaże zagraniczne (Reportage from Abroad)*, Kraków, 1981
- Series: *Dzieła emigracyjne i przedwojenne Melchiora Wańkowicza* (8 titles), Warsaw, 1989–1995
- *Korespondencja Krystyny i Melchiora Wańkowiczów (Correspondence between Krystyna and Melchior Wańkowicz)*, Warsaw, 1992

- Jerzy Giedroyc and Melchior Wańkowicz, *Listy 1945–1963* (Series: *Archiwum Kultury*; Correspondence between Jerzy Giedroyc and Melchior Wańkowicz), Warsaw, 2000
- King i Krolik. *Korespondencja Zofii i Melchiora Wańkowiczów* (*Correspondence between Zofia and Melchior Wańkowicz*), 1 volume: 1914–1939, 2nd volume: 1939–1968; Warsaw, 2004
- Series: *Dzieła Wszystkie Melchiora Wańkowicza* (*Total Works of Wańkowicz*), 16 volumes, Warsaw 2009–2011, the first edition of *Ziemia zanadto obiecana* (*The All-Too Promised Land*), *Posłannictwo i obcość* (*Mission and Foreignness*), *Reportaże wołyńskie* (*Reportage from Wolyn*).

Preface

Melchior Wańkowicz: Polish Hemingway

Considered by many as Poland's Ernest Hemingway, Melchior Wańkowicz and his writing were bigger than life. One of the most popular Polish writers, he always inspired attention, esteem, and also controversy . . . a writer's life that is still rekindled and analyzed.[1]

He was beloved by his readers, who stood in long queues to buy his books, and who packed the auditorium when he gave a speech. For the readers, he was Alpha and Omega, the authority; they trusted him and admired him.

Wańkowicz was the most eminent Polish reporter and was called the "father of Polish reportage" having many followers. He created the theory of his reportage—explaining the "mosaic method"—implanting different events of several people into the life of one person.

He impacted many generations of writers. When he was writing *Bitwa o Monte Cassino* (*Battle of Monte Cassino*), his secretary was Zofia Romanowiczowa (born Górska). Encouraged by him, she started writing, and became the author of many interesting books.[2]

Melchior Wańkowicz and his writing were exceptional. His life and the subjects of his books were extraordinary. He lived in many places and roamed many areas. An eminent literary critic, Krzysztof Masłoń, defined him as "a painter of the panorama of Polish history, a creator of patriotic literature. Readers want to learn about the beautiful, tragic, and heroic events of our history, and such were 'put into words' by Melchior Wańkowicz."[3]

Born in the Kresy—"Borderlands,"[4] a former territory of the eastern provinces of Poland—he lived in pre-war Poland. As a war correspondent of General Władysław Anders's Second Corps, he described the time of World

War II in his books. Wańkowicz is the author of one of the most famous Polish books, which for many became a kind of national treasure—*Bitwa o Monte Cassino*. He had many Polish readers all over the world. Many years after the writer's death, Zbigniew Brzezinski shared his thoughts: "I met Wańkowicz at one point in his career and I was certainly a very youthful reader of his account of the battle of Monte Cassino. Ever since then, his ability to capture the nuances, sounds, and emotions of wartime have been etched in my memory."[5]

After the war he stayed in exile, first in England, then for nearly ten years in the United States. In 1958, he returned to Poland permanently. Sixteen years later he died in Warsaw. His funeral gathered thousands of people and became an unofficial day of national mourning.

Wańkowicz played an enormous positive influence with his presence in Poland from 1958 to 1974. He gave so much to his nation with his return. His books played a huge part in shaping Polish national consciousness: they glorified the heroism of the Polish soldier, they gave citizens strength and comfort to withstand the Communist reality imposed on the nation, and the writer himself set an example by taking his independent stand.

What was the writer's strength that contributed to his isolation and many polemics? His indomitability, tendency to go his own way, cheek, and contrariness. He belonged to no political group or even an official social group, so he was not backed up or viewed as "our man." In that situation, no one nominated him to any award, and no reward was ever bestowed upon the great, popular writer. Many writers agreed to collaborate with the authorities, openly or covertly—the latter is indicated by the security police files found in 1989 in the Institute of National Remembrance (IPN).[6] Wańkowicz was envied for his independence by his psychologically weaker colleagues and opportunists. That feature was valued by the opposition to communism (e.g., Jan Olszewski, Jan Józef Lipski, Marta Miklaszewska), which constantly grew and finally led to establishing "Solidarity" in 1980, six years after the writer's death. He supported the opposition financially. Before his death he gave a substantial sum to a fund to aid people repressed for political reasons.[7]

He was surrounded with jealousy of his fellow writers who did not have such vast popularity and trust among the people. His defenders were the crowds of faithful, devoted readers. Until his death, the dislike and envy of the literary community accompanied him, but the love of the crowds never diminished.

Many years have passed since the writer's death in 1974. His books are constantly re-issued; he is still quoted by journalists and publicists, even by politicians. His neologisms—*kundlizm* (going to the dogs, or more literally, to mongrels), *chciejstwo* (wishful thinking)—have settled in the Polish language for good. Wańkowicz exists in the media.[8] There are streets and schools named after him, including a well-known Warsaw journalist college (Wyższa Szkoła Dziennikarska). There are awards for competition called— "Melchior"—in several categories for the best radio reportage.[9] He climbed high up to the writers' Olympus and remains there on a firmly established pedestal.

The texts that make up this book were written over the years. I am writing of the specific character of Wańkowicz's writing, the style of his storytelling and narration, and the subjects of his books. Serious subjects and issues are often interwoven with lighter topics—in what may be viewed as a tribute to Wańkowicz's principle that you have to "give the reader a break." I write about the writer's family, which he described in several of his books—his daughters Krystyna and Marta, called Tili, and his wife Zofia, called the Bunny.

I also show some images from the life of a man I knew personally: Wańkowicz and his writing, Wańkowicz and his home, Wańkowicz and his environment. I was part of that environment, I worked with the writer in the last two years of his life, and I stayed in his immediate proximity. In any memoirs there is the danger of the recollecting person shifting—consciously or not—to the forefront, as if they enviously granted themselves more space than would follow from the circumstances. I tried to avoid that and instead focus on the atmosphere, the climate of the life of the writer, whose interests turned both to himself and to others, to great causes of the time in which, despite his age, he participated with all his zeal and deep insight. Neither old age nor illness managed to isolate Wańkowicz from life. Vitality and awareness were great gifts of his nature.

Life near Wańkowicz was never dull. Life was always intensive, imbued with color and meaning. There are people who passively let the waves carry them on, and even see a sense of some necessary security in that. Wańkowicz was different. He tried to direct both himself and his environment. Only death was able to snatch that significant and sometimes incomprehensible ability from him.

Figure P.1. Wańkowicz relaxing after a lecture.

NOTES

1. Aleksandra Ziółkowska-Boehm, "Co z polskim Hemingwayem?" ("What about the Polish Hemingway?"), *Rzeczpospolita Daily*, 7/9 April 2007, p. A18.

2. One chapter in this book is dedicated to Zofia Romanowiczowa and Wańkowicz.

3. Krzysztof Masłon, "Kochana Zosieńko Moja, Najdroższe Melisko" ("My Loveliest Zosieńka [Zofia], Dearest Melisko [Melchior]"), *Rzeczpospolita Daily*, 16 December 2004, p. A10.

4. These territories today lie in western Ukraine, western Belarus, and eastern Lithuania, with such major cities as Lviv and Vilnius. This territory was included within the Polish Lithuanian Commonwealth and Second Polish Republic until World War II.

5. Letter to Aleksandra Ziółkowska-Boehm, 2 February, 2010.

6. In 1989, during the revolution movement of the trade union "Solidarity," the Communist state was overthrown and the democratic rule was re-established.

7. Andrzej Friszke, preface to Jan Józef Lipski, *KOR,* (Warsaw, 2006).

8. Television, for instance, shows the writer speaking of the battle of Monte Cassino in a cycle of lectures: "Melchior Wańkowicz—opowieść o bitwie Monte Cassino" ("Melchior Wańkowicz—The Story of the Battle of Monte Cassino") (1971) made by Jerzy Passendorfer. There is Bohdan Poręba's movie on Major Henryk Dobrzański, entitled *Hubal* (1973), whose name was made legendary largely thanks to Wańkowicz. A documentary *Mój pradziad—Melchior Wańkowicz (My Great-Grandfather—Melchior Wańkowicz)* (1998) was made by Piotr Morawski. Jerzy Wójcik made a movie *Wrota Europy (Europe's Gate)* (1999) based on *Szpital w Cichiniczach (The Hospital in Cichinicze). Ziele na kraterze (Herbs at the Crater)* was made into radio readings and dramas.

9. Established by journalist Irena Pilatowska.

Chapter One

Melchior Wańkowicz

On the Man and His Contribution to Polish Reportage [1]

The biography of Melchior Wańkowicz (1892–1974) is one of those fascinating reportages, the hero of which is a writer on the trail of the human adventure. The life of Wańkowicz was very rich and presents material for an entire book, at least. He was a writer, war correspondent, emigrant, globetrotter, but most of all a reporter. His beginnings are to be found in a world in which feudal mores could still be met with, but at all times he lived at the very epicenter of the most important current events. A linguistic biography of Wańkowicz would constitute a mirror for the development of today's Polish language, and his books offer interesting material for the study of Polish usage of the first half of the twentieth century, especially as far as *kresowe* regionalisms are concerned, although they also reflect contemporary Polish usage since 1945.

One might speak of several currents in the writings of Melchior Wańkowicz. I cite the reporter's accounts of World War II (*Monte Cassino, Westerplatte, Hubalczycy*), memoir narratives (*Szczenięce lata* [*The Puppy Years*], *Ziele na kraterze* [*Herbs on the Crater*], *Tędy i owędy* [*This Way and That*]), historical-geographical travel writings (*W kościołach Meksyku* [*In the Churches of Mexico*], *Na tropach Smętka* [*On the Trail of Smętek*], the American trilogy *W ślady Kolumba* [*In Columbus's Footsteps*]), and finally feuilletons and belles lettres (*Zupa na gwoździu* [*Nail Soup*], *Wojna i pióro* [*War and Pen*], *Przez cztery klimaty* [*Through Four Climates*], and *Karafka La Fontaine'a* [*La Fontaine's Carafe*]). However, the main current of Wańkowicz's writing consists of grand literary reportage, from which all his ventures into other genres of prose branch out.

1

The Wańkowicz school of literary reportage grows out of a broad tradition: the creative, rich, colloquial, and flowing prose of Poland's eastern marshes, the so-called Kresy. A generous extravagance of words links together the writers of the linguistic and stylistic aura of that region, if one might put it that way: Mickiewicz, Wańkowicz, Pruszyński. It is a colorful, living language that developed from the contact of two civilizations.

The regions around Mińsk and Kowno both formed the linguistic sensitivities of the future writer. The particularities of the Polish-Lithuanian territories, as well as their subjugation to the Russian Empire during the era of the partitions, shaped the unique, characteristic stylistics of the Kresy area. In later years Wańkowicz would write:

> I was raised in two regions of different linguistic backgrounds. In my mother's house, near Kowno, the foundation was Catholic. Polish and Lithuanian dominated in the church; there was a symbiosis between these languages, many bilingual families, and in these conditions the dialect developed organically. My father's house was in Belarus. The orthodox population came into contact with Polish ways only through the local manor. For this reason, the Polish language possessed a purer form, even unto linguistic subtleties. A coachman, for example, would say *konie się zmęczyły*, whereas his Catholic-Polish counterpart in Kowno said *koni się zmenczyli*.[2]

The Polish language as it was at the turn of the twentieth century, as heard in the house of his grandmother, Feliksa Szwoynicka, played a considerable role in the development of the lexical richness of the future writer. The huge influence of the family hearth, with its specific "kresowy" Polish, on the entirety of the writings of the author of *Szczenięce lata* verifies the rule, that childhood has a great significance for the development of the linguistic habits of the adult.

Wańkowicz's school years passed in Warsaw, where he attended the Chrzanowski (today's Zamoyski) Gymnasium. Wańkowicz attended school during a period of pitched battles waged by the young on behalf of education in Polish. The future author took vigorous part in the activities of youth organizations, first as a high school pupil, and later as a student of the Szkoła Nauk Politycznych (School of Political Science) in Kraków. He participated in many of the varied literary projects of his generation.

A new chapter in the history of the Polish language began with the restitution of the Polish state following World War I. The language received strong support and multi-faceted patronage from the Ministry of Education, Press, and Radio of those years, and the Polska Akademia Umiejętności (Polish Academy of Sciences). As Wańkowicz wrote, *Ja chcę pisać o Polsce, która rośnie jak drzewo, sposobem mówienia, który rósł z nią razem* (I wish to write about Poland, that grows like a tree, by using the manner of speech growing along with her).[3] For this purpose, the writer collected *powiedzonka żydowskie, chłopskie, szlacheckie, księżowskie* (Jewish sayings, peasant, noble, and priestly turns of speech).

Wańkowicz's career as an author followed an original course. His debut consisted of three books, of which the first two, *Strzępy epopei* (*Rags of an Epic*) and *Szpital w Cichiniczach* (*The Hospital in Cichinicze*) were anecdotal reportages from the war years, whereas the third, *W kościołach Meksyku*, was already standard reporter's fare. All of them excited an interested respect thanks to their colorful and indeed gorgeous style. They were praised by representatives of the most different orientations, political camps, and literary groups.

At last in 1935 there appeared two books which confirmed the two-tracked nature of his literary passions. They are the anecdotal *Szczenięce lata* and the narrative of his weeklong sojourn in Moscow, *Opierzona rewolucja* (*The Fledgling Revolution*).

Wańkowicz more than once underscored how much he owed to his background, the land on which he was born and raised. It was for him a font of memories that bestowed upon him the first lines of his rich, colorful personality. This is the source of his closeness to the earth, and nature. The cultural and ethnic borderlands seemed to be uniquely fertile in outstanding individuals. Perhaps it was that collision, that symbiosis of cultures and traditions that created exceptionally advantageous conditions of development? Or perhaps the breaking away from the particular atmosphere of the manor houses of the nobility liberated some hidden energy?

Szczenięce lata, one of his most beautiful books, was born of love and longing for his familial regions. In the words *Źdźbło każde rośnie ku lepszemu* (Each blade of grass grows toward the better), a sentence enshrined on the last page of this book, faith in life, the author's optimism, and old-Polish good humor are united in a modern élan and the cult of labor. Wańkowicz excites reflection on Polish themes, delves into the national consciousness, and by appealing to the past allows the reader a deeper understanding of his contemporary reality.

The book *Opierzona rewolucja* constituted quite an important stage in Wańkowicz's creative career, as it signifies the writer's ability to "enter into his theme" as well as his readiness to describe the world just as he sees it, without bias. From this time on Wańkowicz was to give notice of himself again and again as, above all, a reporter-writer. Works appear which have a specific form. Before the war, they are *Na tropach Smętka* and *Sztafeta* (*Courier*); during the war, they were *Wrzesień żagwiący* (*September Aflame*), *Dzieje rodziny Korzeniewskich* (*The Korzeniewski Family Saga*), *Bitwa o Monte Cassino* (*The Battle of Monte Cassino*), as well as the great reportage from Palestine, *Ziemia zanadto obiecana* (*The All-Too Promised Land*). After the war he was to publish *Ziele na kraterze* in which he returns to his beloved anecdotal style. In the years 1967–1969 there would appear the triptych of his travels in America entitled *W ślady Kolumba*. In his last book, *Karafka La Fontaine'a*, I find a summation of the author's literary wisdom and experiences.

Of the difficulties of assigning Wańkowicz's books to an appropriate literary genre, of their uniqueness, and of their specific characteristics, transcending the set canons of the art, articles were written at the publication of almost each of his works. Already in 1936, at the publication of *Strzępy epopei*, one of the critics wrote that it was difficult to closely define the genre to which the book belongs, as it is neither belles lettres, nor journalism, nor an historical work.[4] This is not literary fiction, but rather living, direct reminiscences, noted down *in flagranti* and given back with the plasticity and color of something fresh, just experienced, and not yet looked back upon with the cool objectivism that finally lends perspective. In turn, Juliusz Kaden-Bandrowski wrote about *Na tropach Smętka* that Wańkowicz's book is neither novella, nor novel, neither report nor typical travel literature, nor is it a new contribution to the literature of travel and leisure. *Nie podpada*, the critic writes. *Nie podchodzi ta praca pod żadne rubryki. Jest bowiem czymś nowym: jest przeżyciem* (It belongs nowhere. It doesn't fall into any category, for it is something new: it is an experience).[5]

Amongst opinions offered on the subject of Wańkowicz's reportages, our interest is aroused by the statements of writers creative in that genre, who described their own accomplishments in more or less precise literary, not publicistic, terms. An example of this is a reporter making reference to the creative methods of a given famous author. Egon Erwin Kisch set the similarity between the reporter's craft and that of the author of realistic fiction in a unique rule which crosses out the differences in their points of departure (for Kisch, Gustave Flaubert in *Salammbô* and Émile Zola, both "naturalists," are reporters). Melchior Wańkowicz was of a similar opinion. For him, not only Flaubert and Zola, but also Herman Melville was a reporter, and he called that writer's parabolic novel *Moby Dick* a "masterpiece of 19th-century reportage."[6]

A common view is that the author of *Na tropach Smętka* himself set the genre of Polish reportage on the broad road toward the literature of fact. His mastery of words, his ability to create fleeting moods, the plasticity of his images, his abbreviations, all testify to the writer's creative predispositions. On the other hand, his reporter's instinct as a hunter of reality, his ability to be literally everywhere where something interesting, worthy of description, was going on, and his gluttony of life's concretes, events, his race with time, all point toward the reporter's métier, in the very best sense of the word.

The creative writer introduces numerous changes to his work; he is somehow uncomfortable in a set convention. Reportages differ, in Wańkowicz's opinion, from belles lettres in that the writer does not invent, but rather combines observed facts and figures, all in the name of typecasting. The novelist can get by without archetypes such as these—he may invent at will.

> Let us say that there exists the same difference between the reporter and the belles-lettrist as between the painter and the mosaicist. The first rubs this or that synthetic color of his choosing on his palette, while the reporter takes his paint straight from the tube, or, more precisely, he composes a factual mosaic. He must search long before he finds the right stone. [7]

Wańkowicz's writings are based on fact. They emphasize the concrete and invest it with special significance. *Tworzywo* includes many real events, statistical data, and human histories; in this book, even the cited letters of one of its protagonists—Bombik—are authentic. We find real conversations, facts, and people at every step. Wańkowicz had a gift for noticing and observation, and on this, along with his ability to synthesize, his art is based. In *Tworzywo,* for the first time in Polish literature, its Polish emigrant protagonists do not only not fall and waste away, but succeed. For however much Henryk Sienkiewicz, Maria Konopnicka, or Jan Wiktor[8] created a literary witness to the horrid misery of the emigrant's fate, Wańkowicz, while not denying by any means the existence of misery, still shows its being overcome in the life successes of emigrants. Of course, his choice of the Canadian "diaspora," an emigrant community flourishing in a rich, virgin country, with much empty space, made it easy for the author to show such success, while had he chosen France it would have been more difficult.

Besides the many critical comments on the genre of reportage that we find sprinkled throughout his books, Wańkowicz dedicated an entire separate study to his understanding of this topic, entitled *Prosto od krowy* (*Straight from the Cow* [i.e., *The Horse's Mouth*]). The matter is also specifically treated in the introduction to the collection *Od Stołpców po Kair* (*From Stolpce to Cairo*) entitled "O poszerzeniu konwencji reportażu" ("On the Broadening of the Conventions of the Reportage") and, above all, in *Karafka La Fontaine'a.* He termed his reportages "the literature of fact." They are, generally speaking, works in which the author spins his own reflections, weaving into them numerous digressions.

To the present time the problems of the functioning, indeed even the existence, of fiction, in reportage have not been fully dealt with (as a matter of fact, Krzysztof Kąkolewski is of the opinion that there is no difference at all between the fictional work *sensu stricto* and the so-called reportage story).[9] The conception of truth in the reportage has been traditionally based, among other things, on the differentiation noted by James Reston between "literal truth," the direct truth of facts, and "essential truth," that is, synthetic, collective truth.[10] The former does not completely satisfy the creator, because there is no way to achieve a fully artistic effect in its limits, while the latter is obtained from facts chosen in a more elastic manner, as if it were distilled in a manner that is not subordinate to the reigning norms of reference in time and space. The concept of "essential truth" allows for the securing of the effect of synthetic truth, linking parallel events distant in time or space. Such operations are well known in literature, for literary creation does not have to signify, does not signify in each case, creation *ex nihilo.* Many authors observe people close at hand and at a distance. A detailed analysis of many authors, such as Dostoyevsky or Conrad (such as we find from the pens of Jerry Allen, Andrzej Braun, Zdzisław Najder, or Norman Sherry),[11] shows that the individual silhouettes of their protagonists, circumstances, events, and geographical landscapes have their equivalents in reality, their patterns in the concrete world which their authors once brushed up against.

The theory of the artistic primacy of essential truth over literal truth draws the reportage based on that theory close to more or less fictional narrative prose, and convinces us of the kinship of these two genres of writing. In contemporary times, as borders between the genres become ever more unclear, along with the clarity of compositional contours, the quarrel that developed between the fictional and authentic camps seems to have become quite dated. Such discussions, which from time to time flare up in today's Poland, seem all the more anachronistic when we consider what is going on in other countries.

In the 1970s in the United States the genre known as *new journalism* appeared, and displayed strong developmental tendencies. The representatives of this movement, such as Norman Mailer, Kurt Vonnegut, Thomas Pynchon, Philip Roth, and Tom Wolfe, carried out a revolution in the area of traditional ideas about literary genres, introducing journalism into the literary sphere. They found the materials for their work in facts taken directly from life, from their surroundings, and they described them with the aid of various literary techniques. The essence of this movement is the loosening of all forms. For them there exists no difference between the techniques of writing a discourse, an essay, the short story, or a novel.

In Poland, Ryszard Kapuściński recognized this approach and worked within its conventions. Wańkowicz's writing, on the other hand, is the opposite of the above-cited theory. His views on the topic, which he expressed in many of his works, as well as his "mosaic theory," can be pointed to in his defense against the attacks of those reviewers who would accuse him of an atypical approach to the writing of reportages.

Wańkowicz introduced to his works fictional elements, and he did weave the fate of authentic protagonists into the histories of fictional characters; he did construct his stories from different pieces, coloring them according to the spirit of his rules. Yet he was constantly fascinated not only by the fate of the individual, but also by larger quandaries. Fiction is not in conflict with the nature of the reportage, as long as it expresses authentic problems in a true way. For example, Wańkowicz himself stated that he crossed the Pacific a full four times, while "compressing" the facts collected on these journeys into the description of one trans-Pacific course.[12] The full picture of his reporter's mosaic is built up from facts sometimes fictive, sometimes brought over from other arrangements of reality, sometimes from probabilities. This makes the mosaic an interesting and purposeful operation, when the element organizing the structure of the text is, for example, a societal, cultural, sociological, or political phenomenon. The protagonist is, in this case, less important, as his function is of a secondary nature. Looking at the matter from the perspective of the use of fiction and the idea of the mosaic, Wańkowicz did not create anything new. Kisch's reportages are a montage of truth and fiction, and the Soviet reporter Valentin Oviechkin groups hundreds of events from the lives of actual people under one name which constantly surfaces in many reportages.[13]

Understandably, in great measure, the reportage is based on the personal relations of witnesses and participants in the events described, which relations the author then links to his own observations and commentary. Usually, however, the author himself touches the concrete he describes directly, inspecting the scene of the action. There must be an autopsy, a personal confrontation with what he wishes to write about. But what can we say, then, of those of Wańkowicz's reportages like *Westerplatte*, *Hubalczycy*, or the second part of *Ziela na kraterze: Wrzesień żagwiący*, which the writer did not authenticate with his own observation, as he was neither in Poland, nor in a POW camp during the Nazi/Soviet occupation? These works awe us all the more for the masterful precision with which, basing his work only on first-person narratives and letters, the author was able to reconstruct a truthful picture of the Warsaw Uprising. Warsaw under the German occupation, its moods and atmosphere, complete with the most elusive details, were rendered in *Ziele na kraterze* with unbelievable realism. The writer was not in Poland at the time of the events he depicts, and yet this book has been cited as one of the best descriptions of the period it describes.[14]

The same is true of *Hubalczycy*, a book based on the accounts of Roman Rodziewicz, a participant in the battles of Major Dobrzański's division, whom Wańkowicz met in Italy. In the writer's archives we find a huge packet of letters from the former Hubal soldiers who, except for a detail here and there, all recognize that this book most faithfully records the climate of those wartime months.

Before World War II, Wańkowicz was known as the author of, among others, the above-mentioned *Szczenięce lata*, books for children, and most of all, his widely renowned reportage *Na tropach Smętka*. The book received much recognition and grew popular not only on account of its interesting form, but above all because in it, the author raised a subject until then passed over in silence: the life of Poles cut off from the fatherland, yet vibrantly displaying their Polishness in the German-held lands of Warmia and Masuria.

I would like to give a broader relation of the reaction that Wańkowicz's *Na tropach Smętka* elicited in Germany. The German reaction to his *Na tropach Smętka* is extraordinarily interesting.

In June of 1935, Wańkowicz set off on a trip, by kayak and automobile, through Masuria and other regions of East Prussia. His goal was to learn something about the life of Poles cut off from the motherland. Before he undertook his trip, he applied for a letter of safe conduct from Hans Schwarz van Berk, the editor-in-chief of the Nazi periodical *Der Angriff*. Van Berk commissioned an article from him, entitled "Ein Pole erlebt Ostpreussen" ("East Prussia in the Eyes of a Pole"). Wańkowicz determined to employ this commission as camouflage in his dealings with the East Prussian authorities. The result of his journey was a reportage rich in political material, and a colorful description of adventure and conversations, a book which won for itself a wide popularity (*Na tropach Smętka*). The writer considered this his first book written with a conscious literary aim; thus he prepared its composition with great care (as the bibliography bears witness). The book was a great success. It went through nine editions in the space of four years. The first two came out in 1936; the last pre-war edition was dismantled on the printers' machines in Bydgoszcz by the Germans in 1939. The book won for itself wide recognition and popularity (Konrad Górski, Adam Grzymała-Siedlecki, Juliusz Kaden-Bandrowski, and many other cultural lights praised it in print) thanks to its interesting structure, but above all, because in it the author took up matters theretofore unknown, displaying lively examples of Polish life in the regions of Warmia and Masuria. What is more, the author foresaw the war to come, and set in the book a timetable describing the course of the invasion from sea, land, and air a full three years before September 1939.

In 1945, on the Pomeranian coast, there was found, in circumstances with which I am not very familiar, a mimeographed copy of this book, among other tossed-away paper. On its first page was printed the caution *Streng vertraulich* ("Extremely Confidential"), which testifies to the character of this publication in German. The copies were numbered (this one bore the number 193), and thus destined only for a chosen few. The motives for its publication were clear. In a foreword we find this note from the publisher (the East German Union):

> A citizen of Polish nationality, Wańkowicz, who in 1935 undertook a trip through Masuria by kayak and toured the other regions of East Prussia by automobile, recorded in this book his impressions from the journey. This work was widely disseminated in Poland and nearly all of the Polish newspapers printed very positive reviews. In a clearly biased form are recorded Polish

views on East Prussia. In the face of the clearly inimical conclusions of the author, the State Secret Police (Gestapo) was impelled to forbid the publication of this book in Germany. However, since it is a valuable aid to understanding Polish methods of nationalist tactics, they have permitted the East German Union to translate the book and distribute it among trusted, concerned persons.

In Wańkowicz's archives may be found photocopies of the correspondence concerning the book exchanged between Erich Koch, president of East Prussia, Von Moltke, the German ambassador in Warsaw, and Theodor Oberländer (president of the Bund Deutscher Osten [BDO]), in which the correspondents strove to identify who was responsible for enabling Wańkowicz's trip, and who arranged his credentials as a correspondent for *Der Angriff*. Upon the appearance of Wańkowicz's book, the borders of the German Reich were immediately closed to him, and the book was placed on that nation's index. Pressure was even put on Warsaw to forbid its distribution in Poland. One of the initiators of this idea was Theodor Oberländer, who in Adenauer's Germany headed a ministry dealing with repatriated Germans. In a letter from 3 March 1937, Oberländer promised to send the German foreign ministry a copy of Wańkowicz's book, suggesting at the same time "that the ministry succeed in as short a time as possible in forbidding its distribution in Poland. For this matter is not only a grave insult to Germany as a whole, but an insult to the Führer himself."

On 5 March the Foreign Ministry wrote back, announcing that it "has not only published its reservations about this book, but has approached the Polish government with the proposition that it be recalled from the market." For his part, on 21 December 1936, Oberländer wrote the following to a BDO activist:

> You will soon be receiving the copies of Wańkowicz's book, which I first had to expedite to Berlin. It has been a long time since I have had in my hands so interesting an example of Polish work. Some of the charges cannot be passed over in silence. In this connection, I request materials concerning the Lanc and Kiwicki matters, and others, as soon as possible. Just think what sort of impression this will have on Germans in Poland, if these sorts of accusations remain without answer.

Of course, nothing was done in Poland to remove the book from the market. The reviews of *Na tropach Smętka* in the German press were, predictably, harsh. In the April 1937 edition of the bi-monthly *Ostland*, Wańkowicz was labeled *ein notorischer Lügner* (a notorious liar), and was generally treated as a dangerous Polish writer, inimical to the Reich.

Na tropach Smętka is an important document of an important era in the life of Poland. An excellent example of the reportage genre, it remains one of the most noteworthy titles in its author's literary opus.

Wańkowicz was also publisher and co-owner of Rój Publishers, founded on his initiative in 1924. In the course of its fifteen-year existence in Poland, this publishing house achieved a signal position amongst the publishers of the inter-war period. One year earlier in 1923, Wańkowicz accepted an appointment as the director of the Press and Entertainments Department in the Home Office. Among other things, this department brought out a monthly bulletin in Polish and French dedicated to the publishing industry.

Wańkowicz encouraged booksellers to print sensational literature, based on actual events. The Arct firm and the Dom Książki Polskiej (Polish Book House) agreed to initiate just such a publishing concern, but on the condition that Wańkowicz himself suggest themes and authors for the series. The publishing series was registered as a journal, and bore the title *Biblioteczka Historyczno-Geograficzna* (*The Historical and Geographical Library*). It had a consecutive numeration and its own editor. Wańkowicz was successful in obtaining the cooperation of a number of interesting personages, such as Julian Tuwim, Zofia Kossak, Maria Kuncewiczowa, Juliusz Kaden-Bandrowski, Ksawery Pruszyński, Wacław Sieroszewski, Juliusz Kleiner, Wacław Borowy, Julian Krzyżanowski, Jan Stanisław Bystroń, Konrad Górski, and Karol Irzykowski. Series were published which dilated on great legal trials, spy themes, inventors and discoverers, famous lovers, and so forth. In time, the journal was transformed into a publishing house on its own. In 1926 its co-owners became Melchior Wańkowicz, with a two-thirds stake, and Marian Kister, with one-third.

If in relation to Polish authors Rój was just one of several serious publishing houses—such as Gebethner, Mortkowicz, Hoesick, and Wende—around which the literary elite was grouped, in the area of translations Rój enjoyed pride of place. Assimilated were both popular literature and the works of the greatest authors. Alongside the books of Jack London, James Oliver Curwood, and Vicki Baum, it published Polish versions of André Gide, and work on a translation of James Joyce's *Ulysses* was only cut short by the eruption of the war.

Rój was first to introduce the Polish readership to such writers as John Galsworthy, Roger Martin du Gard, Aldous Huxley, André Malraux, Thomas Mann, André Maurois, Marcel Proust, Erich Maria Remarque, Bertrand Russel, Upton Sinclair, and Arnold Zweig. On Wańkowicz's initiative a series of great works of the twentieth century was established. Seven of the authors of this series were already, or were shortly to become, Nobel laureates: Sigrid Undset, François Mauriac, Pearl Buck, Mikhail Sholokhov, Luigi Pirandello, Thomas Mann, and Romain Rolland.

Rój also published Soviet literature. Books by Ilya Ehrenberg, Valentin Katayev, Boris Pilniak, Alexei Novikov-Priboy, Mikhail Prishvina, Maxim Gorki, and Alexei Tolstoy were all brought out by Rój.

Many Polish authors debuted under the Rój imprint, such as Jerzy Andrzejewski, Pola Gojawiczyńska, Witold Gombrowicz, Teodor Parnicki, Adolf Rudnicki, Bruno Schulz, Adam Ważyk, and Tadeusz Łopalewski. Rój was first to print Schulz's *Sklepy cynamonowe* (*Cinnamon Shops*) and *Sanatorium pod klepsydrą* (*The Sanatorium at the Obituary Notice*), Gombrowicz's *Ferdydurke* and *Pamiętnik z okresu dojrzewania* (*Memoir from Adolescence*), Gojawiczyńska's *Ziemia Elżbiety* (*Elizabeth's Land*), Andrzejewski's *Ład serca* (*The Order of the Heart*), and Maria Ukniewska's *Strachy* (*Bugbears*). In after years, Wańkowicz recalled with regret that Jarosław Iwaszkiewicz's *Brzezina* (*Birchwood*) was turned down by his house.[15]

The publishing house on Kredytowa Street introduced not only new authors, but new literary genres as well. At Rój's inspiration, Czesław Centkiewicz gave up the electrician's profession in favor of writing. Tadeusz Dołęga-Mostowicz worked at Rój as a typesetter, and was to publish there his *Kariera Nikodema Dyzmy* (*The Life and Times of Nikodem Dyzma*), which was to prove extremely popular. Rój, as Wańkowicz reminisced in after years, was neither afraid of Communist writers, nor of writers from the ONR camp.[16] They feared neither impious atheists nor pious Catholics—they feared only bad writers.[17]

Finally, when the war broke out, Wańkowicz's fled the Germans and found his way to Romania. His wife Zofia Wańkowicz took the helm at Rój, desirous of salvaging its continuity of existence, so that, after the war, her husband could return to work. Then a conflict flared up between Zofia and Hanna, the wife of Marian Kister. This battle is documented among the correspondence collected in the writer's archives, as well as in a book authored by Hanna Kister and published in 1980.[18] In it, the author collects many of her own memories, as well as information about the workings of the publishing house and its continuation—in one sense of the word—after the war in the United States as "Roy Publishers." Melchior Wańkowicz himself, the founder and co-owner of Rój, appears perhaps four times in the pages of Kister's book, as if in passing. Zofia Wańkowicz, who deserves much credit for the upkeep of the publishing house during the occupation, receives no mention whatsoever.

This, in brief, is a thumbnail sketch of the active life of Melchior Wańkowicz up until the outbreak of the war in 1939.

At the outbreak of the war, Wańkowicz was attached as a war correspondent to the armored brigade of General Grot-Rowecki. However, when he arrived at Kurów, where he was to meet up with the troops, he found the town in smoldering ruins and learned that the brigade had since moved off in an unknown direction. The writer made it to Lublin, in which there was already no Polish authority. During the bombardment of the town, he listened to the German radio from Wrocław, which announced, in Polish, *Wańkowicz jest w Lublinie, ale my go tropami Smętka złapiemy* (Wańkowicz is in Lublin, but we're going to hunt him down on the trail of Smętek).

This bitterness explains in part the photostats of the correspondence dealing with his person ("Who provided Wańkowicz with a visa?"), that he received many years later from Bonn, between Hans von Moltke (Reich ambassador in Warsaw) and Erich Koch, the president of East Prussia.

Near the end of September 1939, the writer swam across the Dniester, under fire, carrying with him his typewriter. He recalled this scene many times in later life, and it became something of a symbol to him. He remained in Romania until September 1940.

Later, he was to write about this period:

> So the war began for me on the debit side. I was stuck in Romania, dreaming of being with our boys in France. Any old zero was getting a visa, while my exit was blocked. Later I was stuck for a year on Cyprus. It was the same as "Snake Island" in England—a deportation point for undesirables. Then, I was held for two years in Palestine. I tried hard not to give in. Slipping past the representatives of the government in exile, I traveled about visiting the military camps in Romania. I had some readings, I gathered material, and my two brochures about the September campaign were printed during the occupation. It was on Cyprus that I worked up the materials I'd gathered.[19]

Using the pseudonym Jerzy Łużyc, he also published in Bucharest the book entitled *Te pierwsze walki* (*These First Battles*). This is a collection of reportages written on the basis of facts narrated by Lieutenant Jerzy Lewandowicz, and deals with the battles fought by Polish soldiers in September 1939 on the southern front (Wisła-Soła). In this same year of 1940, also under a pseudonym, he published the brochure *Z Generałem Sosnkowskim* (*Alongside General Sosnkowski*). It contains materials concerning the battles waged by the Second Division of the Polish Army near Lwów, and paints the portrait of the general, the tragic hero of that sad period. Both brochures were smuggled successfully into Poland, where the underground press disseminated them. Later, the writer was to include both narratives as parts of a larger whole, *Wrzesień żagwiący.*

While yet in Romania, Wańkowicz contacted Marshal Edward Rydz-Śmigły and conducted an interview with him. He also spoke with Józef Beck and Henryk Sucharski, the commandant of Westerplatte. Thirty years later, Andrzej Micewski referred to this latter conversation:

> What was Beck thinking in the final years, the final months before the war? What did he foresee? We possess an important testimony in his very own

words, pulled verbatim from his mouth by Melchior Wańkowicz. [. . .] Wańkowicz's conversation with Beck is a very important historical document.[20]

In September 1940, on account of the coming German invasion of Romania, Wańkowicz, along with a group of other people in danger because of their politics, took advantage of a British invitation to travel to Cyprus, where he was to remain for two months. When in turn the Germans invaded Cyprus, he was evacuated to Palestine.

This was a fortunate (in misfortune) turn of events, as Wańkowicz had long been fascinated by the question of how the Jews had succeeded in maintaining their national identity through twenty centuries of dispersal and foreign occupation. To what did they owe this? To what characteristics, what circumstances? In Palestine, he was to write (among other things), the article "Z jakimi hasłami wkraczamy do Palestyny" ("With What Slogans Do We Enter Palestine?"), in which he states:

> If Poland is to be a democracy, that is, if each of her citizens is to have an influence on the country's destiny, then it is necessary for that citizen to be well informed, that he understands what's going on in the world. It has fallen to the lot of us few to see various countries and study their life. Let's not waste the opportunity. Above all, let us consider ourselves ambassadors of our nation. There should be no place among our number for idiots, who confine their knowledge of their surroundings to the addresses of taverns. Abstinence, consciousness of one's own dignity, respect for the efforts of others, and a sincere desire to learn—these are the slogans, beneath which we enter the Holy Land.[21]

In Tel Aviv, Wańkowicz began a series of lectures entitled "Narodziny syjonizmu" ("The Birth of Zionism"). In 1943, he published *De profundis*, the first volume of an intended cycle of books dealing with the martyrology of the Jews and their tragic history. The subsequent volumes of the cycle, *Ziemia zanadto obiecana* (*The All-Too Promised Land*) and *Posłannictwo i obcość* (*Mission and Foreignness*) did not find a publisher.

De profundis appeared in the series *Przez lądy i morza* (*Over Land and Sea*, Pelima), dealing with the history of the Zionist movement in the broadest sense of the term. Wańkowicz collected a rich informative and descriptive base of the history of the blossoming of Zionist thought in the consciousness of both the Jews themselves and the world at large from the nineteenth century through the turn of the twentieth century. With the courage and conscientiousness of a true researcher, the author touches upon many delicate matters, exhibiting even a certain tendency to the most vivid descriptions and formulations.

In the Jerusalem-based *Głos Polski* (*Polish Voice*), Edward Kostka wrote: *Wańkowicz ma wszystkie warunki, aby "odbrązować" (mówiąc stylem Boya) tajemną wiedzę o Żydach i przyswoić tę wiedzę polskiemu społeczeństwu* (Wańkowicz has the complete ability to debunk [to paraphrase Boy-Żeleński] the hidden knowledge about the Jews and to speak of it in a way that Polish society can understand).[22] In Hebrew, there appeared the article, "Oczyma nie-Żyda przez żydowskie okulary" ("Through the Eyes of a Non-Jew, Wearing Jewish Spectacles") in which we read:

> Wańkowicz turns a skeptical eye on life. He always sees both sides of the coin. Now, such a person who looks upon many events in the life of his own nation with great skepticism may be permitted to assume a similar stance in face of the social phenomena of a nation to which he does not belong.[23]

The next stages of Wańkowicz's wartime anabasis led him to Iran, Iraq, Syria, and Lebanon. Of course, the author derived advantage from his post as war correspondent attached to the Polish Army. His further destiny was to be linked with the Second Corps. Along with them he traveled to Egypt, and from thence to Italy. He was at Monte Cassino, which resulted in his three-volume reportage *Bitwa o Monte Cassino* published between the years 1945 and 1947 by the publishing arm of the Culture and Press Detachment of the Second Polish Corps.[24] Along with *Na tropach Smętka*, this is perhaps the most widely recognized work of Melchior Wańkowicz. It is considered a classic of martial reportage. *Bitwa o Monte Cassino* opened a new chapter in the genre of contemporary war correspondence. Wańkowicz entered into the Polish literature of fact with his writing talents and experience as a reporter, and the result was a completely innovative book. He created it, collecting materials "on the fly," while the fighting was still going on. He made his way to each company, each platoon, verifying his facts both at headquarters and among the soldiers themselves. He collected an immense body of documentation. First of all, he had to deal with the basic question of war correspondence, that is, with the simultaneity of various military actions, resulting in an immeasurably difficult composition of time. The book breathes truth, although it is neither a montage nor a historical recollection, nor a simple collection of documents, but rather a carefully composed picture of the great battle. He's no longer painting with synthetic colors, nor is he picking and choosing from the palette of facts to construct the picture he has in mind.

For one example, we may consider the following scene:

> Out of three companies of the Second Batallion, only thirty-four soldiers returned whole. When I visited Lieutenant Brzóska in his dugout, still weak from the pressure of the sandbags, he said with determination:
> "Please remember: it would not be exact to write that the battalion was shattered."

"How then am I to describe it?"

Lieutenant Brzóska's gaze sank into the sandbagged wall: through the narrow slit one could see the bright day, and there, in the open, dark human figures were carrying away the fallen. It all looked so distant now, unreal like shades in a child's Chinese lantern. The lieutenant's lips moved quietly: "Slaughtered."[25]

Some reviewers felt that it was General Anders's opinions that were expressed in *Monte Cassino*, and that Melchior Wańkowicz was the creator of the legend of the battle.[26] For others, the writer was the bard of the individual soldier, a critic of the failures of the staff.[27] Both camps were judging the book, and its author, from their own ideological perspectives. Judgments in Poland differed from those offered in emigration. The readers, however, accepted the book with acclamation.

Earlier still, in 1943, the small work *Dzieje rodziny Korzeniewskich* saw the light of day. In 1944, it was published in Rome and in New York, and was translated almost simultaneously into English, French, and Italian.[28] It also appeared in India. This is a deeply stirring document, which speaks of Polish refugees, forcibly transported into the depths of the Soviet Union in the years 1939–1941, where they slowly died of hunger. It is told through the lips of a woman who survived the tragedy that wiped out her entire family.

In the *Dziennik Żołnierza* (*Soldier's Daily*), Jan Olechowski wrote on the value of this document:

> The value of this literary work is based on its art of presenting a simple account in such a way that it evokes in us a fresh, deep shiver of horror, a shiver of the deepest sympathy. The author has achieved this by reducing the entire story to the maximum of simpliticy. No personal commentaries of the author muddy the stream of this tragic tale. His well-known style has disappeared. There remains nothing but the pure stream of human suffering. [. . . In relating] the story as if it was related with an exhausted, yet calm whisper [. . .] Wańkowicz has displayed in full the art of his writing. Each word is weighed so carefully, that at times we have nothing but an exact relation, and yet just one moment after the dry, official note of the death of the youngest of the Korzeniewskis, when he records the final sentence, "And thus the story of one family, of the Korzeniewski family, murdered," that one word "murdered" hits us like a hammer blow and remains the strongest, most moving experience which will remain, relentlessly, in the memory.[29]

Immediately following the cessation of hostilities Wańkowicz set out to visit shattered Europe. He traveled through Germany, Austria, France, and Italy. In January of 1947 he settled in London, where he lived in Ealing, remaining there until leaving for America in 1949.

In 1947, *Kundlizm* (*Mongrelism*) appeared in Rome. The author himself comments on the genesis of this book: *Z chwilą demobilizacji wraca na nonkonformistyczną ścieżkę. Skoro żołnierz pozostaje na emigracji, nie należy mu dalej podbijać bębenka, tylko przygotować na życie wśród obcych, omawiając wady narodowe* (As soon as he is demobilized he returns to his non-conformist paths. Since the soldier remains in emigration, he shouldn't keep banging on the drum, but rather prepare himself for life among strangers, and point out the flaws of his nation).[30]

The popularity of the author of *Bitwa o Monte Cassino*, garnered during the war, was to fall off dramatically with the war's conclusion. About this time, Wańkowicz learned of the public burning of *Kundlizm* in a Polonian girl's school, as the book was determined by them to be "a shaming of the Polish nation."

In *Parada*, Juliusz Mieroszewski was to write:

> When one takes in hand Wańkowicz's *Kundlizm* immediately after reading the second volume of his *Bitwa o Monte Cassino*, one comes to realize, suddenly, that the doors to the Pantheon have been slammed shut, and we remain outside, among the everyday murmur of foreign streets. We became an "emigration" from the moment when the Second Corps ceased to exist as a unit. [. . .] Our tragedy lies in the fact that we are rich in history and tradition, while dirt poor in possible programs. Still and all, it would be a horrible thing if we—as Wańkowicz writes—allowed the cemeteries of our heroes to become the breeding grounds of the émigré mongrel.[31]

On the other hand, in his comments in the *Orzeł Biały* (*White Eagle*), Tadeusz Nowakowski underscores the writer's ceaseless chase after truth, maugre the consequences.[32]

Kundlizm is an example of Wańkowicz's social passions. A similar example is the brochure *Klub trzeciego miejsca* (*Third Place Club*), published in Paris in 1949. The basic thesis of that book is the statement that Poland lays in the cultural sphere of the West, and the geopolitical sphere of the East. In such a situation, Poles who wish to accomplish something must agree to compromises in both directions. The author declares his own membership in this "third place club."

The book stirred a storm in the year it was published. Two years after, in 1951, Jerzy Giedroyc was to write:

> Even today I would publish *Klub Trzeciego Miejsca* as the best yeast yet produced to stir our thought. The only political evolution that I went through is the road to the conviction, that in the present situation, in the face of a conflict of two empires, we can and must be on America's side, but in no way must we become her blind tool or agent.[33]

Earlier (in 1947), *Wrzesień żagwiący* was published in London. Its 530 pages included the 240-page *Wrześniowym szlakiem* (*On the Roads of September*) first published in 1943, as well as the tale of Hubal, which was later published as a book in its own right as *Hubalczycy* (*The Partisans of Major Hubal*). In a letter to the editors of the *Orzeł Biały*, Wańkowicz wrote:

> This book was written in 1939, when the government *in exile* was just being formed, there was no Polish Army to speak of, and world opinion was not miserly in its bitter commentaries on the defilade of victorious Germans on the Boulevards in Warsaw, taking up the slogan of one of the propagandists of the German campaign, about *Achtzehn Tage in Polen* ("eighteen days in Poland"). I wrote this book from stories told by soldiers, some of them wounded, who made their way through the unguarded frontier. I tried to give back something of their mood, to write in their words. [34]

Juliusz Mieroszewski, who collaborated with *Kultura* in Paris, wrote these words to Wańkowicz about *Hubalczycy*:

> You are at your best as a writer in *Hubalczycy*. There are portions of that book which make me think that, if you had taken upon your shoulders the task of composing an epic in prose, something along the lines of a *Popioły* [*Ashes*] of the twentieth century, this would be without a doubt the greatest work in our historical literature. For you tower above Żeromski in composition, and above Sienkiewicz and Żeromski in the unity of your prose, unsentimentalized and yet at times lyrical, in a masculine way. [35]

In 1952, in London, the Oficyna Poetów i Malarzy (Poets' and Painters' Press) brought out the next title by Melchior Wańkowicz, entitled *Polacy i Ameryka* (*Poles and America*), in which the author gives a succinct sketch of the Polish contribution to the building of the United States. In this book he sets forward the thesis that the epoch of Western culture has come to an end. We live "in between" epochs, and in the United States can be noted traits of a moving away from European culture.

In the United States, the author lived with his younger daughter Marta (Krystyna fell during the Warsaw Uprising). He worked on the chicken farm owned by his son-in-law Jan Erdman, who had fought at Tobruk. In 1950, and then again in 1955, he toured Canada, giving a series of readings in centers of Polish population and collecting materials for his next book dedicated to the Polish emigration.

He wasn't making out too well as an emigrant. As a writer with "sharp edges" he was no critic's darling. He was not well off, and he was in need of readers. Ever more serious differences of opinion were growing between the writer and the emigration in general. These were made apparent first of all by *Kundlizm*, which was like a bucket of cold water tossed on the emigrés' megalomania, which was in essence a singular inferiority complex. Beyond this was his unwillingness to go along with the resolution of the Polish Writers' Conference in exile[36] "not to write to Poland." Wańkowicz declared at the time, *To oni mnie mogą nie drukować, ale póki tylko będę mógł, będę pisał do kraju* (It's up to them to decide whether to print me or not, but as long as I can, I will write for Poland).[37]

All this made matters worse. Wańkowicz looked askance at the emigration, and wrote bluntly his critical opinions, for example, in *Klub trzeciego miejsca*. In that book, the author confessed that he did not believe in the West, in the historical mission of America. He analyzed the situation and set out a prognosis for the future. As mentioned above, he believed that we are living "between epochs." The old epoch was given the coup de grace by Soviet Russia, and the new was just barely coming to be, characterized by the dominance of technology, global communications, and multi-governmental organizations. He wrote:

> In 1949, it is my opinion, that Russia will be victorious, but unable to organize and govern the world. And it will fall apart. To follow the side doomed to lose against Russia is thoughtless suicide, and the struggle for the so-called values of Western culture—the hypocrisy of pundits, who are able to recite Wyspiański from memory, but who haven't read even one basic handbook of political economics.[38]

When, among others, the *Dziennik Polski* (*Polish Daily*) ceased to print his columns, retiring to the quiet of his family home the writer composed *Ziele na kraterze*, which was published in 1951 in New York. Later, the book was reprinted in Poland, and became the spiritual bread for many families. After familiarizing himself with *Ziele na kraterze*, Jerzy Giedroyc was to write:

> I read the book and am quite moved by it. It is a tragical book, and if it were not for a few unnecessary items [there aren't too many of them], it would be splendid. Maybe Rojek or Giertych[39] might be indignant with the last letter. I know nothing more beautiful.[40]

The next title published in New York (1955) was *Drogą do Urzędowa* (*The Road to Urzędów*). Constituting a compilation of belles lettres built upon his own experiences, and those of others, it is an attempt at displaying the variety of "Polish fates" during the last war. Beginning with the September Campaign, through the first partisan struggles and the first mass executions of Poles in their own country, we are led through Romania, the USSR, German internment camps, Cyprus, nearly the entirety of the Near East, with Palestine at the head of all, Iran, Egypt, the Gold Coast, France, and Italy.

The book's main protagonist, Hauke, is a synthesis of the well known from pre-war Warsaw Fiszer (habitué of coffeehouses and font of humorous anecdotes) and Wańkowicz himself, with his wartime experiences, and his judgmental approach to pre-war Poland. We wander with Hauke through Romania and Cyprus; in Palestine, we experience the tragedy of the leaders of the militant Jews. We are present at the readings. We observe how the sharp-edge of criticism suddenly emerges, as well as good-hearted humor at the expense of Urzędów, as well as understanding and love for this quiet little town, this land striving toward better days, which is a symbol for the lost fatherland. The pain of the loss does not become a reason for idealization, and thus Urzędów appears before our eyes just as it was: small, provincial, full of quarrels, perhaps, and shortcomings and blemishes, but still the one and only, the irreplaceable.

An interesting characterization of the book may be found in the *Dzienniki* (*Journals*) of Maria Dąbrowska, who, unlike Jerzy Giedroyc, was delighted by the book:

> Wańkowicz has left us his novel *Drogą do Urzędowa*. He wants to write a cycle of novels entitled *Panorama losu polskiego* [*A Panorama of Polish Destinies*]. I don't know how the whole thing will turn out—a panorama can't be anything but a panorama—a "popular macroimage"—but that *Drogą* is very interesting. And in and of itself it's already a panorama of all the sufferings and adventures of "all Polands" during the war. Palestine (splendid), Italy, Africa, lands and seas, a POW camp in Germany, the conspiracy at home, the destinies of Poles in Russia, and in everything wit, humor, suspense, tragedies that freeze the blood, comical adventures, the excellent, suggestive characterization of the protagonists, surprisingly intelligent reflections on (so to speak) practical philosophy, good dialogues, passionately moving situations. The two chief protagonists—a priest and a Jewish doctor—are certainly two of the best in Polish historical-manneristic literature. It's not well received among the émigrés, and it could only be printed here at the cost of deleting the episodes from Soviet Russia. Despite the fact that neither in the Jewish themes, nor in the Russian themes, nor even in the German themes the traditional "baggage" is not to be found. No resentments, allergies, animosities. Certainly, this is no revelation, no "high art," but rather a novel/reportage. Still, in its form it is pushed to the limits of art of a sort and is quite a departure from the traditional form of novels. Just like the "authenticity" of its plot, characters are pushed to the limits of non-realistic construction. [41]

An interesting testimony of Wańkowicz's relationship to the emigration may be found in his correspondence with Czesław Miłosz. In 1952, he wrote to the poet (who had just decided to emigrate, yet whose letters were full of critical comments on the subject of Poles in foreign parts): *Pan nie ma racji, że "literatura emigracji jest fikcją i właściwie publikować można tylko w obcych językach." Gdyby Pańską formułkę przyjął Norwid albo Cervantes siedzący w więzieniu. . . .Czytelnictwo jest rzeczą pierwszej wagi dla pisarza, a jednak są bodźce jeszcze istotniejsze* (You aren't right, that "émigré literature is a fiction and that one can only publish in foreign tongues." If your

formula had been accepted by Norwid or Cervantes sitting in prison. . . .
Readership is a thing of the first importance, and yet there are impulses even
more elemental than that).[42] And later,

> You write that the atmosphere's too close in emigration that writers have left
> for (Western) Europe only to return. Well, if they left for here, I suppose they
> were searching for something. And if it's no good either here or there, then it's
> better to sit here, where one can make one's living than there, where even life
> is blurred. If it came to that, I'd rather starve writing (even if it was only to be
> the writing of letters), than to starve without writing. [. . .] You write that in
> emigration you feel worse than you did under the German Occupation. How-
> ever, at least here one can work, even if with difficulty. The German Occupa-
> tion didn't enter into our inner world. Didn't you read your verses aloud in our
> own house during the occupation? I'm sure there aren't so many readings there
> these days. Is that because you're free to write all you want? Or is it maybe
> because the "petrification" that Toynbee speaks about has set in?[43]

Three years later, the writer changed his mind. One can follow the matura-
tion of this idea (of his eventual decision to return home) in his private
correspondence with his wife in 1955, from the period of his second—after
five years—reading tour of the Polish settlements in Canada. This he undertook in order to gather material for his next book (the first, *Tworzywo* [*Matter*], entitled in English *Three Generations,* translated by Krystyna Cękalska,
with a preface by Benedykt Heydenkorn was published in New York in
1954) concerning the Polish emigration. In these letters one may find a
number of hints that witness to his developing thought of return. The situation he found in Canada this time was different from that he experienced
before. He did not meet with much resonance, nor even interest concerning
his plans. He wrote to his wife: *Jeszcze nie wiem, czy będę kontynuował
podróż. Sądzę, że jednakże będę pchał póki się da. Atmosfera jednak, która
mnie spotyka, jest nie tyle atmosfera hołdu, ile zniecierpliwienia natręctwem.
[. . .] Sądziłem, że po pięciu latach będzie lepiej: ludzie poczują się pewniej,
poczną wracać do spraw kultury. Jest jednak inaczej* (I still don't know if
I'm going to continue the journey. I think that I'll push on as long as I'm
able. But the atmosphere that meets me is not an atmosphere of homage, but
rather of impatience at my intrusion. [. . .] I had thought that, after five years
it would be better: that people would feel more certain, and would begin to
return to cultural matters. However, the opposite is true).[44] In his letter from
23 March 1955, he writes with directness: *Pamiętaj, że jeśli się nie
wydźwigniemy tu, to jedyna możność życia aktywnego pozostaje w kraju*
(Remember, if we're not able to pull ourselves up here, then the only possibility for active life remains at home).

The above-cited letter is also interesting on account of how Wańkowicz
formulates his questions about the sense of life, meditates on his own writ-

ing, on the generic burden of what he does. So much the more, because during his stay beyond the borders of Poland, although he authored several books, he was not petted by reviewers and did not obtain any of the many and various prizes that others received. This is a noteworthy point. Neither in pre-war Poland, as the author of the important book *Na tropach Smętka*, nor in emigration, where he brought out *Bitwa o Monte Cassino*, nor yet after his return to Poland, did he receive any prize in recognition of his work. In time he came to speak of this as a fact that he valued. He was a writer who aroused unrest and evoked polemics, and could not be fit into any pigeonhole.

His seventeen-year-long sojourn outside of Poland came to an end in the fall of 1956, when he returned to Poland for a few weeks, to Poland, which had just undergone its post-October ferment. Then, for a year, along with his wife, he visited (still by automobile) the United States (collecting material for his cycle of reportages *W ślady Kolumba*). He spent four months in California, at the headquarters of the Hartford Foundation, an organization serving artists.

On 27 May 1958, Wańkowicz returned to Poland for good. Concerning his return he said, *Przeszedłszy przez pęknięcie ziemi czuję, że przyszedłem tutaj swój, że trafiłem na ludzi i ludzie ci dużo mi dają. Nie mogę znaleźć innego słowa jak to, że jestem upojony każdym dniem w Polsce* (Slipping through a crack in the earth, I feel that I have arrived here as one who belongs, that I have contacted with people and that these people give me so much. I can't find other words for it than these, that each day I spend in Poland inebriates me).[45]

One must keep in mind that, in returning to Poland, the writer had to agree to certain compromises with censorship. As an American citizen (since 1956), he consciously took part in the literature of his homeland at just such a price. First of all, he agreed to a censored version of *Bitwa o Monte Cassino*. The deletions, to which he agreed, evoked an expected storm among the Polish emigration in London and elsewhere. A special committee was set up, which was to judge the new edition (the judgment, it turns out, was positive)—after which the writer was castigated in the Polonian press,[46] which tossed his compromise in his face as treason.

At the same time, the author, not seeing the possibility of the publication of his emigration books in Poland, gathered only those passages which could pass muster at the censor's office into other, new publications. And thus fragments of *Kundlizm* and *Klub trzeciego miejsca* were published in Poland in the collection *Przez cztery klimaty*, which constituted an omnibus of his entire life as a publicist. In the volume of his selected reportages entitled *Od Stołpców po Kair* (*From Stołpce to Cairo*), the author placed fragments of his *Drogą do Urzędowa*. Thus, the author's unique *modus operandi* in Poland was born: if an entire book can't be published, at least a fragment can come out somehow.

Wańkowicz took part in public life through his writings, especially through his public readings, that won him a great popularity. His lectures in the Sala Kongresowa of the Palace of Culture in Warsaw drew such a large crowd that room was lacking. And so—as one might state it without exaggeration—the most popular writer in the country came out clearly against the ruling regime when he affixed his signature to the so-called Letter 34, after which he was forbidden the right of printing his works in Poland.

An essential event in the life of the then seventy-two-year-old writer was his trial in 1964. It gave Wańkowicz the occasion to present his perspective on the realities of the Polish state. On 5 October 1964, he was imprisoned to be tried. The background of the trial was the tense situation in the relationship between the regime and the cultural elite in the last period of the rule of Władysław Gomułka. The importance accorded the letter of thirty-four writers and scholars (February 1964) by the West, who were protesting against the restrictions placed upon scholarship and culture in Poland, as well as the publication of their repression on this account through the press, caught the regime off guard and forced it to change its tactics. The signing of Letter 34 by this unusually popular writer had a strong echo in Polish society and increased the resonance of the protest.[47] Robert Kennedy, the senator from New York and former U.S. attorney general, published a special declaration concerning the Wańkowicz Affair. He also had a conversation with Edward Drożniak, the ambassador of the Polish People's Republic in Washington. Both the American and the Norwegian Pen Clubs sent letters of protest. Wańkowicz's trial was the most celebrated political trial of the 1960s.[48]

CONCLUDING REMARKS

How long does a writer's popularity last after his death, especially in the case of a writer who drew crowds because of his extraordinary personality? Wańkowicz is the author of many books, several of them quite splendid, and they should certainly stand the test of time. During his life, he evoked great interest and emotions, and, not infrequently, controversy. Such controversies remain until today, and can especially be seen in certain circles far from Poland. I had the occasion to meet with this phenomenon during readings and author's evenings among American Polonia. The so-called wartime emigration does not pull punches in its criticism. They continue to bear a grudge against Wańkowicz for his allowing the censor to excise portions of *Monte Cassino*. Above all, this concerns the first chapters, which deal with the formation of the Second Corps. The book *Monte Cassino*, as published in abbreviated editions up until the 1980s, begins with the battle itself. The untrue assertion given in a posthumous article by Tadeusz Katelbach in *Kultura*, suggesting that Wańkowicz crossed out the name of General Anders in

Polish editions of the book, has never been corrected, despite the letter written to the editors of *Kultura* by the writer's daughter, and despite the ease of verification. A sort of stubborn bindweed has attached itself to Wańkowicz's name in this regard and has not been rooted out even today. And yet the name of General Anders *did remain* in all editions of *Monte Cassino*, even though other deletions were indeed made. The later emigration, however, made up today of people in their forties and fifties, has stressed that it was thanks to this very book that knowledge of the legendary battle has been handed down. What sort of role would this book play today, if it were published for the first time in Poland? How many readers would it have reached?

It is good that Wańkowicz returned to Poland. If he had remained in emigration, he would have died a bitter man, in poverty, and quarreling with the Polonian establishment. I myself, while harboring deep, due respect for the perspective of the political émigrés, cannot judge with the same yardstick the people of culture who returned to Poland after the war. One must judge their perspective in Poland, and their achievements. I know that there has existed a certain codex of émigré behavior, which was formulated by Juliusz Mieroszewski at one time on the pages of *Kultura* and clearly separated the political emigration from Polonia per se. Demanded of political émigrés was that they not accept the citizenship of their new country (while rank-and-file Polonia was "allowed" to do so). The political activist, the publicist, and the writer should be distrustful vis-à-vis the endeavors and advances of the PRL (People's Republic of Poland) regime. According to this perspective, people who belong to the elite of the political, scholarly, or artistic emigration should not visit Poland, whereas such visits by "Polonia" were accepted without hesitation. According to Grażyna Pomian, the returns of both Cat Mackiewicz and Wańkowicz were, so to speak, successes for the Communist régime.[49]

Both during his life and after his death, Melchior Wańkowicz awoke emotions, often controversies, with his exceptional personality. Some harbored a grievance against the writer for his decision to return to Poland. Even now you can sometimes hear the accusation that Wańkowicz returned "not to Poland, but to the People's Republic." I will always stress that he returned to his homeland, to his readers, and to his Poland. He didn't allow himself to be entrapped into any action or game. Wańkowicz was sued and had a political trial, which became the most famous political trial of the 1960s. After that the writer was deemed a hero by the generation of my parents: he embodied moral courage, independence of opinion, and obviously great talent and the art of the word.

I wonder, if the writer had remained in emigration, to what extent his *Monte Cassino, Ziele na kraterze, Hubalczycy, Westerplatte,* and *Tworzywo,* like the other titles, would be well known. Would they have had their place in the libraries of Polish homes? How valuable and large a role these books played in the formation of the consciousness of many generations is difficult to measure, but incontestable. Would these books, published earlier in small editions by émigré houses, have made it into the hands of readers in Poland? How many people, how many libraries, possess the first, émigré editions of the above-mentioned books? To what extent may one take seriously the currently popular, public demonstrations of people, who state that they grew up on books published beyond the borders of Poland? Only the intellectual elite had access to, and interest in, certain titles, published after all in tiny numbers. Miłosz, when he was awarded his Nobel Prize, was not widely known even among students studying the humanities at universities in Poland. When queues formed in Warsaw late in the night before bookstores opened, in order to buy his books, for most standing therein this was their first contact with his name. I don't dare to estimate how well he would be known today, had the Nobel not swept people toward the bookstores.

Thus, I wonder what would have happened with the books of Melchior Wańkowicz, had he remained and died in emigration. A popular writer before the war, known as the author of *Szczenięce lata* and *Na tropach Smętka*, might have awaited a renaissance. *Monte Cassino* would have appeared in small editions, along with *Ziele na kraterze* and *Tworzywo*, and these would perhaps have elicited a few reviews and articles reminding their readers by the way of his pre-war titles as well.

Meanwhile, his presence in Poland from 1958 to 1974 played a hugely positive role. After his political trial in 1964, the generation of my parents held him in honor as a hero. For everyone, he was the incarnation of civil courage, independent judgment, and of course great literary talent, the artism of the word. I found a similar summing-up in *Kultura*,[50] where Bogusław Włodawiec noted:

> Against the background of the literary circles in Poland and beyond its borders he was conspicuous by the independence of his judgments, his style of writing, and his political vision. [. . .] He was able to make contact with simple people, informing them of quite sophisticated content. As it seems, this is not a universal ability among Polish authors. Unfortunately, his works, in which he developed his political visions, were not published in Poland. If, however, he had lived longer, or had Solidarity arisen some ten years earlier, Wańkowicz would have had a great chance to become one of the spiritual fathers of the Polish revolution, and its symbol; Polish literature on the other hand would have been much richer for a reportage of the August strikes, written by the master of this literary type.

Figure 1.1.   Wańkowicz as a student.

Figure 1.2.   Wańkowicz with his Leica.

NOTES

1. Published in: "The Polish Review," vol. 48, no. 2, 2003: 131–40; "The Polish Review," vol. 48, no. 3, 2003: 253–75.

2. Melchior Wańkowicz, *Karafka La Fontaine'a* (Kraków: Wydawnictwo Literackie, 1983), I:258.

3. Wańkowicz, *Przez cztery klimaty* (Warsaw: Państwowy Instytut Wydawniczy, 1973), 133.

4. See S. Czosnykowski, in *Pion*, 6 October 1936.

5. Julian Kaden Bandrowski, *Gazeta Polska* no. 38, 1938.

6. Wańkowicz, *Od Stotpców po Kair* (Warsaw: Państwowy Instytut Naukowy, 1971), 17.

7. Wańkowicz, *Od Stotpców po Kair*, 7.

8. See, for example, Sienkiewicz's short stories *Za chlebem* and *Latarnik*, Konopnicka's verse novel *Pan Balcer w Brazylii*, and Jan Witkor's *Wierzby nad Sekwaną* and *Na paryskim bruku*.

9. Vide Krzysztof Kąkolewski, *Wańkowicz krzepi—wywiad rzeka* (Warsaw: Czytelnik, 1977).

10. See, for example, his *The Artillery of the Press* (New York: Harper & Row, 1967); *Prelude to Victory* (New York: Knopf, 1942); *Sketches on the Sand* (New York: Knopf, 1967).

11. Jerry Allen is the author of *The Thunder and the Sunshine: A Biography of Joseph Conrad* (New York: Putnam, 1958). Andrzej Braun has been publishing Conrad criticism for some twenty years. Most recently, he has brought out *Szkoła Conrada* (Warsaw: Abakart, 1995). Among Zdzisław Najder's works, most apposite are perhaps *Conrad under Familiar Eyes* (Cambridge: Cambridge University Press, 1983) and *Życie Conrada Korzeniowskiego* (1980). See also Norman Sherry's *Conrad's Western World* (Cambridge: Cambridge University Press, 1971).

12. Wańkowicz, *Od Stołpców po Kair,* p. 17.

13. Egon Erwin Kisch was a Czech journalist and publicist creative in German. Oviechkin's work is cited by Wańkowicz in *Od Stołpców po Kair.*

14. In 1959, the readers of the *Życie Warszawy* newspaper recognized it as the best publication dedicated to the Warsaw Uprising.

15. It was finally published, along with *Panny z Wilka*, in a volume of that same title by Gebethner and Wolff in 1933.

16. ONR—Obóz Narodowy Radykalny (the "National Radical Camp"), a right-wing organization.

17. See M. Wańkowicz, "Wspomnienia wydawcy" in *Za i przeciw* no. 5, November 1968.

18. Hanna Kister, *Pegazy na Kredytowej* (Warsaw: Państwowy Instytut Wydawniczy, 1980).

19. Melchior Wańkowicz, "Pisarstwo" ("Writing"), *Kultura (Culture)* no. 32, 1969.

20. Andrzej Micewski, *Życie Warszawy (Warsaw Life)*, 23/25 August 1969.

21. A clipping from the writer's archives, with incomplete bibliographical information.

22. Edward Kostka, *Głos Polski (The Polish Voice)*, Jerusalem, no. 15, 1943. As is the case with many of these citations, I am quoting clippings from the author's archives. As such, the bibliographical information for many is unrecorded or incomplete.

23. A citation from the Polish translation of the article published in *Hemashkit*, 22 October 1943. Both the translation and the original are in the writer's archives.

24. In Polish, Wydawnictwo Oddziału Kultury i Prasy II Polskiego Korpusu.

25. Melchior Wańkowicz, *Bitwa o Monte Cassino (The Battle of Monte Cassino)* (Rome: Wydawnictwo Oddziału Kultury i Prasy Drugiego Polskiego Korpusu, 1945–1947), vol. 1, p. 289.

26. See Bohdan Czeszko, *Przegląd Kulturalny (The Cultural Review)*, 27 October 1957, who writes: *Uchylam kapelusza przed wynikiem pracy prowadzonej w najtrudniejszych do pomyślenia warunkach* (I tip my hat in praise of the results of work undertaken in the most difficult conditions imaginable). Olgierd Terlecki, *Kultura*, 13 October 1968 writes: "Wańkowicz's work constitutes a unique position in Polish military literature. It is colorful, passionately and sensitively written, anything but banal stylistically, and at the same time particular, containing a rich analytical and even critical material base. No other of the belligerents in this war can boast such a panorama of battle. The Battle of Monte Cassino has become the first monument that Polish literature has erected to the efforts of her soldiers."

27. See Jan Hubert, *Polityka (Politics)*, 2 January 1967 who writes among others: "The legend of the battle of Monte Cassino is a harmful legend, like every legend of all bloody hecatombs, on which whole generations are raised. [. . .] The book has no psychological finesse; it has only and exclusively the pathos of heroism, the pathos of the victim."

28. See, for example, *Golgotha Road* (New York: Knapp, 1945).

29. Jan Olechowski, *Dziennik żołnierza (Soldier's Daily)*, Italy, 20 May 1945.

30. Melchior Wańkowicz, *Autożyciorys (Autobiographical Sketch)*, from the writer's archives.

31. *Parada (Parade)*, Rome, 1 December 1946.

32. Tadeusz Nowakowski, "Na tropach kundla" ("On the Mongrel's Trail"), "Orzeł Biały" ("The White Eagle"), London, 26 June 1948.

33. Jerzy Giedroyc, letter to M. Wańkowicz, 9 November 1951.

34. Melchior Wańkowicz, letter to the editors of the *Orzeł Biały*, London, 26 June 1948.

35. Juliusz Mieroszewski, in *Jerzy Giedroyc—Melchior Wańkowicz. Listy 1945–1963 (Jerzy Giedroyc—Melchior Wańkowicz. Letters 1945–1963)* ed. and note Aleksandra Ziółkowska-Boehm (Warsaw: Czytelnik, 2000), p. 183.

36. In Polish, Zjazd Pisarzy Polskich na emigracji.

37. Melchior Wańkowicz, "Sprawa wydania książek w kraju" ("The Matter of Publishing Books in Poland"), *Kultura*, Paris, 1956 4/102, p. 159.

38. Wańkowicz, *Klub trzeciego miejsca (Third Place Club)* (Warsaw: Wydawnictwo Polonia, 1991), 15–16.

39. Jedrzej Giertych (1903–1992)—political activist and author of several books. Marian Rojek (1905–1968)—journalist and publicist.

40. Jerzy Giedroyc, letter to Wańkowicz, 28 November 1951. See *Jerzy Giedroyc—Melchior Wańkowicz. Listy,* p. 235.

41. Maria Dąbrowska, *Dzienniki (Journals)*, ed. and adnot. Tadeusz Drewnowski (Warsaw: Czytelnik, 1988), vol. 4, 291.

42. Melchior Wańkowicz, letter to Czesław Miłosz, 18 January 1952, in *Twórczość*, 1981/10.

43. Wańkowicz to Miłosz, 5 February 1952.

44. Melchior to Zofia Wańkowicz, 3 March 1955.

45. A. Wróblewski, "Spotkanie z Wańkowiczem" ("A Meeting with Wańkowicz") *Prasa Polska (Polish Press)*, 1959/5, p. 18.

46. Press published in Polish outside of Poland

47. "Letter 34" was written about in *Time*, the *New York Times*, the *Washington Post*, the *Washington Evening Star*, and the *Christian Science Monitor* in America; in France: *Le Monde*, *Combat*; in Great Britain, the *Times*, the *Guardian*; in Italy, *Avanti*, *Il Quotidiano*, *Il Messaggero*; in Switzerland, *Neue Zürcher Zeitung*; in West Germany, *Frankfurter Allgemeine Zeitung*, *Frankfurter Rundschau*; in Denmark, *Politiken*, *Berlingske Tidente*; in Sweden: *Handelstidning Justitia*. Wańkowicz's trial was described in magazines with circulations in the millions, such as *Time* and *Die Zeit*, among many others.

The next chapter is dedicated to the 1964 Wańkowicz Trial.

48. For more information, see Aleksandra Ziółkowska-Boehm, *Proces Melchiora Wańkowicza, 1964 roku* (Warsaw: Nowe Wydawnictwo Polskie, 1990).

49. See Grażyna Pomian, *Kultura i jej krąg (Culture and Its Milieu)* (Lublin, 1995).

50. Bogusław Włodawiec, "Melchior Wańkowicz," *Kultura*, Paris, 1995/1–2 str. 178–85.

Chapter Two

The Trial of Melchior Wańkowicz

1964

PART A: "LETTER 34"

In 1964, the trial of Melchior Wańkowicz was one of the most sensational court cases in Poland of the 1960s.

The "Wańkowicz case" played out against a background of inflamed relations between the authorities and people of culture in the last period of Władysław Gomułka's[1] rule. At the Twelfth Plenary Session of KC PZPR[2]—the Central Committee of the Party (15–18 October 1958), Gomułka called for a general attack on the artistic intelligentsia. The intelligentsia was supposed to return to being an agent between the party and the masses, as it used to be in the years of Joseph Stalin's rule. Putrament asked, "How do we make press and literature fight for the party's line again?"[3]

The recipe seemed plain and simple. "We need to identify a few writers," Professor Adam Schaff recommended, "designate people [. . .] of unstable balance and [. . .] push them in the right direction."[4]

Gomułka claimed that writers had to face a choice: either to "break their pens, leave, and seek a new job for themselves" or convert to the party's positions. "Comrades," said the first secretary, "we need to use all those possibilities to attract all valuable writing people [. . .] bind them to the line of our party."

The new methods favored self-censorship. The "culture spreading" policy allowed decisions from the censorship office on Mysia Street to shift onto directors of publishing houses, and also onto the authors themselves. During the next few years, the feelings of dissatisfaction grew. The attitude of Władysław Gomułka toward national culture was shown by the limited paper allotment for publishing houses and weeklies. In 1960, two papers were closed: *Przegląd Kulturalny* (*Cultural Review*) and *Nowa Kultura* (*New Culture*) (they were replaced by the weekly *Kultura* [*Culture*]). In July 1963, the Thirteenth Plenary Session of KC PZPR adopted the motto of an ideological fight against the "imperialist propaganda coming to Poland on the waves of Radio Free Europe."

The general meeting of the Polish Writers'Association (ZLP) planned for 1963 was to be combined with the twentieth anniversary of the People's Republic on 17–18 January 1964. Instead, the main board of the association called an extended plenary session, where the agenda's main item was the paper by Professor Jan Zygmunt Jakubowski on post-war literature. The session became an occasion for harsh criticism by the writers. The criticism concerned the decrease in the production of literature. Antoni Słonimski stated that for the first time, book production in Poland had fallen to last place in the socialist bloc and resulted in the closing of two papers. *Nowa Kultura* and *Przegląd Kulturalny* became victims of modern literature's trouble with censorship. Beside Słonimski, the other writers and academics included Stanisław "Cat" Mackiewicz, Paweł Jasienica, Stefan Kisielewski, Paweł Hertz, Melchior Wańkowicz, and Mieczysław Jastrun. The charges were answered by Jarosław Iwaszkiewicz, Jerzy Putrament, Tadeusz Hołuj, Helena Zatorska, and others.

In the months following, the attitude of the authorities toward culture exacerbated the tension. Among other things, two scripts of Andrzej Wajda were not allowed to be filmed. Even the president of ZLP, J. Iwaszkiewicz, complained that he had been unable to gain an audience with the prime minister for the last year, nor with Kliszko[5] for the last five years.

In early March 1964, at the initiative of Antoni Słonimski, writers and academics decided to write a letter to the prime minister, Józef Cyrankiewicz, of the following content:

> Limiting the amount of paper allotted for printing books and papers, and tightening censorship give rise to a situation which threatens the development of national culture. Considering the existence of public opinion, the right to criticism, free discussion, and reliable information to be necessary elements of progress, and driven by civic concern, the undersigned demand the cultural policy to be changed in the spirit warranted by the State Constitution and in accordance with the nation's best interest.

Jan Józef Lipski[6] took it upon himself to collect signatures. On 14 March 1965, Słonimski submitted the letter in the secretariat of Cyrankiewicz in the presidium of the Ministers' Council. The letter had been signed by thirty-four people. In alphabetic order, these were Jerzy Andrzejewski, Stanisław "Cat" Mackiewicz, Maria Dąbrowska, Stanisław Dygat, Karol Estreicher, Marian Falski, Aleksander Gieysztor, Konrad Górski, Paweł Hertz, Leopold Infeld,

Paweł Jasienica, Mieczysław Jastrun, Stefan Kisielewski, Tadeusz Kotarbiński, Anna Kowalska, Zofia Kossak-Szczucka, Jan Kott, Kazimierz Kumaniecki, Julian Krzyżanowski, Edward Lipiński, Maria Ossowska, Jan Parandowski, Stanisław Pigoń, Adolf Rudnicki, Artur Sandauer, Wacław Sierpiński, Antoni Słonimski, Jan Szczepański, Władysław Tatarkiewicz, Jerzy Turowicz, Melchior Wańkowicz, Adam Ważyk, Kazimierz Wyka, and Jerzy Zagórski.

In Maria Dąbrowska's[7] *Journals,* I found the following fragments concerning the collection of the signatures:

Warsaw. 15 III [March] 1964. Sunday.

Young Lipski (the one from the "Krzywe Koło" ["Crooked Circle"] discussion club) brought a short text requesting the Government to extend the freedom of speech secured in the Constitution. There were many signatures already there of academics and writers of very famous names. I am not keen on such "petitions," because they bring no results, but I constantly refuse everything and always in the end something happens that I cannot refuse simply by the rule of the law of numbers or probability. Thus, I decided to sign it in the order my name came, without discussion. Lipski said: "I wanted to ask you— to sign here under Prof. Infeld where a space was left—maybe you could sign here to fill in the space."

(Infeld's signature was first.) I signed without thinking. Mindlessness is my biggest fault. Because that was a very naive maneuver to get my signature in a "prominent" position. I should have said: "No, Mr. Lipski, it's a bad move. The addressees will immediately think that the others signed the letter on seeing my signature." And it was quite the opposite. I signed on seeing so many signatures.[8]

On 23 March, the Security Service detained the former secretary of the "Krzywe Koło" Club—Jan Józef Lipski—on the charge of collecting signatures. Słonimski, Kisielewski, and Ossowska immediately intervened, asking about the reasons for detention. In the end, within twenty-four hours Lipski was released. Dąbrowska wrote:

27 III [March] 1964. Friday.

[. . .] In connection with submitting that modest petition for increasing paper allotment, Lipski—who collected the signatures—was arrested. Słonimski not only submitted the petition personally in the presidium of the Council of Ministers, giving his address, but when Lipski was arrested, he immediately organized a delegation consisting of himself, Ossowska, and Kisielewski. They went to the prosecutor of the city of Warsaw and stood up for Lipski (and Słonimski again took the responsibility), so that in twenty-four hours he was released—and the presidium sneeringly noted he had been "detained" in a different case.

"Letter 34" (titled from the number of its signatories) was broadcast in Radio Free Europe. The whole Western press also commented and debated the event. The Polish authorities reacted quite quickly and harshly. Many of the signatories (eleven, to be exact) were forbidden (for an indefinite time) to appear on radio or television, or publish anything in the press. Passports were withdrawn. Certain people were particularly persecuted. Among others, the interview with Professor Sierpiński was withdrawn from publishing, the announcement of Andrzejewski's lecture was called off, Kott's article was withdrawn from *Twórczość*,[9] Słonimski's articles from *Szpilki*,[10] also Cat Mackiewicz's features from *Słowo Powszechne*.[11] Wańkowicz's cycle on Kennedy in *Kierunki*[12] was stopped. Cat Mackiewicz's and Wańkowicz's books were withdrawn from sale. Printing of the Polish volume of Estreicher's bibliography was stopped. Kott and Kisielewski were denied passports. For the signature of Turowicz, the circulation of *Tygodnik Powszechny*[13] was cut from forty thousand to thirty thousand.

At the same time, *Życie Warszawy*[14] published an article by Maria Dąbrowska submitted much earlier by the author. Dąbrowska, who was not among those persecuted, sent the author's fee back in a gesture of solidarity with her protesting colleagues. She wrote in her *Journals*:

27 IV [April] 1964. Monday.

[. . .] I received a letter from Korotyński. [. . .] At the end of the letter, he thanks me once again for the article and asks to remember him in writing, meaning more articles. I answered with a letter, and put a copy of it in my file with copies of letters important at that time. In short, I announced in the most courteous manner that as long as the writers who had signed the letter to the Prime Minister were discriminated against, neither did I feel entitled to publish anything and receive any author's fees, and thus I asked not to be paid the fee for the article *Nie to i nie tak* [*Not This and Not Like That*].

Next day, he called me saying he was very troubled by my letter, and could he come the next morning. [. . .] He sat here until one o'clock. The conversation was lively and with appearances of honesty, though who knows what the man might have been hiding. My "thesis" was that the foreign publicity in the press and the radio was the fault of the bodies immediately replying to the letter to the Prime Minister that started the repressions. In my opinion, the press should have given a notice about "Letter 34" and opened a public discussion about it. Then, the foreign press or Radio Free Europe could only reprint or transmit domestic messages. I said that the repressions were more harmful for the state interest, as they blew the matter up to undue proportions. He seemed to agree with me that the means used were not quite thought out, but he tried to downplay the repressions. Actually there were none, just a recommendation by the Prime Minister not to contact such and such writers for a time "until the matter was cleared." As a matter of fact, he later came to show me the letters that most academics and one writer—Jan Parandowski, of course—had written to the Prime Minister, bemoaning the publicity of the matter abroad that was caused "nobody knows how." [. . .]

And the thing is the West likes sensations about the East, just as the East likes the ones about the West. Isn't it so that here any news unfavorable for the European or American West is immediately blown up by the radio, TV, and the press to extreme proportions?

How the news about "Letter 34" reached Radio Free Europe, we can learn from the book of the then director of its Polish section, Jan Nowak-Jeziorański, *Polska z oddali* (*Poland from Afar*) (London, 1988). According to what he wrote, the first news came to London to the Radio Free Europe (RFE) correspondent in London, Zbigniew Racięski. On 26 March, a woman returning from Warsaw gave him a letter from Melchior Wańkowicz, right there at the airport, in which the events were described in detail. Names of the signatories were given. Jan Nowak writes that he asked Reuters and UPI to check the news (mainly to avoid the appearances that the letter's authors worked together with Radio Free Europe). The agencies confirmed the information and then RFE broadcast the text of the letter and names of the writers and academics who had signed it. Further news on the topic came from Cat Mackiewicz, who sent the full text of the letter. At the same time, both the letter and the whole issue around it spread worldwide, thanks to Reuters and UPI. Western press was buzzing, protest letters of writers were published, Polish culture's situation was discussed and compared to the situations in other countries of the Soviet Bloc. Polish authorities were determined to hush up the whole issue. The main emphasis, that is, drainage of Polish culture was blamed on the alleged cooperation of the instigators with Radio Free Europe. In answer to *Time*'s correspondence from Warsaw and a statement of twenty-one British intellectuals, the Polish authorities demanded that Polish writers sign a letter to *Time* that was aimed at ending the protests in the West. The letter was published in *Time* on 28 April 1964, with ten signatures. It said among other things:

> We regret that the issue gave an occasion to organize a campaign against our country, based on false information published particularly in the West German press and broadcast by Radio Free Europe. We state that it is not known to us that any of the people who have signed the letter to the Prime Minister be currently deprived of the right to hold lectures or publish their books.

The letter was signed by the following professors: Aleksander Gieysztor, Konrad Górski, Leopold Infeld, Kazimierz Kumaniecki, Julian Krzyżanowski, Edward Lipiński, Wacław Sierpiński, Jan Szczepański, Władysław Tatarkiewicz, and Kazimierz Wyka.

From the thirty-four signatories of "Letter 34," Professor Konrad Górski withdrew his signature, and wrote a letter to Prime Minister Cyrankiewicz, where he put the blame for involving him in the case on Jerzy Turowicz. His letter was read out by Kliszko at the meeting of the Writers' Association.

After some time it seemed the matter had died down—repressions were canceled, and the name of Kisielewski and others began to reappear in the press. Yet Wańkowicz and Słonimski were still blacklisted. Soon it turned out that the authorities hadn't forgotten the case. On 4 May 1964, Władysław Gomułka met a delegation of the Polish Writers' Association led by Jarosław Iwaszkiewicz. A result of that meeting was the party's protest to show that the group who had signed "Letter 34" was isolated and the community was not identifying with it. After gathering the first signatures, among others those of Auderska, Bratny, Bartelski, K. Koźniewski, Przyboś, and Żukrowski, the Basic Party Organization (POP PZPR)[15] of writers issued an appeal to ZLP. The appeal asked members to sign a statement protesting against the "organized campaign slandering the People's Republic of Poland that is run in the Western press and in the sabotage radio station Free Europe."

The statement had the following content:

Dear Colleagues!

In Radio Free Europe, in Western European press, and recently also in the United States, a malicious propaganda campaign has been unleashed against the People's Republic of Poland. The pretext for the campaign were the circumstances related to a letter to the prime minister of the Republic which was sent by thirty-four academics and writers. In reply to that foreign political campaign, about 150 Polish writers from Warsaw, Kraków, Katowice, Poznań, Szczecin, Lublin, Bydgoszcz, and other units of ZLP decided to sign a statement which is also an act of our political demonstration.

The executive of the Party Organization in the Warsaw Unit of ZLP hereby makes an ardent appeal to all our colleagues and comrades, party and nonparty writers, including also the authors of the letter to the Prime Minister, that they kindly support with their voluntary signature the stand taken in that statement. We are convinced that the mass character of our demonstration will be the right reply to the hostile propaganda. We have various views, different opinions on the issues of our community and on the issues of culture and art—but we all have one thing in common: we do not wish our internal problems and concerns to be an excuse for harmful attacks on Poland.

Here is the text of the said statement:

We, the undersigned Polish writers, express our decisive protest against the organized campaign slandering the People's Republic of Poland which is run in the Western press and in the sabotage radio station Free Europe. We object to any foreign interference in our internal issues, in our cultural policy, which is a common concern of the creative intelligentsia and the political and state authorities of the country. Please notify us of your decision in the shortest possible time with an express letter or a telegram to the secretariat of ZLP

Main Board (Warsaw, 87/89 Krakowskie Przedmieście Street) or sign your name personally on the list kept in the secretariat of ZLP Main Board.

The executive of the PZPR Party Organization in the Warsaw Unit of ZLP, Warsaw, 9 May 1964.

The text of the "protest," signed by over 150 writers, was published in *Życie Warszawy* (no. 113, 1964). Further lists of signatures (over six hundred in total) were published in the press.

The statement was signed among others by the following people: from Warsaw, H. Auderska, A. Braun, J. Brzechwa, A. Bocheński, R. Bratny, A. Bukowska, L. Bartelski, Cz. Centkiewicz, A. Centkiewiczowa, W. Dąbrowski, S. R. Dobrowolski, B. Drozdowski, S. Flukowski, J. Hen, K. Iłłakowiczówna, J. Iwaszkiewicz, J. Jurandot, E. Kabatc, K. Koźniewski, H. Lepecki, L. Lewin, A. Lisiecka, J. Lenart, T. Łopalewski, A. Maliszewski, A. Minkowski, I. Newerly, B. Nawrocka, A. Olcha, L. Pasternak, J. Przyboś, J. Putrament, J. Rogoziński, L. Rudnicki, M. Rusinek, W. Słobodnik, E. Szelburg-Zarembina, S. Szmaglewska, S. Wygodzki, W. Zalewski, St. Zieliński, W. Żółkiewska, S. Żółkiewski, and W. Żukrowski; from Kraków, J. Broszkiewicz, K. Filipowicz, J. Kawalec, T. Kwiatkowski, Wł. Machejek, W. Maciąg, J. Meissner, S. Otwinowski, J. Lowell, W. Szymborska, H. Vogler; from Katowice, T. Różewicz, A. Wydrzyński, W. Szewczyk; from Łódź, L. Gomolicki, St. Czernik, J. Koprowski, M. Piechal, Wł. Rymkiewicz; from Bydgoszcz, Wł. Dunarowski, A. Kowalkowski, Wł. Turwid; from Szczecin, I. G. Kamiński, M. Misiorny; from Poznań, T. Kraszewski, B. Kogut, J. Korczak; and from Lublin, M. Bechczyc-Rudnicka and K. Bielski.

Fifty-six Communist Party members did not sign the protest. The ones who refused their signatures included F. Bieńkowska, J. Bocheński, K. Brandys, M. Brandys, T. Konwicki, J. S. Lec, J. Pomianowski, J. Stryjkowski, A. Wirpsza, W. Woroszylski, and A. Wróblewski, as well as Catholic writers—J. Dobraczyński, W. Grabski, A. Gołubiew, J. Zawieyski, and others. It was said that many Communist Party members refused to sign the statement, saying that they had never listened to Radio Free Europe so it was difficult for them to protest against its program. The writer Adam Grzymała-Siedlecki supposedly said that he was deaf and wasn't even listening to Polish radio. The editorial team of the literary monthly *Twórczość* did not sign it, either, adopting a critical attitude toward the stand of the ZLP president and editor-in-chief of the monthly—Jarosław Iwaszkiewicz.

Dąbrowska wrote in her *Journals*:

14 V [May] 1964. Thursday.

A protest letter was announced against Free Europe. The executive of POP [Basic Party Organization] in ZLP invites us to read it beseechingly. It's a letter that—similarly to the letter of the professors to *Time*—will fuel the anti-Polish campaign anew.

"Letter 34" was the first important event—the first joint action of Polish intellectuals—and it started a new protest form. Jan Nowak in his memoirs *Polska z oddali* writes:

> Indeed the case of "Letter 34" was a crucial moment in the history of RFE. Intelligentsia found us to be a valuable ally. From that moment on, we didn't have to fish for news from Poland. We had news thanks to the help of the society itself. People came to us and to our correspondents constantly and on their own initiative. . . .
>
> Thus Wańkowicz was right as he wrote that "the clumsy actions of the authorities contributed to great popularization of Free Europe."

The case of Melchior Wańkowicz was a sequel to "Letter 34." The common opinion concluded that Wańkowicz was arrested on a clear order of Władysław Gomułka, but Zenon Kliszko played a great part in making that decision. Reportedly, the prosecutor's office had objections that the date of the process was set too early, and that the prosecution would not be sufficiently prepared. Yet there were some authorities guided by their own reasons, who demanded a quick trial. That version would indicate intrigues within the party.

Paul Wohl, a correspondent to the Boston *Christian Science Monitor* (December 1964) thus wrote about the case and its basis:

> It seems that the initiative "of the politically nonsensical" arrest of Wańkowicz was taken by police authorities behind the backs of Władysław Gomułka and his successor as the secretary of the Communist Party, Zenon Kliszko.
>
> That reappearance of the secret police as a deciding authority on the political scene is—in the opinion of the correspondent—the most alarming sign of the current reality in Poland. This seems to mean that the regime authorities have considered the "policy of moderation and common sense" applied so far to be insufficient against the increasing tension.

At the Seventh Meeting of Writers from Western and Northern Poland, Zenon Kliszko voiced a speech accusing "Letter 34" signatories of "devious intentions." He said:

> Those two or three organizers of the case of the letter did not wish to discuss those or other postulates. They wanted a demonstration into which they dragged several writers and academics, abusing their trust and goodwill. Those few instigators, guided by rather dubious intentions and unfulfilled ambitions, addressed the letter in fact not to the state authorities of our country, but to

foreign centers, finding their way to them earlier than to the official address-ee.[16]

In Dąbrowska's *Journals* we read:

9 V [May] 1964. Saturday.

> [. . .] In whose interest is this nasty inflaming of the case? All the time, the mysterious party bodies play a role here. Someone really wishes to cause discord among writers, to evoke chaos and confusion.

In the face of the approaching June meeting of the Polish Writers' Association, some of the "Letter 34" signatories were considering how to use it to defend their rights. Melchior Wańkowicz suggested that some writers prepare projects of their speeches, and the best would be chosen or they would be compiled. Before the meeting he visited—together with Antoni Słonimski and Paweł Jasienica—Maria Dąbrowska in Komorów. She noted:

2 III [March] 1964. Tuesday.

> [. . .] The gentlemen from "Letter 34" wish me to present the case at the meeting of the Warsaw Branch. The mere thought of that stupefied me and worsened my physical condition so that yesterday I took to bed for almost the whole day. I gathered the last reserves of my strength to order the materials concerning the case that has unnecessarily poisoned and paralyzed over two months of my time, has eaten up more health and life, of which I have so little left.

At the general meeting of the Warsaw Branch on 12 June 1964 (where delegates to the meeting in Lublin were elected), Maria Dąbrowska gave her speech. She took part in the discussion and presented—after Zenon Kliszko's public accusations—the case of "Letter 34" and the conflict around it. (It was the last public appearance of the writer in her life.) Dąbrowska presented the content, course, and behind-the-scenes of the whole case, protested against stigmatizing anonymous organizers of the letter ("if our authorities know it"—she said—"let them say openly and out loud who did it, and present the evidence"). She believed that the "Letter" had arisen from the plenary session of the Polish Writers' Association of 17–18 January 1964. In her view, it would have been possible to avoid the publicity in the West, had the matter been treated openly from the beginning. She expressed her hope that "we will end this Polish second difficult twenty-year period in a less quarrelsome manner," and asked to have the repressions and discrimination abolished. She also sustained most charges expressed in "Letter 34" as well as her signature. She criticized the interview given by the ZLP president, J. Iwaszkiewicz, in *Życie Warszawy* (no. 119, 1964), who "failed to use the chance to relieve the confusion arisen."

The meeting turned out stormy. The speakers included, among others, Cat Mackiewicz and J. Grzędziński. Jarosław Iwaszkiewicz accused Dąbrowska of not appreciating his services for the association. Jerzy Putrament spoke of the complicated situation of the authorities after October 1956. [17]

Dąbrowska's speech was received with great enthusiasm. It was considered to exude personal dignity and moral courage. The assembled company rewarded her with spontaneous applause (K. Koźniewski would tell me later, "I wasn't clapping!").

In her *Journals*, the writer recalled that day twice:

15 VI [June] 1964. Monday.
Only today I'm finishing the so-called "memories from the present."

So I read, trying to say it as if I were speaking, because I always know my texts almost by heart. At first I was sitting, but after a few sentences I noticed that it was more difficult to speak out when sitting, and my voice was failing me anyway. My God, where is my great voice, with which I could always speak effortlessly in the greatest, the least acoustic rooms.

As I was reading I thought of what to skip. [. . .] But the room, previously noisy and unruly, listened so quietly and without the least murmur that in some natural flow, so to say, I read almost everything, leaving out only one paragraph. I was interrupted a few times with applause, which somehow didn't please me. I rather felt embarrassed. When I finished—there was long, great applause. Later I learned that everyone present stood up, but I didn't notice, I wasn't feeling quite conscious, and I was already regretting that I'd had that speech at all, that I hadn't said more warm words, but only at the end, that I hadn't left out more. Then, to my ultimate horror, Mackiewicz took the floor. He had assured and promised me that he wouldn't speak. He praised me to the heavens; dear God, save us from "allies." I prefer opponents a thousand times. I forgot to add that Putrament spoke first, right after me. He spoke very well, loyal, couldn't find a fault with it. [. . .]

I should have actually gone out, when Mackiewicz started speaking, and he was interrupted with some very hostile exclamations. But I felt very faint, I was afraid my legs wouldn't carry me. [. . .] I must also add that Iwaszkiewicz got the same applause as I. [. . .]

Inside I feel terrible. Terribly disgusted with myself and everything I do, with that blasted Free Europe, with all my co-signatories, with life and with death. [. . .]

Clinic. 24 X [October] 1964 Friday.

[. . .] I return to the meeting of POP of 5 X [October]. Well, Kliszko spoke the most severely against Słonimski, and so everyone was afraid for him. But he also mentioned that Wańkowicz in response to my question of 12 IX [September] said: "If there are any charges, we ask you to provide names and facts." So he gave a fact: that an investigation had been started against Wańkowicz.

Reportedly it was about some memorandum, written by Mel,[18] which was to be read out by Andzia. But it was sent abroad. [. . .] Anyway, Mel had led us, and me in particular, up the garden path. I undertook presenting the case of "Letter 34" in the conviction that no one had sent anything abroad.

During Maria Dąbrowska's speech, Zenon Kliszko, who was present in the room, admitted that the authorities had made certain mistakes and not all responsibility for the existing tension fell on Polish intellectuals. But he stressed that on the other hand, based on the police report, "it is unacceptable" that documents not meant for print were "smuggled" abroad.

Wańkowicz was absent from the meeting. On the next day, the daily of the Polish Communist Party, *Trybuna Ludu*[19] informed its readers that he had been arrested. In the same daily, an article by Maria Dąbrowska was published in connection with her seventy-fifth birthday, as well as information about Zenon Kliszko participating in the writers' conference. Due to those contradictions, in analyzing the gist of the writers' dispute, rumors appeared that the political police on their own account ordered Wańkowicz arrested on the same day that Kliszko went to the writers' conference. At that time, the vice minister for domestic affairs was Mieczysław Moczar.

The Case of Wańkowicz

What was the post-war life of Melchior Wańkowicz? After the war, he first visited Poland in 1956. In 1958, he returned to Poland permanently. With an American citizenship (since 1956), he consciously joined in domestic literature production, paying for it with numerous compromises with the censors. He published many books, including emigration reprints (among others, *Monte Cassino, Ziele na kraterze*, and *Tworzywo*). His pre-war titles were missing, for example, *Strzępy epopei, Szpital w Cichiniczach, W kościołach Meksyku, Opierzona rewolucja*, and *Sztafeta*, as well as some of the books published while he was in exile, for example, *Drogą do Urzędowa, Kundlizm, Klub trzeciego miejsca, De profundis, Dzieje rodziny Korzeniewskich*, and *Wrzesień żagwiący*. From the latter, two texts were taken—*Westerplatte* and *Hubalczycy*—which were published in large numbers, but the full text of *Wrzesień żagwiący* was not published until 1990. Krzysztof Zajączkowski, author of a book on Major Słaby, a doctor from Westerplatte,[20] writes:

In the imperfect state that the People's Republic was, rationed disputes were conducted based on incomplete historical knowledge; inconvenient facts and names were forgotten. In this case, the debate was eradicated of anything that might be related to the "stab in the back" from the East, i.e., with the Soviet aggression on Poland on 17 September 1939. That was why *Wrzesień żagwiący* was not published as a whole.[21]

Wańkowicz took part in the public life with his literary work, most notably lectures, with which he gained much popularity. His talk in the Congress Hall in the Palace of Culture and Science gathered such a large overflowing audience that there weren't enough seats. Hence the most popular—and that is no overstatement—Polish writer of the time gained incredibly greater popularity by his open addresses against the authorities. When he signed the protest "Letter 34," he was banned from publishing anything in Poland.

What did the course of events directly related to the trial of Wańkowicz look like?

In the files of the Regional Court (Sign. IV k 151/64), I found documents dated before 5 October (when the writer was arrested) which may illustrate the rapid pace of preparations for the trial.

Warsaw, 28th September 1964
To the Minister of Domestic Affairs

REPORT

I report that while performing professional duties I have obtained unofficial, hard information that a document of several dozen pages, slandering social and political relations in Poland, entitled "Speech Project—J. A." was sent abroad. The said document was sent in June 1964 in a manner so far not established, by Melchior Wańkowicz, U.S. citizen, residing in Warsaw, to be used by Free Europe and other radio stations of the capitalist states. Enclosed is a photocopy of the said document.

Senior Inspector of the Ministry of Domestic Affairs
Maj. Tadeusz Cibor

3rd October 1964
Minister of Domestic Affairs
General Public Prosecutor of the People's Republic of Poland
Comrade Kazimierz Kosztirko

Enclosed I am sending a report of Senior Inspector of the Ministry, Maj. Tadeusz Cibor, of 28th September 1964, together with a copy of "Speech Project—J. A. (or a substratum for successive speeches of 4–5 speakers)" sent abroad by Melchior Wańkowicz, U.S. citizen, residing at Warsaw, 10 Puławska Street, flat No. 35, to be used against Poland by the station "Radio Free Europe." I am ordering an investigation in the case.

I enclose the following to be used as needed:

1. Fragment of a photocopy of the above-mentioned "Speech Project—J. A.,"
2. Note of 28th September 1964,
3. Monitoring reports of Radio Free Europe of 1 VII [July] and 14 VII [July] 1964,

4. Copy of the Free Europe monthly *Na antenie* [*On Air*] of 2 VIII [August] 1964.

Minister Władysław Wicha

In the files of IPN (Institute of National Remembrance)[22] there is a copy of the answer:

3rd October 1964

Director of III Department of Ministry of Domestic Affairs
Comrade Col. Stanisław Filipiak

In reply to the writing of 30 IX [September] 64 [. . .] after researching I inform that:

1. The typed document beginning with the words "Speech Project—J. A.," the photocopy of which (29 pages of photo paper in A-4 format) I present—was not typed on the typewriter from which typing specimen were sent as reference material.
2. The handwriting (in corrections and notes on particular pages of the photo-copy of "Speech Project—J. A."), except a few spelling corrections on page 23—belongs to the person who has filled in the questionnaires pre-sented for research as reference materials. The questionnaires were ad-dressed to the Regional Militia Chief in Warsaw, dated 27 VIII [August] 1956, 7 VII [July] 1958, 26 VIII [August] 1959, and filled in for the name of Melchior Wańkowicz (asking for a resident visa).
3. The writing in the corrections on page 23 of the said document cannot be identified.

Also, as requested, we are sending photocopies of selected fragments of the document—photocopy presented to us: Comparative research.

Head of the Criminology Dept. of the Citizens' Militia[23] Headquarters
Col. H. Zelszański, Ph.D. (*name illegible—AZB*)

Warsaw, 5th September 1964
General Public Prosecutor's Office
of the Department of Supervision
over Investigation and Inquiry
No. DSD, 086/64
To Citizens' Militia Headquarters
of the City of Warsaw

In connection with the commenced investigation I am ordering to have U.S. citizen Melchior Wańkowicz, born 10th January 1892, detained and brought to the General Public Prosecutor's Office in Warsaw, room 104.

Vice Director of 2nd Department
Edward Sanecki
Deputy General Public Prosecutor

On 5 October, Wańkowicz and his wife were coming back to Warsaw from Kraków by car. On the way he was stopped several times, supposedly to check documents. Right after they entered the flat at 10 Puławska Street, the bell at the door rang and officers of the Security Office appeared with a search and an arrest warrant. His papers were raked over carefully, some things were confiscated, among them his private notebook, his correspondence with his daughter—Marta Erdman, who lived in the United States— and his "Hermes" typewriter. Wańkowicz was arrested and brought to the General Public Prosecution building in 25 Krakowskie Przedmieście Street. He was then brought to the Mostowski Palace, where he was remanded in custody for five weeks until he was temporarily released after the verdict of the first instance that is. In IPN files[24] there is a report from the house search:

Memo
From the house search conducted on 5 X [October] 64 in the flat of M. Wańkowicz
Warsaw, 6th October 1964

The search lasted from 6:00 p.m. to 9:00 p.m. It was led by public prosecutor M. Rataj, who except for supervision took no direct part in searching for crime-related documents.

The other members of the searching group followed the public prosecutor's orders and searched through the desk and wardrobes. Wańkowicz behaved appropriately for all that time.

After 8:20 p.m. comrades Chlebicki and Rapała came with the order to bring M. Wańkowicz to the General Public Prosecutor's Office before 9:00 p.m. Public prosecutor Rataj told them the man would be brought there in 20 minutes, i.e., at 8:40 p.m.

The search had actually been completed when comrades Chlebicki and Rapała came, only writing the protocol remained. Because of Wańkowicz searching for a stamp to seal the case with the seized documents, and because of entering the garage to take the pistol left in the car, and then entering corrections in the protocol, all the procedures were not completed until 9:00 p.m.

After the writing of the protocol started, the public prosecutor decided not to take Wańkowicz to the General Public Prosecutor's Office and to finish writing the protocol in his absence. As the procedure extended in time, the public prosecutor was not able to bring Wańkowicz to the General Public Prosecutor's Office before 9:00 p.m.

Capt. H. Walczyński

On the same day—as I had written—an open meeting of the Basic Party Organization of the Warsaw branch of the Writers' Association took place, at which Zenon Kliszko was one of the speakers. He condemned the "Letter 34" signatories, but made no mention in public about Wańkowicz being arrested. It was said that the president of the Polish Writers' Association, Jarosław Iwaszkiewicz, had been informed about the operation of the Security Services, and allegedly intervened, though in vain, in Wańkowicz's defense. Other writers learned only later in town that the author of *Na tropach Smętka* had been arrested.[25]

Stefan Kisielewski recalls in his *Abecadło*[26] (1990) the day when

> late in the evening Mrs. Wańkowicz, the wife of Melchior Wańkowicz, came, saying they'd had their house searched, that her husband had been taken, and to notify the Association. She said: "Maybe call Iwaszkiewicz." I said: "No, no, I won't." "Then maybe Putrament." I said: "Alright." I found his number and called: "I wanted to tell you that Wańkowicz has been locked up." There was a long stretch of silence by the call's recipient; then he said: "Listen, I was having such a nice day, sunny, did some fishing, I was content, and you spoil it all with such news. What's going to happen if they start to hunt down such old bisons."

An official PAP (Polish Press Agency) note of 27 October 1964, reprinted in the daily press, said as follows:

> Trial against M. Wańkowicz.
>
> On the 26th of this month, a trial commenced before the Regional Court for the City of Warsaw against Melchior Wańkowicz, accused of sending abroad materials slandering the People's Republic of Poland for the purposes of publication.
>
> After the initial procedural matters and reading the bill of indictment, the court acceded to the defendant's request and motion by the defense and adjourned the trial until 3rd November this year.

Two days later, probably on the advice from defense lawyers, Zofia Wańkowicz submitted an application to the then minister of justice, Marian Rybicki, asking him to ensure good conditions of imprisonment for her husband.

7th October 1964
Zofia Wańkowicz
Warsaw
10 Puławska Street, flat No. 35

Ministry of Justice
Mr. Marian Rybicki

On 5th October 1964, the study of my husband, Melchior Wańkowicz, was searched, and my husband was taken to the General Public Prosecutor's Office in Warsaw.

Until now my husband has not returned, and I am deeply shaken with that fact. Taking into consideration his age (72)[27] and poor health, I am submitting an ardent request that you kindly ensure to my husband conditions that are suitable for his health and age, and provide medical care for him.

Zofia Wańkowicz

I found a separate letter by the deputy general public prosecutor, Edward Sanecki, concerning conditions that the writer was exposed to, written no doubt after some intervention from the authorities. In fact, as he told me years later, handling such issues was not his job.

7th October 1964
Headquarters of the Citizens' Militia
of the City of Warsaw

Enclosed I am sending a copy of the decision to remand Melchior Wańkowicz, son of Melchior Sr., in custody. The said man was handed a copy of that decision.

Please detain Melchior Wańkowicz in the Militia Headquarters not in the cells for the arrested, but in a separate, light room which would ensure maximally good living conditions.

Edward Sanecki
Vice Director of 2nd Department

The "maximally good living conditions" were a separate room on the ground floor of the Mostowski Palace, with a bed plus bedclothes and basic furniture. The windows were barred, the harsh light of a bare bulb glowed day and night, two police officers were on duty in the room at all times. Zofia Wańkowicz had to ask permission to give her husband a food parcel. In the court files there is her application of 21 October:

21st October 1964
Zofia Wańkowicz
Warsaw
10 Puławska Street, flat No. 35
To Regional Court for the City of Warsaw
4th Penal Department

I would like to request permission to hand over a food parcel for my husband, containing

1. one pack of "Nescafe" coffee
2. sugar
3. tea
4. some meat
5. fruit
6. a bar of chocolate

Zofia Wańkowicz

The public prosecutor had the then deputy public prosecutor of general prosecution, Stefan Dzikowski, go to the Mostowski Palace and see for himself in what conditions the defendant was staying.

"I went upstairs," he recalled years later, "had a look at the room. It was an office modified for living purposes, with a nightstand and a bed. The bed was wide, not such as you see in cells. The bedclothes were clean and quite nice. I came back and stated that I had no reservations to the place where Wańkowicz was staying."

As we talked further, he added: "Ma'am, the prosecutor [general public prosecutor—note by AZB] probably knew at that time that it was a mistake to conduct that trial, but I don't suppose he wanted it himself or that it was his decision."

On 17 October, the defense attorneys submitted a motion to revoke the remand, enclosing appropriate medical certificates and the justification that "Melchior Wańkowicz suffers from generalized atherosclerosis with particular involvement of the brain vessels and the central blood circulation system with secondary heart muscle degeneration during cardiac insufficiency," "chronic inflammation of the gallbladder and inflammation of the lymph vessels of both lower limbs with edema and pain." "Considering the advanced age of the defendant Melchior Wańkowicz (seventy-two) such illnesses may be dangerous for the defendant's life" (see court files).

The motion was turned down. Consent was granted, however—after two interventions—for the consul of the American embassy in Warsaw to visit Wańkowicz.

Warsaw, 16th October 1964
Consul
Walter B. Smith II

As the consul of the United States of America authorized by the Council of State of the People's Republic of Poland—I request permission to visit the American Citizen Melchior Wańkowicz.

Walter B. Smith

The visit was short. When asked by the consul whether he wished any help from the U.S. Embassy, Wańkowicz replied in the negative.

The trial started on 26 October—three weeks after charges were brought against Wańkowicz. Forty people were admitted to room 15 in the Regional Court in Warsaw, including the defendant's wife and sister-in-law and a few members of the Writers' Association. Representatives of foreign press and others were told that they could be admitted only with a "ticket," which could have been procured a week earlier. When the procedure was protested against with the chief judge, Henryk Kempisty, he replied briefly: "I do not have to give explanations." At first, the U.S. consul was not admitted, either. He had to intervene a second time to be allowed in.

News about what was happening in the courtroom spread throughout Poland. Foreign press wrote extensive articles on the trial—expressing esteem for the stand of Wańkowicz. Domestic press limited itself to short PAP messages with only procedural information.

The charges against Wańkowicz were based on article 23 of the decree on crimes posing particular danger during the country's reconstruction. The article said:

Who spreads or for the purposes of spreading prepares, keeps, or transports written or printed materials or images that contain false information which may bring considerable harm to the interests of the State of Poland, or which may lower the dignity of its highest authorities, is subject to imprisonment for no less than 3 years.

Thus the minimum punishment for such a "crime" was three years of imprisonment. The decree on "crimes posing particular danger," commonly called the Small Penal Code, came from 1946 and was a product of Stalinist "law and order." It was applied during the height of Stalinist terror.

In the period of 1959 to 1962 three cases are known of the authorities referring to that paragraph to subdue representatives of cultural life in Poland. By virtue of the decree, Anna Rewska was sentenced for distributing the Paris *Kultura*, Anna Rudzińska for concluding a contract with the same monthly for a translation of Feliks Gross's book, and the writer Jerzy Kornacki for allegedly circularizing anonymous anti-government lampoons.

The indictment contained the charge that Wańkowicz had prepared a twenty-nine-page typescript of a speech project that supposedly contained "false information slandering the People's Republic of Poland," and sent it to his daughter living in Washington. The material was to be used by Radio Free Europe. In the case files there is a photocopy of Wańkowicz's typescript (or more exactly, photographs), stenographic records of several broadcasts of Free Europe (of 1 and 14 July), with quoted fragments of the writer's text allegedly used by RFE next to the material, and a copy of the periodical *Na antenie*, issued by RFE. They were to confirm the similarity of the materials prepared by Wańkowicz and those used by the Polish section of Radio Free Europe.

Below I quote the full bill of indictment (see court files). Enclosed was a list of evidence and prosecution witnesses—namely one, Major Tadeusz Cibor.

Figure 2.1.   Wańkowicz signing autographs for readers. Poland 1960s.

PART B: GENERAL PUBLIC PROSECUTOR'S OFFICE

10th October 1964

BILL OF INDICTMENT against Melchior Wańkowicz, suspected of crime under art. 23 paragraph 1 of the decree of 13th June 1946 (Journal of Law No. 30, item 192 as amended).

I. ACCUSED

1. Melchior Wańkowicz, son of Melchior and Zofia born Szwoynicka, born 10th January 1892 in Kalużyce (USSR),[28] writer, of gentry descent, citizen of the United States of America, of Polish nationality, with higher education, married with 1 adult child, no estate, no criminal record, resident of

Warsaw, 10 Puławska Street, flat No. 35 (remanded since 7th October 1964—Card 37).

Of:

Writing in June 1964 in Warsaw a 29-page typescript "Speech Project—J. A. (or a substratum for successive speeches of 4–5 speakers)" which included false and slandering information about the situation of culture in Poland, and then sending the text to the United States of America to have it published by a center of hostile propaganda, Radio Free Europe, by which actions he caused significant harm to the interests of the Polish State, which constitutes an act defined in art. 23 par. 1 of the decree of 13th June 1946 (Journal of Law No. 30, item 192 as amended).

Under art. 15 and 20 par. 1 of the code of penal proceedings, the above case will be heard by the District Court for the City of Warsaw.

II. JUSTIFICATION

Card 1. In a writing of 3rd October 1964, the Ministry of Internal Affairs notified the General Public Prosecutor's Office that Melchior Wańkowicz had sent to the United States of America "Speech Project—J. A. (or a substratum for successive speeches of 4–5 speakers)" to have the paper used by the Free Europe radio station.

Cards 2–14. It follows from the materials enclosed hereto that the paper "Speech Project—J. A." was used in Free Europe broadcasts on 1st–14th July 1964 and in articles published in the monthly of the said Radio, *Na antenie* of 2nd August 1964.

Card 3. It has been stated that in the said paper, describing the situation in culture and literature in Poland, the author has included expressions which present the attitude of the authorities toward national culture development in a falsified manner.

Card 15. On that basis, an investigation was initiated. The investigation established that the paper "Speech Project—J. A." mentioned above has been written by Melchior Wańkowicz.

Cards 30–31, 43. The above findings are based on comparative research of the typescript and handwriting, performed by the Criminology Department of the Citizens' Militia Headquarters. The research has shown that the typescript has been typed using a "Hermes-Rocket" No. 5405841 typewriter, owned by Melchior Wańkowicz, and the corrections and supplements made in the typescript have been made in his hand.

Cards 20–23, 35–36, 44–45. The above statements agree with the explanations of Melchior Wańkowicz, when questioned as a suspect. He pleaded not guilty and stated that he had written the said "Speech Project—J. A." himself, and then, after corrections, he had sent it to the United States to his daughter who is living there permanently. Melchior Wańkowicz also stated that he had enclosed a handwritten letter to his daughter with the typescript. The letter told the addressee that the sender, i.e., Melchior Wańkowicz, not only did not object to using the sent text abroad, but even wished for it to be used, with one reservation—that his name not be given while using the said materials.

Deputy General Public Prosecutor
Edward Sanecki

List of people to be summoned to the hearing:
Defendant: Melchior Wańkowicz—Militia Headquarters of the City of Warsaw
Witnesses:
1. Tadeusz Cibor, Warsaw, 2 Rakowiecka Street,
List of other evidence:

1. "Speech Project—J. A." typescript copy
2. The monthly *Na antenie*
3. Expert analyses from criminology departments of the Militia

Headquarters
for inspection:

1. Fragment of a photocopy of "Speech Project—J. A."
2. "Hermes Rocket" No. 5405841 typewriter

Deputy General Public Prosecutor
Edward Sanecki

In the first hearing, on 26 October, Wańkowicz made a motion that the hearing be postponed and he be released from custody to be able to take the notes and materials he might need to prepare his defense. He was denied the possibility of searching for those materials himself. His wife was supposed to bring them to him. In that case, the writer refused to answer any questions and stated he could talk only with Gomułka himself or with the minister of domestic affairs, Mieczysław Moczar.

The trial was recorded. Twelve magnetic tapes were recorded, and from them, protocols were later written. It is certain (so claim, for example, the defense attorneys) that the protocols in the court files are not full and faithful records. With that reservation, I am still quoting them here. Following are the words of the prosecutor, Edward Sanecki, in response to the writer's motion: "Before I address the motion, I must say here that the guarantor of reliability in the People's Republic of Poland is the court before which the defendant appears."

The case was adjourned. Meanwhile an unprecedented thing occurred—granting the prisoner's wish, Mieczysław Moczar came to talk to him. The meeting is said to have lasted nearly four hours, and for many years caused many various comments, as the information that circulated about it was sometimes plain contradictory. Edward Sanecki told me years later that during the meeting the two men "nearly fell in each other's arms in greeting."

The writer told me personally about the "rather friendly attitude of Moczar" toward him, and Mieczysław Moczar himself—in memoirs issued in 1983 in Kraków *Życie Literackie* (issues 49 and 50)[29]—stressed the nearly cordial relations which in his account existed between him and the writer. In some fragments, one may have the impression that the men were on a first-name basis—which was not true, but Moczar's clever, deceitful trick.

Władysław Pociej, the defense attorney, on reading the said memoirs of the general, sent a protest letter to the weekly's editor-in-chief, Władysław Machejek. The letter evoked no reaction. I am quoting here its contents after the weekly *Stolica* (*The Capital*) of 26 March 1988 (I was given both the text of the article and of the letter by Władysław Pociej in person):

> I did not think there was a need to speak up about the suit that was filed against Melchior Wańkowicz for a crime under art. 23 par. 1 of the Small Penal Code (to explain: the provision was repealed by provisions introducing a new penal code—act of 19 IV [April] 1969), consisting in writing material with false information that might cause considerable harm to the interest of the Polish State, punishable by imprisonment for no less than 3 years. I thought the matter could be put in the memoirs I might write. I was induced to take up my pen and write a letter to *Życie Literackie* by reading a fragment of the memoirs of Gen. M. Moczar, published in the said *Życie Literackie*. I make no claims to edit those memoirs in any way; however, it seems to be my duty to depict those same matters in a slightly different way, on behalf of Melchior Wańkowicz, so to speak, whom I had the honor to defend along with two of my colleagues.
>
> From the memories published in *Życie Literackie* one could surmise that M. Wańkowicz was surprised with the suit filed against him, that he wished to avoid the unpleasant consequences in the form of criminal proceedings. According to historical truth, it must be said that Wańkowicz did not try to escape criminal responsibility, but in a sense he even provoked. He gave me an account of his talk with Gen. M. Moczar, or rather of its final conclusion, that came down to the simple statement: "So you will do f***ing time," to which Wańkowicz reportedly gave an equally succinct answer: "So I will do f***ing time." This was a result of Wańkowicz's tenacity, as he did not want to make any concessions.
>
> In his defense, Wańkowicz never denied having written the article published in the bi-weekly of Radio Free Europe, *Na antenie*, and did not even deny that arranging for the article to be published conformed (in the sense of a possible design) with his intentions. He explained it to me in his own unique manner: "You know, it was something like: I wish but I'm scared, but more of the 'I wish' part." When establishing his line of defense, he did not want to weaken that statement to make it more favorable for him, and so it stayed until the end.
>
> M. Wańkowicz believed that in the dispute with the authorities he was in the right. As a matter of fact, it was about the right of a whole group of intellectuals, and that he had acted from necessity, so to speak, as no speeches held in the country brought any results. [. . .]

That dispute, besides its political aspect, also involved his own private issues. Wańkowicz's works were not printed or re-issued. This was explained as being because of lack of paper, which excuse he considered a trick and hypocrisy of the authorities. With agitation, he told me about J. F. Kennedy's biography that he had written but which was not printed. In six weeks after the assassination of the U.S. president in Dallas, working day and night ("I felt sick with exhaustion, caffeine sustained me"), Wańkowicz sent the manuscript of the book entitled *Kennedy na tle międzyepoki* [*Kennedy against the Background of the Interperiod*]³⁰ [. . .] to the editor.³¹

So much for the words of Władysław Pociej, who further in his article corrects other things erroneously related by General M. Moczar in his memoirs, among them those concerning the verdict itself.

According to the case protocol (court files), Wańkowicz himself said in the hearing:

I refused to testify until I could speak to a high-ranking party official, I even named him—General Moczar, and he finally came, and we talked. We were talking for some three and a half hours in a very nice atmosphere. I finally understood that someone talks to a writer in a kind tongue at last. I felt the influence of the talk with General Moczar, and I was predisposed to cooperate.

The trial was reopened after eight days. The case was transferred from the small room number 15 to a bigger one, number 16. The trial lasted three days. The prosecutor was still (and remained so until the trial's end) the deputy general public prosecutor and vice director of Second Department, Edward Sanecki. Chief judge was Wiesław Sikorski; defense attorneys were Władysław Pociej (above quoted), Józef Domański, and Jadwiga Rutkowska. The trial was conducted *in camera*, therefore, credible details were missing.

In the court files that were made available to me after twenty-six years from the trial, I found interesting fragments of the testimony records. During the hearing, Wańkowicz stated that the materials brought to him by his wife to use for his defense were incomplete, and he asked to have the hearing adjourned again and to allow him to search his archives by himself. Prosecutor Sanecki replied:

Prosecutor:

This is either a misunderstanding or you are trying to make a demonstration. I can't understand this attitude of the defendant. A whole range of documents were brought to you, and thus the court gave you the possibility to reply to a range of facts from the investigation. You refuse to give explanations under a pretext of hindering your defense. Or, the court will treat this attitude like that seen in other cases, where the defendants—who I don't intend to compare you to—make, or try to make unnecessary demonstrations to cause cheap sensation and make themselves pseudo-heroes. In this case, there are no heroes.

Defendant Wańkowicz:

> I must strongly emphasize that I was not guided by a wish to demonstrate anything with my statement, quite the contrary. Otherwise, I would not use up so much time to prepare my defense. I do not want to narrow the case, even if it may seem like this now. The People's Republic is trying a writer who during his entire life has walked the route of this nation. [. . .] I am an American citizen, and I would like to explain in the proceedings how and why this came about. I am at my most positive toward what is happening in the Polish Republic, which is proven by the fact that I not only praise, but also criticize what is wrong.

In the hearing, adjourned until 3 November, the defendant (D) answered the court's (C) questions. Below is a fragment of the records (see court files):

C: How did you send that writing to your daughter?

D: Through someone.

C: Was that a normal way of communicating with your daughter?

D: No.

C: Why was that writing sent through someone and not in such a way as you normally communicated with your daughter?

D: Because I received a cable—it was after the "34" case—an anxious cable, and since the speech would not be useful—just lay there—an opportunity came up suddenly, so I sent it. I didn't send it by mail because I was afraid it would be lost.

C: What do you mean by saying you were afraid it wouldn't get there by mail?

D: I was afraid it would be confiscated.

C: Why did you think so?

D: Because that's quite a common practice.

C: Was it because of the content of the script?

D: Yes, because of the content.

A witness for the prosecution was Major Tadeusz Cibor, a rather mysterious figure. Until June 1964, he was a secretary of the Polish Embassy in Washington, DC, at the same time being a Security Service officer. He testified fully *in camera*, with no one from the audience present, while witnesses for the defense testified in different, more open conditions. The defense witnesses were Bohdan Czeszko, Igor Abramow Newerly, Kazimierz Koźniewski, and Stefan Kozicki.

As the attorneys wrote when suggesting the witnesses to be called (writing of 22 October 1964), the indicated witnesses "know the defendant well and their testimonies may contribute to explaining the culpability, in particular by presenting the character and ideological profile of the defendant, visible in his works and personal activity in the inter-war period, in exile, and after returning to Poland."

Below I quote the hearing records from witness testimonies—for the prosecution and for the defense. (I do so with a repeated reservation that the records are incomplete. The divergence between the preserved records and the actual questioning concerns, for instance, the testimony of Kazimierz Koźniewski—thus it follows from, for example, comparing the memories that Koźniewski shared with me and Wańkowicz's reaction to his testimony—called *Pitaval*.)

> Interrupted 3rd November 1964
> on 4th November 1964
> Protocol of the main hearing
> Regional Court for the City of Warsaw, 4th Penal Department
> case of Melchior Wańkowicz
> charged under art. 23 par. 1 of the Small Penal Code
>
> Present:
>
>> Chief Judge, Regional Court Judge: Wiesław Sikorski
>> Judges, Regional Court Judge: Anatol Derkacz
>> Lay Judges, Regional Court Judge: Stefan Kaciczak
>> Prosecutor: Edward Sanecki
>> Stenotypist: Teresa Niemojewska
>> Defendant—Melchior Wańkowicz—appeared.
>> Attorneys present—Jadwiga Rutkowska, Józef Domański, and Władysław
>> Pociej.

The chief judge ordered an evidence hearing and informed the defendant that the latter was entitled to make comments and explanations concerning each piece of evidence (article 295 of the code of penal procedure).

On calling witness Tadeusz Cibor to the courtroom—based on article 277 of the code of penal procedure—the court decided to hold the hearing *in camera* during the part concerning testimony of that witness due to state security reasons.

Warned by the chief judge about criminal liability for false statements—article 140 of the penal code—and asked for full name, occupation, and relationship to the parties, the witness (W) stated:

> TADEUSZ CIBOR, aged thirty-eight, unrelated, Major in active service, officer of the Ministry of Domestic Affairs.

W: Until summer this year I was staying for some time on duty in the United States of America. At the end of June this year, while performing my professional duties, I obtained from a confidential source a document to look at. The document was a typescript of several dozen pages, and its title started with the words "Speech Project—J. A." At the same time, I learned from the same source that the document had come from Poland, had been written by the writer Melchior Wańkowicz, and was meant to be used by Free Europe. I read the document on-site and judged both the document and the information given to me to be noteworthy. Of course I mean "noteworthy" from the point of view of my professional interests. In August this year, when I was back in Poland, I came to Warsaw after reporting to my original unit, and I initiated an investigation according to the adopted principles and as provided by the law.

Prosecutor (P): Did that typescript have any handwritten notes on it?

W: I forgot to add that since I obtained the document only to read it, I have made a photocopy of it.

The document had both typed corrections in it, like crossing-outs and some corrections, and handwritten corrections of that kind.

The court presented the document entitled "Speech Project—J. A."—a photocopy of it from the envelope on card 4 of investigation files—to the witness.

On being presented the document, witness Cibor said:

W: These are undoubtedly fragments of that document. Of course, a photocopy may be copied multiple times, as we know. This photocopy has certainly been made from the negative of the photocopy made by me.

P: Was there in that typescript, on those pages any note that looked like a letter or guidelines addressed to a specific person, or not?

W: I do not recall anything like that, except notes which introduced corrections to the text itself.

Defense Attorney (DA): Did you leaf through the whole text?

W: Of course.

DA: Was the last page of that typescript whole, or had a part of it been edited out?

W: I have not paid particular attention to that, but I think it seemed whole. I do not recall anything to be incomplete or cut.

DA: Did the person who made that document available to you have to return it?

W: I cannot say that. I had to return the document, as I could only read it. I cannot give any explanations concerning the source of information.

The chief judge restored openness of the hearing.

Witness BOHDAN CZESZKO, aged forty-one, unrelated, writer

The chief judge warned the witness about criminal liability for false statements—article 140 of the penal code.

Witness Czeszko: Mr. Melchior Wańkowicz I know from his writings, and I have also met him on some occasions. I am not a literary critic. I have expressed my opinion about his works several times; I've had the possibility to give my opinion on the topic in my publications. I believe him to be a writer of great stature, an excellent reporter, a man who has done a great deal for the school of Polish reportage—both with his works and by supporting the work of his younger colleagues—Ksawery Pruszyński, for instance. His works were always related to the history, the current history of the Polish nation. That is what I can say on the topic. I wouldn't like to start any far-going analyses here because I don't feel an expert therein.

DA: When did you last meet Mr. Wańkowicz and talk to him directly?

W: I think this was the only direct conversation I had with Mr. Melchior, as before the war I was too young to be an interesting interlocutor for him, and after the war, it so happened there was no occasion to talk. I had this one conversation with Mr. Melchior some time—I can't exactly recall right now—after his signing the 34 manifesto, and after I then published an article on that in *Kultura*. Mr. Melchior invited me then to meet him. I visited him in Konstancin in the ZAIKS[32] home and there we talked about that incident.

DA: Did Mr. Wańkowicz then have any critical attitude concerning certain phenomena in the sphere of cultural life in Poland? Did he express it toward you? What was his attitude toward those phenomena?

W: Well, I think that by signing the 34 manifesto, Mr. Melchior defined his attitude toward the phenomena in Polish cultural life. Just like I believe that his signature under that manifesto, actually just like the signatures of the other participants of that incident—that was, at least for me, of some political nature.

DA: Of what content was your conversation with the defendant?

W: We talked about the manifesto, I mean this was the gist of our conversation. I explained my stand on the matter, and Mr. Melchior said that he'd made this gesture of signing the manifesto as a Polish writer who was concerned with the best interests of Polish culture.

DA: In the conversation—beside moments of criticism—were there also affirmative moments, like the wish to reach some sort of agreement with the party or, say, with the censors? Were there only negative moments, or were some things positive?

W: It's difficult for me to judge those things. I think that his coming back to Poland and starting to publish his books here, by participating in the life of this country—that alone seems to be some sign of his attitude toward Poland.

DA: Do you know any details from the life of Mr. Wańkowicz?

W: No, I don't.

DA: And do you know his attitude toward the emigration in America?

W: No, I don't know it.

DA: You have taken a specific stand toward what you called an incident. I understand each of you took a slightly contrary stand, right?

W: We took completely opposite stands.

DA: In your dispute with the defendant, did you sense—as concerns his point of departure for the conversation—was it hostility, or was it concern, but some positive stand?

W: The question is so unspecific that I cannot answer it, forgive me.

Defendant Wańkowicz (D): In that conversation, which had a rather aggressive tone on my side, did the stands I took express concern for Polish culture, or simply idle negation of the whole system and so on?

W: Judging by what I heard from Mr. Melchior, and taking it in good faith, I believe you cannot find negation of the People's Republic of all the phenomena related to the notion, neither in his activity nor in his words.

DA: Did you, in your analysis of the defendant's works, note the style, vocabulary, temperament?

W: If I may state an opinion at all about anyone's command of the Polish language—since I am not a literary critic, as I have already said—I personally consider the language of Mr. Melchior to be one of the better varieties, and anyway, to be an interesting phenomenon considering literature in general.

DA: Does the earthiness, or bluntness of expression in Mr. Wańkowicz's writing diverge from the average?

W: Yes, that's for sure. Mr. Melchior is an eminent writer and uses the Polish language in an exceptional manner. His command of the language, awareness of the word, awareness of the weight of the words he uses, is great. The bluntness is great, and Mr. Melchior's writing temperament is great, which obviously constitutes his value as a writer.

Witness IGOR ABRAMOW NEWERLY, aged sixty-one, unrelated, writer

The chief judge warned the witness about criminal liability for false statements—article 140 of the penal code.

Witness Newerly: I myself met Mr. Wańkowicz several times. As a writer he has given his opinion in his works. He's a writer of great stature.

D: Did you have the impression when talking to me that you were conversing with someone who gives idle criticism? Or was there in the conversations in which I spoke with excitement and an underlayer of acknowledging the reality and trying to improve it? What impressions did you have after the conversation?

W: That is right. I had the impression that you talked with a much excited air. Certain tender matters excited you very much. Sometimes you exaggerated—someone else might see it in a slightly different aspect, but I certainly sensed some concern, civil concern and protest in that.

Witness KAZIMIERZ KOŹNIEWSKI, aged forty-six, unrelated, writer

The chief judge warned the witness about criminal liability for false statements—article 140 of the penal code.

Witness Koźniewski: I know Mr. Wańkowicz; I have been a friend of his daughters since 1937.

D: What stance did I take toward the People's Republic of Poland?

W: This is a very general question and it is difficult to answer it in a specific way. When you came to Poland and for a long time that you stayed here, you were certainly a man, a writer who tried in the maximum active way, the maximum loyal way, to understand our political situation today. Yet I must say that in the last period, the controversies between us multiplied and that clear-cut stand from the beginning was later disturbed in some way. In the beginning, you certainly came here to Poland with a strongly positive attitude, which is proven in some way by the mere fact that you came. The divergences of ideas between us arose in the matter of "Letter 34." You took a stand that is known by your signing the letter. During this whole case, you had a most critical attitude toward the cultural policy pursued in Poland.

Defense Attorney (DA): What was Melchior Wańkowicz's point of departure in those conversations?

W: Like I said, Mr. Wańkowicz's stand on coming here and later was very positive. And then later, in the recent time, his stand went very much toward the critical and so it underwent some change.

DA: From what position came the criticism?

W: Well, from the position of a citizen who is somehow engaged here in this existing reality, and who raises a whole range of critical opinions toward it.

P: Were you in Vienna together with the defendant in 1963?

W: Yes, I was.

P: Did the defendant continue this journey you started together, somewhere farther?

W: Yes, we separated in Vienna and Mr. Wańkowicz went farther, to West Germany and Switzerland.

P: Did Mr. Wańkowicz tell you anything about the conversation he had in Munich with Mr. Tadeusz Nowakowski, head of the Polish section of Radio Free Europe, and what was it that he said?

W: I find it difficult to recall everything in detail now, but in any case it was some report, some information. He spoke of a few hours spent with Mr. Tadeusz Nowakowski, about some dinner they had together, and exchanging information—I think, concerning what Mr. Wańkowicz told Nowakowski about his literary situation. I can't recall any more details right now. In any case, they spent some time together, and Mr. Wańkowicz told me about it right after we met in Vienna.

DA: Does the expression "centripetal writer," referring to Wańkowicz's writing stand, come from you?

W: No, not from me, because I haven't prepared any printed study. This is an expression with which Mr. Wańkowicz defines himself, and referring to his writing stand, at least in some periods, it is definitely very appropriate.

DA: How shall we understand this expression "centripetal writer"?

W: In the light of Melchior Wańkowicz's works, I understand that it means a writer who quite willingly applies to creating in every political situation—I think it needs to be stressed: in every political situation—to creating those state-positive values, for the benefit of the state.

DA: Have you ever concerned yourself with Wańkowicz's book *Tworzywo*?

W: Yes, I have.

DA: What is your opinion about the novel? What did Wańkowicz want to say in it?

W: It is a novel in which Wańkowicz presents the history of Polish emigration in Canada from the beginning of this century until the outbreak of World War II. He shows there the whole process of Poles leaving Poland and then joining the American-Canadian society. I believe it to be one of the most interesting titles in the literary output of Wańkowicz.

DA: When did the June meeting of the Writers' Association, combined with a discussion on the 34 matter, take place?

W: Between 15 and 20 June this year.

DA: Could you describe Wańkowicz's style?

W: It is certainly a somewhat very emotional style. Although it must be said that when he wrote his *Sztafeta*, that is in 1937–1938, *Sztafeta* was written very precisely, considering its journalistic value. I have the impression that in a later time, the style of Mr. Wańkowicz yielded to a certain dominance of emotional elements over journalistic rationalist elements.

DA: Do you know such publications by Wańkowicz as *Kundlizm*, or *Klub trzeciego miejsca*?

W: *Kundlizm* is a collection of features of a rather lesser weight. It held a discussion on some relics of a rather minor nature, relics in the attitude of emigrants, sort of post-nobility relics, if I may say so. And as concerns *Klub trzeciego miejsca*, its thesis was such that there is a great dispute in the world between communism and capitalism, between the Communist and the capitalist way of thinking and activity. The book was written in 1949. The author took a stand toward the two worldviews, the two political practices. He tried to take a neutral stand, a stand on the sidelines, one as a third-party observer, hence the title of a Third Place Club. The thesis was such that in twenty-five years more or less they would somehow unite, probably the two systems of thought would meet somewhere midway, and then become the third-party people. Wańkowicz advised all intellectuals to reserve places for themselves in that third-party club—and then they would have a lot of scope for activity that right now is possible in neither one nor the other system.

DA: And have you heard how the publications were received by the emigrants?

W: Well, quite variously. On the one hand, the reactions were very negative, and on the other, the very fact of publishing this *Klub trzeciego miejsca* was viewed in some positive way. But the emigration from General Anders's group had a negative attitude toward it. There were and still are various groups among the emigrations, various reactions, also to that.

DA: Were there any frictions between Wańkowicz and the emigration in connection with his return to Poland?

W: There were various reactions to that. There was a very negative reaction, which was expressed in some peer tribunal on publishing a shortened issue of *Monte Cassino* in Poland. There were even some very critical reactions, expressed at some point in an article by Mieroszewski, where Wańkowicz was criticized under the cover of some pen name—this was in 1961 or 1960. But there was also a positive response. I think the group that understood Mr. Melchior Wańkowicz's intentions in returning to Poland, was the team of *Kultura,* that played host to him then.

DA: And what were the relations of Mr. Wańkowicz, back when he was still in America, with Radio Free Europe?

W: I only know that for some time, I don't know how long, he held a Free Europe scholarship, and then he renounced the scholarship, because it was 1956 or 1955. Well, I think it had some connection with his intention, if not of returning to Poland, then of establishing publishing and personal contacts with Poland.

DA: And what about Wańkowicz's personal relations with the team of Free Europe?

W: I don't know.

DA: Were there any controversies between you concerning lectures held by Wańkowicz in Poland? Did you have any reservations as to them?

W: Well, I listened, twice I listened to the lectures, or author's meetings, once it was some time after Wańkowicz returned permanently in 1958, in the Congress Hall, and another time in Vienna, when I listened to a lecture for the circle of Poles in Vienna, a year ago. Those lectures could evoke no reservations.

DA: Do you know that Mr. Wańkowicz has had certain difficulties publishing his works?

W: There were difficulties, true, but they were rather average and quite normal. They could concern any writer and did concern each writer. Each of us has some difficulties publishing books. I know of three particular titles, but it's difficult to say here that they were kind of very serious—anyway, I think that the publishing house has a right to take some negative kind of position on an author's proposal. And besides, in one case out of the three, as I see it, the publishing house was right.

DA: Can you say what the defendant's attitude was toward Nazism and Germany?

W: Most negative.

DA: Do you know the book *Walczący Gryf*?

W: I know it.

DA: What do you think of that book?

W: The most important is, of course, the political significance of the book. The book's function is very positive when you consider assimilating, adapting in the readers' consciousness the issue of Kashubians and Pomeranians fighting for freedom during the occupation.

DA: Do you know what role the defendant played in the case of Sergiusz Piasecki's writing?

W: Once, a long time ago, Mr. Wańkowicz helped discover a criminal's literary work—and then for a long time he was sent manuscripts written by prisoners in jail. Among those manuscripts there came one particularly interesting, a very extensive manuscript by Sergiusz Piasecki, titled *Kochanek Wielkiej Niedźwiedzicy* (*The Lover of the Great Bear*). Mr. Wańkowicz prepared the manuscript for print, and it was a literary success—the greatest of any literary successes of that writer, whose later fate is rather dreary.

Witness STEFAN KOZICKI, aged forty, unrelated, journalist

The chief judge warned the witness about criminal liability for false statements—article 140 of the penal code.

Witness Kozicki: I met Melchior Wańkowicz not so very long ago, in 1961–1962. Yet I have known his works much earlier. I believe him to be a Nestor of Polish reportage, and I value his great contribution to Polish literature. I think, and I've expressed this belief in what I've written, that his return to Poland had enormous propaganda significance simply due to the extensive readership of his books. I have also known Wańkowicz from private contacts. We would sometimes meet and talk about various topics. I sometimes had the impression that particularly when he had some doubts or there was something he didn't understand—because he gladly contacted young journalists and writers, saying, "Teach me this new Poland"—that Mr. Wańkowicz placed me in a kind of polemic position. When he had some doubts, he asked for some rational arguments, and accepted those rational arguments when they were reasonable and right. I think that what was most typical of Wańkowicz and my contacts with him was shown by a certain trip we jointly made to ZMS[33] camps in 1962. When Wańkowicz went there, he was taking the name a little too literally—socialist youth—and therefore had some doubts and was a little anxious. When we came there, those young people started asking him about the exotic. That first surprised Wańkowicz, and then he was indignant and said, "Listen, you are socialists; you should ask me about different things. I won't be telling you about the exotic. We can talk about what is courage and heroism." He then started talking about the relations in the United States. He spoke long and was notably critical. So critical, in fact, that I was surprised that an American citizen could judge America in such a critical way. My relation toward Melchior Wańkowicz was somehow predetermined by the fact that I come from a younger generation of reporters, the generation that has taken the works of Melchior Wańkowicz for a certain model. Once Mr. Wańkowicz showed me copies of the letters he had been sending to people managing our cultural policy. The letters were written like "Dear Sir, Dear Minister, I allow myself to"—and the letters' endings also held such very polite formulae. Wańkowicz was surprised and asked me to explain why he had no reply to those letters, and when he called, the secretaries dismissed him. I was that polemicist—I gave such arguments as I could find, such as I could manage. Mr. Wańkowicz belongs to those stubborn discussants who always stick to their opinion.

DA: Did young reporters, like Górnicki, Wolanowski, have a similar attitude toward Wańkowicz as your attitude?

W: Yes, it was similar. Mr. Wańkowicz is undoubtedly a Nestor of Polish reportage and his work in that area is enormous.

DA: What was the attitude of Wańkowicz toward those writers?

W: Teach me Poland!

DA: Have you ever held any lecture titled "Od Prusa do Wańkowicza" ("From Prus to Wańkowicz")?

W: Yes. I traveled through Lower Silesia with a lecture on the history of Polish reportage, which was entitled "Od Prusa do Wańkowicza."

DA: Have you talked with Wańkowicz on controversial topics as concerns the view on the cultural situation in Poland?

W: Yes, I have.

DA: Were Wańkowicz's words marked with hostility or maybe some sort of concern?

W: Why, of course, with concern.

DA: Could you describe the style of Wańkowicz?

W: It is immensely animated, a unique style, a style full of certain noble vigor, full of neologisms.

After years, Wańkowicz spoke many times about the witness testimonies. He particularly remembered the testimony of Kazimierz Koźniewski, who had been friends with his daughters, on a first-name basis with them, and who testified against him in the trial. He later wrote:

> K. Koźniewski, a friend of the house from back before the war—maintaining the friendly relationship he had with me and which allowed him some benefit before we parted as I took him in my car to Vienna—was (next to Kozicki, Czeszko, and Newerly) one of the four witnesses I called in my trial. They all belonged to the party, but while I can't complain about the conduct of the latter three, K(anary)[34] Koźniewski informed that I had met Tadeusz Nowakowski in Munich (of which he learned from me as I spoke with Ambassador Kuryluk). He concealed, in spite of the judge asking, the aim of my trip, which was to repair my car in Stuttgart (a repairman was traveling with us), and thus insinuated that the aim of the trip was to meet with Free Europe people. He assumed the role of an expert—while the judge never asked or called him to do that—stating that my books shouldn't have been published. And what is most sickening—when I didn't shake his hand after the process, K(reep)[35] Koźniewski didn't dare try and explain the matter.

From police custody, where he was still kept, Wańkowicz sent a letter to the head of the Fourth Penal Department of the Regional Court. In the letter he supplemented his testimony and took a stand toward witness testimonies. He never received a reply to it. The letter's content is given below:

6th November 1964
Melchior Wańkowicz
Custody in the Headquarters

of the Citizens' Militia of the City of Warsaw

To President of the 4th Penal Dept.
of the Regional Court for the City of Warsaw

In my testimony on the last day of the trial I focused on answering the Prosecutor's questions and therefore overlooked some facts that the Prosecutor passed over, yet which may be of significance for the Court.

I have no more possibility to see my lawyers to ask them if giving any explanations after the case is provided for in the procedure. Thus I am giving the explanations not knowing if they are sent via the right channel, if they can be attached to the files, or even if they will be considered by you at all.

This additional testimony concerns my meeting with T. Nowakowski and my American citizenship.

1. The meeting with Nowakowski.

On the spur of indignation that witness Koźniewski, who is a writer himself, could present the mere fact of talking to a writer in exile as incriminating evidence to the Prosecutor, I only gave a sharp reaction to defend that right of mine. Since the Prosecutor did not draw conclusions from the fact in his speech, I limited myself to that, without reflecting that the fact had been actually given, and even if it was not used by the Prosecutor, it might have some impact in the matter. Since the case revolved around the charge of contacting Free Europe, with which Nowakowski collaborated, then my meeting him may be viewed as an incriminating circumstance.

Hence I must state the following:

a. Since I came to Poland, I have never had any direct or indirect contacts with Free Europe, either in Poland or abroad. I use the word "indirect" with the reservation that I have been meeting Polish emigrant writers, and it rarely (if at all) happens that any of them does not somehow earn a living, more or less occasionally, in that institution.

b. I have visited Munich, where the seat of Free Europe is located, four times after the war: twice as a war correspondent after the Allied Army entered it—that was in 1945. The third time was when I was returning to Poland in 1958 and I went to the factory in Stuttgart to buy a car. I stopped then in Munich and saw Nowakowski. I told him then I thought he should return to Poland. I was in Munich the fourth, and last time in November 1963.

The aim of my trip was to go to the factory in Stuttgart again. I brought there a cylinder to be repaired, which couldn't have been done in Poland. As I have no knowledge of engines, TOS [Technical Car Service] (on Omulewska Street) allowed their foreman to go and see to the work for me. We had calculated the time necessary to stay in the factory for three days and, according to that schedule, Ambassador Kuryluk set the date for my lecture in Vienna.

The plan did not include stopping in Munich, even though it was not much out of our way.

Yet we had not considered All Souls' Day, that required us to stay in Stuttgart longer than the time set earlier. I did not want to fail appearing at a date that had already been publicly announced in Vienna, and I accepted the offer of the factory to exchange the old engine block for a new one for some additional payment. In this way, we were done in Stuttgart in two days and that gave us one day to spare. That allowed me to stop in Munich.

What was stated by witness Koźniewski about the trip to Switzerland is true only so far that we went about a hundred kilometers out of our way, going to Stuttgart not through Munich, but through the Allenstein Duchy and Zurich. This was due to a request of the foreman, who had never been in the West and wanted to have as many as four countries visited during our 10-day trip.

The conversation with Nowakowski gave me much interesting information about the lives of particular writers. I had first met Nowakowski in Italy when he was a novice writer, and I judged his talent very highly. I knew his family story. In Munich, he brought his wife and son to the restaurant. At the end of the dinner, he asked if I would have liked to talk to Nowak, the head of the Polish section of RFE. Bending down to his ear, so that his wife wouldn't hear me, I gave him my usual reporter's formula: that as a reporter I had some different rights and would always gladly go to every opium den, brothel, or thieves' dive. But Nowak did not take me up on the offer, and I had no time to see anyone beside Nowakowski, not only anyone from RFE, but even anyone from the Polish community. I really wanted to have some hours to spare for visiting Salzburg, a city I love. And so I made it to the lecture at the very last minute. I suppose I talked about the meeting with Nowakowski to Ambassador Kuryluk over a dinner, and certainly I talked of it at length with Koźniewski.

1. American passport. Again, as something not mentioned by the Prosecutor, it escaped my notice. However, it can also have some significance.

I took the passport to go to Poland. I left 10 days on receiving it. When I discussed the matter of my possible return to Poland with the Ambassador in Washington, and then with the authorities in Poland, I emphasized the fact that I wanted to keep the passport as I intended to go to the USA for a longer time with lectures. And indeed, I stayed in the USA and in Mexico from December 1960 to January 1962. On my return, without any efforts on my part, and not knowing that such a form existed, I received a "permanent resident card," which I first considered a privilege granted to me. I learned later that several thousand people were staying in Poland with such a card. I took into account that if I died, my wife—having renounced her passport—would not receive permission for permanent residence in the USA, where our daughter would be taking care of her.

When the "34" conflict arose, the passport started to be a burden to my mind, as something an immunity against the authorities of my own home country. Thus motivated, I submitted a written application to have my Polish citizenship restored, on 22nd July 1964.

(M. Wańkowicz)

After nearly forty-five years—in 2007—Krzysztof Masłoń wrote:

> For five weeks before the trial he was kept in the Mostowski Palace. When he refused explanations on the first day of the hearing, and made those dependent on talking to a high representative of the authorities, Mieczysław Moczar met him. The meeting was no use, the writer didn't want to agree to any concessions, and Moczar finally said: "So you will do f***ing time." "So I will do f***ing time," answered Wańkowicz. He was most afraid that he'd be released but forbidden to continue with his profession. "I prefer prison," he said in his final word. "Because if I am in jail, I will still remain in the saddle of Polish consciousness. I will be useful."[36]

The hearing lasted three days. Wańkowicz had a two-and-a-half-hour speech. He pleaded not guilty. He stressed that loyalty toward the authorities cannot exclude the right to criticism. He also spoke of the "reptile fund," a kind of slush fund, created from the revenues of classics and used to "pay twofold, or even threefold fees to licensed writers." The writers who received fees higher than the maximum ones specified in the act were Władysław Broniewski, Maria Dąbrowska, Jarosław Iwaszkiewicz, Leon Kruczkowski, and Jerzy Szaniawski.

The lawyers of Wańkowicz emphasized that the writer's actions can in no case be considered a "dangerous crime" and that there was no evidence for Radio Free Europe using materials sent to them directly by Wańkowicz.

In his final word, Wańkowicz not only didn't engage in polemics with the prosecutor, but he also dissociated himself from his own lawyers when they put forward "mitigating circumstances."

PART C: REACTIONS TO THE TRIAL

On Radio Free Europe, Jadwiga Mieczkowska concerned about the case of Wańkowicz, stated the following on 5 November 1964:

> Nobody knows what is happening in the court council room and how the discussion between the professional judge and the two lay judges went or will go. We know that it is not enough to pronounce a sentence, but it needs to be justified, and precisely in this trial the justification will be a puzzle for the judges, regardless of the sentence. Naturally, it will be a different problem with a guilty verdict, and a different one with an innocent verdict, but in both cases the judges' situation will be difficult. The judges' decision will be difficult to render under the existing circumstances, even more so due to the conditions in which a trial against Wańkowicz could come about at all, and also due to the conditions in which the trial is conducted.
>
> The trial is conducted, as we know, *in camera* in administrative terms, although not in the sense of procedure. Within the last four days, only skimpy information on what has been happening in the courtroom reached the press

correspondents waiting out in the corridor. According to the reports from the UPI correspondent, in the defense speech one of the defense lawyers stressed that Melchior Wańkowicz was only expressing his opinion, and that those opinions could in no case cause harm to the State. Furthermore, giving such opinions could not be subsumed as a particularly dangerous crime, and such crimes are described in the Small Penal Code. [. . .]

According to the reports of the Reuter Agency correspondent, Wańkowicz spoke his final words with great dignity and courage. He firmly denied the charge that he'd intended to slander Poland and sent the material abroad to have it published. The hearing is closed. We are waiting for the verdict. Hopefully the verdict, which is to be announced on Monday, will not multiply the list of questions and doubts concerning the principles of the system of justice in the People's Republic of Poland. (RFE monitoring report)

On 10 November, the Regional Court of the City of Warsaw sentenced the writer to three years in prison under article 23 of the decree of 23 June 1946. The punishment was reduced under amnesty to a year and a half (Decree of 20 July 1964 on amnesty Dz. U. No. 27, item 174. According to information from the attorney Edward Sanecki, it is the date of perpetration of the act that counts).

In the verdict's justification, the judges stated that it was falsehood to say that, in their cultural policy, the authorities used repressions, and that the government resorted to police means. At the same time, the court did not deem the deed of Wańkowicz's direct intention of making the typescript available to Radio Free Europe as proven. But it was ruled that the defendant could have taken that possibility into account.

Maria Dąbrowska wrote in her *Journals*:

10 XI [November] 1964. Tuesday.

Today the verdict has been announced in this ridiculous trial that has compromised the interests of People's Poland. No one in the world is going to believe that Wańkowicz was sending abroad materials slandering Poland. And anyway, what does the charge mean at all? If I were a party apparatchik and wanted to "destroy" any editor, I would collect cuttings from *Trybuna Ludu* and *Życie Warszawy*. Based only on the articles printed there about malpractice, defective work, and any other forms of evil plaguing Poland—articles available to the whole world—one could most easily form a charge of slandering Poland. Wańkowicz has been sentenced to three years, and amnesty was applied to shorten it by half, i.e., to a year and a half. The parties have the right to appeal. Due to "among other factors his advanced age and his state of health, the defendant was released from custody." I don't know what that means. Is it for the time of submitting appeals?

Wańkowicz is among the most popular writers. Information about his trial and the verdict immediately went around all Poland and the world. Today, after the verdict, he's one of the world's most famous people. Furthermore, even those who know nothing about "Letter 34" or who don't listen to Free

Europe, nevertheless repeat a distorted version of the trial. Society's distorted version has become "It was allegedly some bigger case, with many writers involved in it, but all were clever enough to extricate themselves from it and only Wańkowicz got caught." And there you have historical truth!

Directly after the verdict was announced, the Regional Court revoked the remand and released Wańkowicz, due to his bad health. Wańkowicz was released from imprisonment before a potential appeal against the verdict from his defense lawyers or from the prosecutor was heard.

The U.S. magazine *Time* reported on the closing of the trial of Melchior Wańkowicz who was sentenced to three years in prison for "slandering the People's Republic of Poland." *Time* stated that the closing was accompanied by a manifestation in the writer's honor in front of the District Court in 127 General Świerczewskiego Street in Warsaw. Three hundred people, mainly students and writers, cheered him. "I think all the nice people came here," said Wańkowicz, named by *Time*—just like by Dąbrowska—the most popular Polish writer. He added that "some not so nice people in room 16 sentenced him for 'defamation of the People's Republic of Poland.'" The case of Wańkowicz was seen by *Time* as a symptom of what was happening with the "once relatively liberal regime of the party head Władysław Gomułka."

Ever since Wańkowicz was arrested, the whole Western press published extensive comments on the event. From the beginning of October, from the start of the trial, several dozen articles concerning the writer's case appeared in the Western press. As I wrote in the previous chapter, these included widely read dailies, like French *Monde* and *Combat*; American *New York Times*, *Washington Post*, *Washington Evening Star*, and *Christian Science Monitor*; British *Times* and *Guardian*; Italian *Avanti*, *Quotidiano*, and *Messaggero*; Swiss *Neue Zürcher Zeitung*; West German *Frankfurter Allgemeine Zeitung* and *Frankfurter Rundschau*; Danish *Politiken* and *Berlingske Tidende*; and Swedish *Handelstidning Justitia*. The trial of Wańkowicz was also discussed in weeklies whose circulation counted in millions, like the American *Time*, West German *Die Zeit*, and many other periodicals. The case was also discussed, as could be expected, by all Polish papers abroad.

In a Polish restaurant in London, "Ognisko Polskie," a protest meeting against "new repressions in Poland aimed at suppressing freedom of speech" took place. The meeting was called by three emigrant organizations embracing people of science and of letters: Polish Society of Arts and Sciences Abroad, Association of Polish Writers Abroad, and Polish Journalists' Union. The speakers were Professor B. Hełczyński, J. Bielatowicz, General Z. Bohusz-Szyszko, and R. Zakrzewski. Then on the motion of W. Wohnout, the assembly passed unanimously a resolution where we read among other sentiments:

Poles abroad express deep concern for the fate of Polish literature in the country and generally for the fate of Polish culture choked by censorship and repressions against writers for their professional work.

Accusing and sentencing writers for "contacts with foreign countries"— proven, e.g., in the case of Melchior Wańkowicz with writing a letter to a daughter staying in the States, and in the case of Jan Nepomucen Miller with allegedly sending an article to London *Wiadomości*—are symptoms of police methods of ruling, unknown in any civilized country.

We, the assembled, view those practices as a new attempt to terrorize creativity, and lodge a most fervent protest against that.[37]

A senator from New York and former general prosecutor Robert Kennedy issued a special statement in the case of Wańkowicz. He also talked to the ambassador of the People's Republic of Poland in Washington, Edward Droźniak.

One of the manifestations of solidarity with the stand of the Polish artistic community in defense of civil liberties was protests of Western literary unions. The American and the Norwegian Pen Club sent letters to the Polish Pen Club. The Norwegian Authors Union sent a protest to the Polish Embassy in Oslo, with the following content:

We, the Norwegian Authors Union, are sorry to learn that a Polish writer, Wańkowicz, has been sentenced to imprisonment. The course of the trial against Wańkowicz gave us the impression that the Polish authorities, considering the current Polish state to be ideal, view a different opinion of Polish writers as non-patriotic. Such a stand surprises us, because neither in Poland nor in the world are there people who could believe that the current Polish state is perfect and above criticism. Equally imperfect are other countries in the world. We believe the actions of the authorities toward Wańkowicz to be harmful for the interests of Poland.

The American Pen Club, in turn, sent a cable concerning the issue of Wańkowicz to Michał Rusinek, secretary of the Polish Pen Club in Warsaw. It said:

Being aware that defending freedom of speech tends to confront the government in Poland, which—to the regret and indignation of writers from all democratic countries—has in the last two years been intensifying their combat against that freedom—nevertheless we, the American Pen Club wish to express our sympathy toward the Polish Pen Club and all the Polish intellectual world in the face of those newest manifestations of indignity it had been subjected to, i.e., Stalin's decree—a muzzle for freedom of speech.

We mean, "the cruel persecution of Melchior Wańkowicz, a citizen of the United States, residing in Poland, a 72-year-old writer, whose life is one great hymn honoring the Polish nation, which fact had also evoked hatred of Nazi invaders against him and his family.

His persecution was based on a Stalinist decree of 1946. Because he signed the well-known "Letter 34," and because he supposedly sent a copy of an undelivered speech, connected with the said letter, to his daughter in Washington, that Wańkowicz was charged with "disseminating false information slandering the state and the prestige of its authorities."

At the end of the cable it was stated: "We have heard that an appeal was lodged against sentencing Wańkowicz to imprisonment. We have no doubts that the Polish literary world wishes to have Wańkowicz acquitted in the Court of Appeal. This agrees with our opinion that the provision of 1946 is tantamount to the feudal notion of *lèse majesté*, violates civil rights, and is a barrier for writers acting as the conscience of their nation."

The cable was signed by the president of the American Pen Club—John Farrara. It was sent on 16 November 1964 from New York to Warsaw.

In Poland, after the sentence only a Polish Associated Press (PAP) message was published. Yet in *Prawo i Życie*[38] (22 November 1964) its editor-in-chief, Kazimierz Kąkol, published an article under the title "Spór o metodę" ("Dispute on the Method"). The author of the text identified himself fully with the prosecution and acted almost like another prosecutor in the case against Wańkowicz. Kąkol devoted a large part of his article to judging the writer's deed—and very much from the prosecutor's point of view. He did not present the readers with the content of Wańkowicz's typescript, but he pre-qualified its contents as thoroughly false and smearing the Polish reality. According to Kąkol, the writer's text was "slinging mud at the cultural achievements, slandering Poland abroad, tarnishing its good name."

In the March issue of Paris *Kultura* (1965), an article by Gaston de Cerizay entitled "Konwencja międzynarodowa" ("International Convention") had a fragment reacting to the above-discussed article by Kazimierz Kąkol. The fragment said: "It was announced in the weekly *Prawo i Życie* . . . that the photocopy of Wańkowicz's letter (which was the subject of the trial) had been made in Free Europe rooms in Munich. The information will certainly be of interest to collaborators of the Munich radio, and in this way, one of the secrets has been revealed."

The then director of the Polish section of Radio Free Europe, Jan Nowak, answered the article in the Polish emigrants' paper *Nowy Świat* (*New World*) (11 March 1965), as he fully denied the possibility of Wańkowicz's text being stolen from RFE rooms.

Twenty-four years later, Jan Nowak wrote more about the case of Wańkowicz.[39] He wrote how the said typescript got to RFE. A fragment follows:

[Wańkowicz] sent his undelivered speech in the diplomatic bag through the U.S. Embassy to his daughter, Marta Erdman, to Washington, with the instructions to give it to Free Europe. I received a fragment on five pages with an instruction that heaven forbid us to broadcast it in one piece. I followed the instruction meticulously. A few most apt excerpts were weaved into news programs: *Panorama* and *Fakty* [*Facts*]. We also broadcast the list of the party members who refused the so-called counter-protest. We published a comment and the list in our monthly *Na antenie*. The names on the list were not given alphabetically, and no one thought to change their order. [. . .] Wańkowicz was charged with sending his speech to Free Europe. Where could the Secret Service learn that from? Except for Marta Erdman, me, my two secretaries, and the Erdmans' friend Wojtek [Wojciech] Trojanowski, no one knew that the writer's daughter gave me a fragment of his speech. Neither was it possible for any agent to get to the document in our building. I kept all confidential papers in the cellar, which was all in one armored safe. Any attempt to get inside by a person who didn't know the opening combination automatically activated alarm devices. Thus we immediately announced a denial. The same was done by Marta Erdman. Wańkowicz acted brash in the hearing and denied everything. A certain Tadeusz Cibor, Secret Service major, was questioned as a witness in the trial *in camera*. The man was put on the list of diplomats in Washington as second secretary and returned to Warsaw five days after Marta received the letter from her father. In this way they wanted to create a conjecture that Wańkowicz's speech was photographed at Erdmans' home in Washington. Mrs. Erdman immediately realized that Cibor's appearance as a witness in the trial was a show. Attached to her father's letter was a piece of paper with handwritten instructions to hand the text of the speech over to RFE. If the Secret Service had really got to those papers, they would have had the *corpus delicti* in their hands.

Meanwhile, in the hearing the prosecutor presented the text of the document without the compromising note and the article in *Na antenie* in which certain fragments of the speech had been published. Wańkowicz's guilt was supposedly proven by that same non-alphabetical order of names of party members who refused to sign the counter-protest. Wańkowicz defended himself with the argument that at least two copies of his non-delivered speech were circulating in Warsaw, so he was not responsible for one of them reaching Free Europe. He also indicated that the most anti-government fragments had not been repeated by us, which proves that we didn't have the whole text.

Right after Wańkowicz was released, his daughter decided to visit him in Warsaw. She sent me a cable that on her way back she would stop at the airport in Copenhagen. I understood that as an invitation to meet her and came there at the appointed time. We had barely said hello to each other, and she was already asking if, except for the fragment she'd sent me, I had got the full text of Wańkowicz's speech from another source. My denial was enough proof for her that we were in no way responsible for her father's imprisonment. As I mentioned, in the trial the prosecutor quoted fragments we had never broadcast.[40]

And so the case that was the subject of the trial of Melchior Wańkowicz—the typescript getting to Radio Free Europe—was explained when Jan Nowak's book was published, as were some other issues. How the text got into the hands of the Secret Service authorities, is still unknown. Wańkowicz himself suspected that the U.S. diplomatic mail with which he had sent the materials abroad had been photographed.

Wańkowicz did not lodge an appeal, and neither did he allow his lawyers to do so on his behalf. He did not consent to going to the appointed meetings of medical boards, a certificate from which could have allowed the authorities to grant him a pardon. In December, he sent a letter to Władysław Gomułka:

21st December 1964
To the First Secretary,

As proven by the attachment, the sentence has just come into effect.

Thus I may now write not as a person who solicits something: in such case, the intention for that letter would have been wrong. Now I am writing not to the authorities, but to a man whose special feelings are thoughts of this country. I am writing to citizen "Wiesław," a prisoner of 1932, 1936, 1951. I am trying to enter into what he was then thinking. I understand the distance of the achievements, but I have also served this country as honestly as I could.

My pre-war *Opierzona rewolucja* was born from the impulse of pushing the cart uphill against the people in Moscow. How much more intensively did I dream of returning to help my countrymen. After all, I have renounced my American citizenship[41]—which I'd first kept due to reasons known to the party—after the case of the 34 arose, as I didn't wish to use any immunity.

Shutting me off from engaging in the issues of life is harder for me than any prison, suffering and not being able to write. That forces me to write about my anxiety concerning the settling of publication issues.

The court has convicted me not only on the offense of sending a message to Free Europe, but even of such an intention. In spite of that, my stand has been distorted by publicly quoting fragments taken freely out of the text, fragments which I did not intend to publish in any form and which had not been broadcast by Free Europe.

If I am paying with a year and a half in prison for my experiences, I believe that my thoughts on publication issues deserve to be considered.

To that purpose, I enclose the text of my speech and a notice to the Court in which I renounce my right to lodge an appeal.

I remain yours truly,
M. Wańkowicz

On 8 January 1965, he was received by Władysław Gomułka for an audience (no note on this topic has been found in the writer's papers). After some time, articles by Wańkowicz started to reappear in papers, and his books were published again.[42]

The writer said that it was only possible in Poland that a person sentenced to a year and a half in prison lived normally, moved about freely, and even traveled abroad. The comment stressed the paradoxes and inconsistency of the authorities. In the end, thanks to the trial, Wańkowicz became even more popular; he became a kind of a hero. People stopped him in the street; he received flowers and letters from readers. Commonly known was an event when he came to the theater, he sat in the first row, and in middle of the act one of the actors recognized him, came up to the footlights, bowed to Wańkowicz, and only then resumed acting. The gesture was acknowledged with applause from the audience.

International opinion showed interest in the name of Wańkowicz and his trial for some time afterward. Often stressed was the awkward situation that the authorities had placed themselves in.

Dziennik Polski (London, 18 January 1965) published an article titled: "Regime Won the Trial—Lost the Case." The author quoted an article by an American correspondent of the *New York Times* who stated that in sentencing a seventy-two-year-old writer to prison, the regime had won the trial, but lost the case. The case returned like a boomerang to hit the initiators. In such a situation, the authorities didn't want to risk the prestige they still had in the country and abroad and refrained from sending Wańkowicz to prison.

In RFE, Jadwiga Mieczkowska informed listeners that the authorities were looking for a way out of the situation in which they had placed themselves by filing a suit against Wańkowicz and allowing a conviction. In view of the repercussions the trial had in the Polish artistic community and the whole society, as well as abroad, the government and the party had to compromise due to the stand taken by the writer. Jadwiga Mieczkowska said: "We can even assume that Wańkowicz will not go to prison, and if the information from foreign correspondents is confirmed, he may even hope for amnesty concerning publication of his works. He would then be in a better situation than before the trial."

The party stressed the stiff principles of its cultural policy with tenacity. It was quite right to say that the authorities had won the trial but lost the case. They had dealt with the case of Wańkowicz in a clumsy manner which provoked unnecessary harmful reactions. There was no clever way out of the situation. The only thing left was embarrassment.

In 2004, Stanisław M. Jankowski returned to the matter of Wańkowicz's trial. Based on declassified materials, he wrote in the New York *Przegląd Polski*:[43]

> In January 1965, general public prosecutor Kazimierz Kosztirko directed a request for a decision concerning the convicted writer to . . . Władysław Gomułka, the then First Secretary of the Party. The prosecutor was worried by the "ostentatious aversion of the convicted toward appealing against the sentence," as in that situation—as he wrote—it would be possible to consider a conditional suspension of the sentence. "In addition," he stated further, "Wańkowicz quite ostentatiously does not intend to ask the State Council to display clemency to him." The possibility of the public prosecutor moving *ex*

officio for a display of clemency was out of the question. Neither should an extraordinary appeal be lodged in favor of the convicted, because such steps would be "politically inadvisable." Not knowing in what mood secretary Gomułka might be, prosecutor Kosztirko had two different ideas to offer him. Let court-appointed doctors—he suggested—examine the man's state of health and, remembering the writer's advanced age, give an opinion to justify deferring the sentence.

If comrade Gomułka did not plan a deferral, they could, wrote the prosecutor, "abandon carrying out the sentence and expel Wańkowicz from Poland as a troublesome and undesirable citizen of a foreign country."

On 21 January 1965, it turned out that comrade Gomułka would not expel citizen Wańkowicz, undesirable in the People's Republic, from the country. Maybe he was influenced by the wording of the cable from the American Pen Club about "cruel persecution and Stalinist muzzle" imposed on the writer? Maybe he was alarmed by the news that the former U.S. general public prosecutor, New York senator Robert Kennedy, intervened in Wańkowicz's case? Or maybe he was simply in a good mood in January? Then maybe he just dismissed the threat to the People's Republic impersonated in the convicted Wańkowicz, who remaining at large—as was heard on the grapevine in Warsaw—had supposedly already knocked a few times at the gate of the prison in Rakowiecka Street with a toothbrush and warm underwear packed in a briefcase.

On the letter received by Władysław Gomułka one can still read, despite the years, the note "suspend," which meant that no one could open the gate of the prison in Warsaw or anywhere else for Wańkowicz. The prosecutors Rybicki and Kosztirko had three days to word the conclusions, and this time they had to inform secretary Władysław Wicha about them. They were to attach relevant paragraphs to Gomułka's decision. They had learned from the writer's lawyers that Wańkowicz did not wish a suspension of the sentence, because he believed, and feared it the most, that it would make it impossible for him to travel abroad.

"He wants to go to prison, hoping for a conditional early release," was the precise explanation given by Jadwiga Rutkowska during the meeting with Judge Sikorski. Also the Administrative Department of the Regional PZPR Committee in Warsaw voiced their opinion. "We cannot," wrote the comrades, "in any circumstance allow the sentence against Wańkowicz to be carried out due to his age and bad health." Prosecutor Kosztirko knew in advance what the decision of a court-appointed doctor would be, or—as he wrote in the letter to secretary Wicha—the decision issued by a medical board of any Warsaw prison. "Ailments related to his advanced age make us expect that the findings of an examination will call for adjourning the sentence *ex officio*," he wrote.

In the rehabilitation trial, on 16 March 1990, the Supreme Court—composed of the chief judge, the judge of the Supreme Court, Władysław Ochman, and the judges of the Supreme Court, Leopold Nowak and Maciej Szczepański—acquitted Wańkowicz. In the verdict's justification, the judges stated that it was not the intention of Melchior Wańkowicz to cause harm to the State of Poland, and the information sent to his daughter in the letter and the speech project was not false. One of two defense lawyers of Wańkowicz in the trial of 1964—Władysław Pociej (Jadwiga Rutkowska was also present; Józef Domański had died by then)—said that back in 1964 he was aware that the verdict against Wańkowicz had been issued before the indictment was ever read out and that defense had been impossible, and he was now ashamed of that. The trial was a moral victory for Wańkowicz, and in the area of culture it helped the Polish society. The sentence against the writer itself, said Pociej, was a bad monument to the judiciary.

Figure 2.2.   Wańkowicz in late 1950s.

INTERVIEWS THAT ALEKSANDRA ZIÓŁKOWSKA-BOEHM
(AZB) CONDUCTED WITH THE PROSECUTOR AND WITH
DEFENSE WITNESSES

Interview with Edward Sanecki (ES) conducted on 1 and 13 March 1990

AZB: Are you still working as a prosecutor now?

ES: I've been a prosecutor for thirty-six years. Now I no longer work as a prosecutor. I work as a defense lawyer in Działdów, but I live in Warsaw.

AZB: In your opinion, what is the difference between the two functions?

ES: The prosecutor is a watchdog of the regime, and the defense lawyer defends. It was the same before the war and after it—the prosecutor executes governmental policy (now Minister Bentkowski does that). As a prosecutor, I sought a basis for indictment; as a defense lawyer I check if there is proof of the guilt.

AZB: How did you become acquainted with the case of Wańkowicz?

ES: Władysław Wicha, who was then the minister of domestic affairs, sent a letter to the public prosecutor, Kazimierz Kosztirko. On 5 October 1964, at about 8 or 9 p.m., I was called to the office of the said prosecutor. I was given materials to read immediately and to give my opinion on. On reading the presented materials I said that formally, legally, there was formal basis to start an investigation against Wańkowicz. The deed was punishable, and the lower threshold of statutory penalty was three years. In such cases the code of penal proceedings demanded arrest. I asked: Do we—the state—need such a trial? The question is, even if a sentence is passed, can it be executed?

The public prosecutor's answer to that was "Mr. Melchior Wańkowicz is currently speaking in Radom . . . and you ask me about a sentence . . ." I understood that Wańkowicz was already being watched.

AZB: So you realized the significance of the trial and its consequences?

ES: I'm no literary critic, but I was aware of the caliber of Wańkowicz's writing and his position as a writer. And so I realized that this case would arouse much interest, which could turn against the country.

AZB: Who—in your view—made the decision to initiate the trial?

ES: I do not know who made the decision of Wicha handing the case over to Kosztirko, but it could have been Zenon Kliszko himself. Still, this is only my guess. Those were such times that the minister of domestic affairs literally sat on such papers—files were bursting, but they were not touched without a political decision.

History shows that people who stand lower in the hierarchy, like I did, saw matters more broadly than those at the top. Much later I learned that Kliszko suffered from Parkinson's disease. I don't know if you know that, but such people are particularly touchy and difficult for others. Also, much was then said about trouble with the literary community. There was surely a conflict between the literary community and the state authorities.

AZB: Why were you appointed for that case?

ES: I was told to take the case. There were about two thousand prosecutors in Poland then, and I'd only had penal and economic cases before. I never had any other political cases—either before or after that one. I couldn't say no—I'd have been told, "Then quit."

AZB: What did your contact with Wańkowicz during the interrogations look like?

ES: I don't know if this is found in your archives, but, at the end of the case, Mr. Wańkowicz paid me a compliment. "Sir," he said. "I don't like this People's Poland, but as a Pole I'll tell you that I'm happy that Poland has fostered such officials as yourself."

The atmosphere of our conversation was always good; he understood that I had to carry out my duties, and I treated him with extra attention, not like a criminal. . . . After all, his services to literature were so great . . . I myself had a humanistic, liberal education, and literature always interested me.

AZB: You say that you treated him with great attention. There are certain divergences in the protocols. . . .

ES: I engaged in polemics with him. He defined himself as a centripetal writer—meaning that regardless of what was happening, he believed a climate desired for the society should be built. I'd read *Na tropach Smętka* during the Nazi occupation. For me, this was one of the catechisms in literature. Yet in some period Wańkowicz wrote articles some of which didn't fit my notions of him. These were articles published in papers for Poles abroad. . . .

AZB: Did you have access to them?

ES: In the Domestic Affairs Ministry there was a special department concerned with culture, I don't know its exact name, and they collected all the materials. I told them, "Give me everything written by Wańkowicz." During the investigation I read the materials given to me very thoroughly.

AZB: What did your first meeting with the defendant look like?

ES: As I said, I was called to the prosecutor's office at about 9 p.m. At 10 p.m. they brought Wańkowicz to the public prosecutor's office in 25 Krakowskie Przedmieście Street. I was waiting for him. I said: "Mr. Wańkowicz, due to the late hour we won't be talking today, but you are still detained. We will start the interrogations tomorrow."

AZB: Why wasn't Wańkowicz detained the next morning? Why was he brought in practically at night?

ES: Do you really think the decision was up to me?

AZB: Wasn't it awkward, arresting an elderly man at night, like a criminal?

ES: Sure it was awkward! They could have summoned him by mail, or sent a messenger! But the whole matter resulted from the "uncovering" done by the Secret Service. What things they'd said about Wańkowicz, and to whom, I know not.

When I watched Wańkowicz for the first time, he made an impression as if he was glad that something happened to him. That was my impression. I would say he had the mentality half of a country squire, half of a scout.

AZB: In what conditions was he kept?

ES: He was placed in a normal room in the Mostowski Palace. I asked him personally on the next day about the conditions. "They're good. I got breakfast," he replied. It was a room with a bed and clean bedclothes.

AZB: But there were bars in the windows, light burned day and night, two militia officers were always in the room . . .

ES: As I recall, he was content. The prosecutor doesn't decide in what way a detainee is to be guarded. I suspect those were Moczar's orders.

AZB: Do you remember the meeting of Wańkowicz and Moczar?

ES: I remember that my superior phoned me and said: "When you're done talking to Wańkowicz, take him to another room, but don't tell him why. Minister Moczar will be waiting for him there. . . ." I told Wańkowicz that someone was waiting for him. "Who?" he asked. I gave him no reply. When they met, they fell in each other's arms. I remember Moczar saying: "Mr. Melchior, what have you done now!" I was not present as they talked, so I can't say any more.

AZB: How did that trial differ from other ones in your career?

ES: I was forty then. I didn't look at that trial from the viewpoint of a professional career. I was aware that the trial of Wańkowicz was a political sort of game. How much material concerning other people was there in Rakowiecka Street, I could only guess. Sometimes, knowing about certain things can be trouble.

Ma'am, each interrogation report was made in two copies, then signed by me and by Wańkowicz. One copy ended up on the desk of the general public prosecutor. Thus the general prosecutor had precise information and could give it to whom he chose.

AZB: Was that a normal practice?

ES: No, this wasn't usual. I can't remember it being done in other cases.

AZB: What did the interrogations look like?

ES: At first Wańkowicz seemed to have a kind of negative attitude toward me. Maybe he thought I'd treat him badly, be rude. He seemed surprised that I didn't interrupt him, that I was polite.

I told him once: "You will have a visit from the U.S. consul." The Maestro got angry. "What for!" "You can tell him yourself," I said. They talked short and polite. "On behalf of the ambassador, I am asking you what kind of help can be offered to you by the U.S. Embassy." "Thank you for the visit. I don't need anything," replied Wańkowicz.

Once he asked: "May I make a phone call?"

"Excuse me, do you want to call the 'Bunny'?" I asked. I knew he called his wife "Bunny." "That's right," he said. "Forgive me for calling your wife with that name," I said, "but I've read your books." "You may call her; just don't drag out the call." Any time Wańkowicz was in the prosecutor's office, he always phoned his wife.

I think his wife, Zofia, also thought she'd see some bully. One day she came, knocked at my door, and came in. I got up and introduced myself. We talked some. Whenever in my practice I talked to the families of the defendants, I told them the bad times would pass.

I think Mrs. Zofia Wańkowicz was pleasantly surprised with my behavior, the forms. You know, there are stereotypes. . . .

AZB: How do you remember the course of the trial?

ES: I remember many things from the trial. I remember preparing carefully. After all, I was dealing with a defendant who was master of the word. The defense was headed by Władysław Pociej (with whom I was on a first-name basis), also an eminent orator, and the people present in the room were the *crème de la crème* of the Polish literature and journalism of the time. I remember the testimony of the journalist Stefan Kozicki. He was the party's man through and through. He said: "We, people of letters, see Wańkowicz as the father of Polish reportage."

I also remember other moments. When Wańkowicz said he'd fought censorship all his life, I told him I had documents which said that he'd been head of censorship before the war. . . . I remember that Wańkowicz felt piqued with that reminder. I wouldn't have said it if he hadn't been emphasizing his exemplary stand like that. . . . He seemed to feel it acutely, though. . . . When Wańkowicz spoke about the difficult situation of writers, that they were not being published, I asked in what numbers his books were being published. That also annoyed him. . . .

I remember that there was certain friction when I was told to write down what I was going to say in court. "Please prepare the speech for the prosecution and give me it for approval." "No, I can't," I said. I never wrote down what I was later going to say. Kosztirko said: "The word is important. If they make a fool of you, we'll get even with you." I dare say that it ended up well. I offended no one. I have always believed I've been speaking good Polish language and properly performing my duties as a state official.

That whole trial was a great embarrassment to some. In the case of Wańkowicz, I was maximally focused. I did my best to be prepared and not fall into ridicule. I was also afraid they would tell me to demand a draconian sentence. I didn't know what punishment I'd be told to demand for Wańkowicz. He got the lowest sentence specified in the decree of 13 June 1946. The court commuted it by half—to a year and a half. Right after the verdict was passed, arrest was repealed.

It wasn't about punishment, although it's only speculation on my part, but about showing a specific community that those authorities would not refrain from using such means. . . . Socially re-educating Wańkowicz? Ridiculous!

AZB: Was Wańkowicz's trial conducted *in camera* like the Western radios said?

ES: No, I don't consider it an *in camera* trial. Such trial may be ordered by the court in certain situations, for instance due to state secret or decency. Beside advisers to the defendant, there may be only two people present in the hearing in such cases. In the trial of Wańkowicz, I remembered the room always full.

AZB: I'll ask you again—why do you think you were chosen by your superiors to conduct the case?

ES: I had the opinion of a reliable man. I am convinced I was chosen because they knew I wouldn't do anything foolish. They knew I could say much without offending anyone.

Now I've been defending one of a group of young men. The oldest is twenty-one, and the youngest eighteen, sentenced for manslaughter and robbery. They've been sentenced for twelve years. . . . They can't even show remorse; I have to persuade them. I notice a certain degeneration of higher emotions. After several decades, I am not emotionally affected by the cases anymore. I analyze them dispassionately to see what I can do for the person I am defending.

The case of Wańkowicz was exceptional back then. There were no political cases at all in that time. I was even astonished to be chosen for that particular case. I've told you about it before, and now you're asking again. I think I've already quoted Wańkowicz's compliment to me. Maybe that was why I was unchanged during the trial. I remember that always, when I went to talk with the general prosecutor after a hearing, I gave him an oral account, and he already had all the information. From whom, I don't know. When the sentence was passed, I also went there. He told me everything was fine; he had no general comments. . . . That was the end of my role.

AZB: How did you later receive the news that Wańkowicz didn't do time after all?

ES: That wasn't my responsibility anymore. The fact that Wańkowicz did not go to prison, was a matter of the court ordering execution of the sentence. . . . However, another piece of news made a great impression on me, you know—that later, after the trial, Wańkowicz was received by Gomułka himself. Gomułka didn't even receive the general public prosecutor in his office, but he received Wańkowicz. I had a private satisfaction that my question before the trial—the one I'd been scolded for— "Who needs that trial? What is it all for?"—was right. I had been right in my doubts.

AZB: Was any pressure exerted on you to take the case?

ES: No, no one forced me; I wasn't going to be persecuted, I dare say. I agreed to take it, because I was a prosecutor and I had to do my job.

I never saw him after the trial. He could have found me; he had the phone number to the prosecutor's office. Later other prosecutors, when they heard I'd conducted the case of Wańkowicz, asked me about him. I know it has been an interesting case in my career. I am glad that not only did Wańkowicz not hold any grudge against me, but he even judged me well.

The trial was an official order. I believed that there was basis to initiate it. I did my job as a prosecutor as well as I could.

Interview with Stefan Kozicki (SK) conducted on 30 January 1990

As the result of my conversation with Kozicki, he gave the following statement:

SK: I was nervous, stressed. I can't remember the situation in detail. It was my first time speaking in court, first time ever. I can't remember what I said, but I do recall that there was no question which would place me in an awkward position.

That trial was a critical point in my relations with Wańkowicz—since that time, I began to have friendly relations with him. Earlier I'd been at a youth camp. Wańkowicz came in his Mercedes and talked to us, young people, about America and other things. I was astonished then that he didn't view America, the whole West, the political emigration, uncritically.

I think that no one in the community of journalists and writers actually believed that Wańkowicz sent the materials to Radio Free Europe himself. We thought someone did it without his consent.

When I was summoned to court, the journalist community showed extreme interest in that. Some people said I ought to back out. Later, after the trial, when everything seemed to be in favor of Wańkowicz again, they even congratulated me.

Interview with Kazimierz Koźniewski (KK) conducted on 7 February 1990

AZB: Did you know the text of the "Speech Project" by Wańkowicz?

KK: I knew its fragments from Free Europe monitoring records. It wasn't nice to learn that those texts broadcast on Radio Free Europe had been written by Wańkowicz. One of the fragments was about me, as well, and I felt upset. Wańkowicz included there a sentence that was unpleasant for me. It gave a negative opinion on my address in the Writers' Association. That hurt me. But that was all back before the case, before the trial.

AZB: What associations do you have with the trial of Melchior Wańkowicz in 1964?

KK: I associate the trial of Wańkowicz with Mel's[44] general attitude— and it's a bad association. Wańkowicz decided to return to Poland in 1958. Someone who decides to return to their country, decides also to choose the political conception of that country. Also Cat Mackiewicz decided to return. Both of them acted similarly, and their actions were incomprehensible for me, and I reject them completely! Cat had trouble for writing to Paris *Kultura*, and Wańkowicz, for cooperation with Free Europe.

I think there was no need for him to send the text to Free Europe. It was a text that concerned our home matters. He had no right to do that. I condemn both Cat and Wańkowicz. I think that in Poland, Wańkowicz could sign protest letters, and that was all right. However, writing to RFE was wrong. But there was no occasion to say that to Wańkowicz. I still can't forgive him that. If he were sued again, I'd act the same.

AZB: As you know, Wańkowicz couldn't forgive you your testimony in court. . . .

KK: Wańkowicz held a grudge for two things I'd said in court. Ma'am, I have always been a loyal citizen of this state. Whenever I am in court, I believe it to be my civic duty to say the truth. I was asked back then if I'd known that Wańkowicz had met Zygmunt Nowakowski in Vienna. I corrected them that Wańkowicz had seen not Zygmunt, but Tadeusz Nowakowski. Later a colleague told me I should have only said he hadn't met Zygmunt, and I should have said nothing of Tadeusz. Yet I don't think it right to sham, to hush things up, to resort to lying. [45]

Anyway, I knew—everyone did—that the whole case would end up well for Mel. . . .

AZB: Why did you think so?

KK: Because that trial was a farce. . . . The other thing that Wańkowicz held a grudge for, and I have a certain sense of guilt myself . . . but that was just a stupid thing . . . Mel's lawyer asked what I thought about *Tworzywo*. I started talking what an excellent book that was. I value it greatly. I've written about it in *Nowa Kultura*. I talked for about three minutes. My stupidity consisted in the fact that both the judge and Mel's lawyer wanted to hear about something else. They wanted me to repeat what I'd written in the review—that the book showed Mel's pro-Sanacja[46] attitude evolving, that Wańkowicz identified himself with the protagonist's political evolution. You have the same protagonist in *Strzępy epopei*—he emigrates to Canada there. However, I talked not of the book's political significance, but of its literary value. Had the lawyer helped me with another question, I would have said what was expected. Mel meant the book's political values. . . .

As to Mel's first grievance—about Nowakowski—I believe I acted right. As to the other—I got plain confused. And that's actually it about the whole trial; it's all that I have to say about the subject now.

My views were known; I haven't changed them. I don't change my views.

AZB: You were friends with the daughters of Wańkowicz—Marta and Krystyna—so your stand must have surprised Wańkowicz.

KK: Ma'am, after the trial Marta came to Warsaw, called me, we arranged to meet in the "Świtezianka" café. When we were talking, she told me that Mel's texts had really been broadcast in Free Europe, that he had sent them to her in a letter. The Voice of America and Free Europe were one thing to me, and Jan Erdman, Marta's husband, was working in the Voice of America. I asked Tili: "How did the texts get in Nowak's hands?" "I won't answer that question," she told me. I believe that either she or Erdman—according to her father's wish—brought the materials to Nowak.

AZB: After your appearance in court, were there any attempts to renew your relations? Did you get in touch with Wańkowicz?

KK: I owed him a hundred zloty. Right after the trial he wrote me a bitter letter, and I sent him the money.

AZB: How did you receive the news that Wańkowicz had been sued?

KK: All that, in my opinion, stemmed from the fact that at some point Mel went paranoid—I can't give it a different name. I still don't understand many people reacting that way. The head of the party's central committee culture department of that time, Artur Starewicz, didn't like Wańkowicz, and I think he made sure that Mel wasn't invited to make appearances on TV anymore. And for Wańkowicz, those appearances were extremely important. He liked being popular. He was annoyed. I didn't understand it then. I told him: "Cool down. If they don't invite you to TV, so what. . . ." Wojtek [Wojciech] Żukrowski, when a book of his wasn't published, also jumped down your throat. Wańkowicz believed he wouldn't be published. He was having a bad time and couldn't wait patiently. And there are just such waves, and writers often get that—they can't view themselves dispassionately. In such a period of discouragement, he signed the protest of "Letter 34," and then sent the letter to Tili, suggesting that she use it.

AZB: This is your opinion on what Wańkowicz was motivated with? Do you think there were no other, basic, important motives? That is quite a low opinion of him that you present, and yet earlier, for many years, you expressed great respect for him as a man and a writer in your letters. It's been said you'd almost become his son-in-law.

KK: Mel had great influence on me; I owe him a lot. But he was a difficult man. He judged others easily, but didn't apply the same rules to himself. He had both great and not-so-great pages in his history. For instance, Cywiński's case is a large stain on his life. I remember him telling me once that before the war writers signed a protest in connection with Brześć,[47] and he didn't sign it. In 1968[48] he didn't protest, either.

AZB: Is that your indirect reaction to Wańkowicz's lampoon *Pitaval IX*, which after the trial he sent to his friends and in it treated you in an explicitly harsh manner?

KK: You're right in that Mel wrote that lampoon against me, as you've called it. I didn't know the text. I was first shown it by Michał Radgowski, already after Wańkowicz's death.[49] On reading it, I learned among other things that I was a Secret Service agent. That was ridiculous. I didn't react; the whole matter was no longer current.

AZB: You didn't engage in polemics with him. You didn't even attempt to explain your stand from the testimony in the trial.

KK: No, I didn't engage in any polemics with Wańkowicz. I would have done it with any other person, but not him. After the trial we acted like two strangers, didn't greet each other on meeting.

Once I met Zofia in a bank. We greeted each other warmly. I remember that between October 1939 and middle of January 1940 I was working as "Rój's" storeman. Did you know, for instance, that Krysia had buried my underground archives in their garden but two days before the Uprising? . . . They were lost. I remember being in their "Dear Home" in spring 1945. I got a few copies of nicely bound *Sztafeta* from under the ruins.

AZB: After what you've just told me, your stand in the trial is even more surprising.

KK: Ma'am, the farce with that trial did Mel good! The trial disgraced the authorities. I think that was why later Cat Mackiewicz wasn't sued. He also published his works under a pseudonym, so did Stefan Kisielewski. . . . Anyway, back to Wańkowicz, his books were later published; he even went on a bus trip with a group that included Moczar.

AZB: You have a peculiar way of looking at the events. . . .

KK: Yes, I must say that everyone has their own view on events, their own interpretation. Wańkowicz felt some resentment, but the literary community had no grudge against me. And I was not told about that lampoon for many long years, either. . . . I repeat, if I'd known that Mel had appeared on Radio Free Europe, I would have broken off relations with him. I felt deeply hurt to learn that Free Europe was reading his text. For instance, Janek [Jan] Strzelecki didn't publicly speak abroad against what he didn't like here in the country. . . . I was also friends with Stefan Kisielewski, despite our political differences. . . . I believe, and I'm going to repeat that by returning in 1958 Mel chose those authorities. His return was also a political decision. I repeat—if the situation were repeated, I would have acted the very same.

PART D: KOŹNIEWSKI—AN AGENT WITH
"*CON AMORE*" SERVILITY

In the above-printed, authorized interview with Kazimierz Koźniewski, when I asked him what he thought about Wańkowicz's lampoon about him (the writer had entitled it *Pitaval IX*), he said, "I didn't know the text. I was first shown it by Michał Radgowski,[50] already after Wańkowicz's death. On reading it I learned among other things that I was a Secret Service agent. That was ridiculous. I didn't react; the whole matter was no longer current." In that short statement, the truth was concealed no less than three times. The first concealment: "I was a Secret Service agent. That was ridiculous." Koźniewski's revelation sounds like a parody, since files of TW "33"[51] show him to be one of the most devoted employees of the Security Office and then Security Service in the history of Communist Poland. Wańkowicz had discovered back in 1964 that Koźniewski had an "agent's mind." He wrote that the latter mainly had a need of *con amore* servility. To quote,

> It must be considered whether it is only an agent's mind. That would be too simple. It is easy to find much more explicit types with agent's minds. That is only a need for servility *con amore*. Perhaps it is best explained by Koźniewski himself. He writes in his memoirs: "Thus I was for my own self one big ambiguity. Anyway, I dampened any disquiet easily. Essentially, I yielded to my surroundings [. . .] a man who functions like that is subject to the law of mimesis.[52]

The second "concealment of truth" in the short quote is the statement told to me[53] that Michał Radgowski showed *Pitaval IX* to Koźniewski only after the writer's death. Already after my interview with Koźniewski was authorized, I showed Radgowski the text and he gave me some correcting information of the facts to put into a footnote. I quote again below:

> In the account of Michał Radgowski, Melchior Wańkowicz—interested in Kazimierz Koźniewski's reaction—asked Radgowski to show Koźniewski the text of the lampoon. That was back when the writer was still alive.

In IPN files, there is a long list of people and institutions where Wańkowicz sent his *Pitavals*. They contain addresses of people of various political views, editor's offices, and associations. There was also the address of the editor-in-chief of *Polityka*[54] Mieczysław Rakowski. Radgowski was the assistant of the said editor, and he received them too, he confirmed. In total, there are 212 places listed. Among the names of addressees were Tadeusz Drewnowski, Andrzej Miłosz, Ryszard Matuszewski, Kazimierz Brandys, Marian Brandys, Andrzej Braun, Professor Witold Kula, Professor Bogdan Suchodolski,

Igor Abramow Neverly, Leon Lech Beynar, Zofia Kroh, Szymon Kobyliński, Wiesław Górnicki, Aleksander Ścibor Rylski, and Antoni Słonimski.

The third concealment and actually a "distortion of truth" in Koźniewski's short statement I quoted is his sentence: "I didn't react; the whole matter was no longer current."

Meanwhile, in a report (as is documented in the archives of IPN) he wrote Koźniewski reacted to the *Pitaval* concerning him:

> For a long time, Wańkowicz has been preparing for himself short *pitavals*, or features against various people. However, when talking to people about them, he stressed they were not for publication purposes. A few months ago, he showed Radgowski a feature against Koźniewski, and asked the former to show the text to Koźniewski. The text is venomous, vitriolic. Extremely violent. Wańkowicz was obviously provoked by what Koźniewski had written about his reportage from the Zaolzie[55] annexation in 1938.

What is noteworthy, Koźniewski writes about himself in the third person. This technique was often utilized by him and by many other agents. In their reports, they often used the third person to talk about themselves, for example, "Koźniewski noticed."

In his report, he stated that the *Pitaval* concerned the matter of Zaolzie from back in 1938, not wanting to reveal openly that Wańkowicz reminded him of his betrayal during the writer's trial in 1964. Maybe for some reason he did not want to recall the incident?

Almost any issue raised in the interview turned out to be distorted. For instance, Koźniewski talked to me about his testimony in court during the trial against Wańkowicz:

> I was asked back then if I'd known that Wańkowicz had met Zygmunt Nowakowski in Vienna. I corrected them that Wańkowicz had not seen Zygmunt, but Tadeusz Nowakowski. Later, a colleague told me I should have only said he hadn't met Zygmunt, and I should have said nothing of Tadeusz. Yet I don't think it right to sham, to hush things up, to resort to lying.

The words sound simply pathetic. Koźniewski dissociated himself from "lying," while the IPN files hold his own reports. There is a report he wrote immediately upon learning that Wańkowicz was going to Vienna. In the report, Koźniewski proposed to accompany him. Exactly two days on returning from Vienna, he wrote another report, where he informed about the writer meeting Nowakowski—and he used the correct name. To quote,

Classified
Abstract, source "33" of 7th November 1963

From 26th October to 5th November 1963, M. Wańkowicz was staying in Vienna and Munich.

In Munich, he saw Tadeusz Nowakowski. Nowakowski was said to be friendly. The conversation had the following topical points:

1. Nowakowski asked very little about the matters in Poland. Wańkowicz had the impression of the man having generally little interest in the country. Yet Nowakowski—according to Wańkowicz—has much knowledge of our domestic matters. He said, e.g., that Kuryluk would be recalled from Vienna, Morawski was to come in his place, and Kuryluk was to become editor-in-chief of *Kultura*. The same information is actually said by other Poles in Vienna—those from the embassy circle.

Nowakowski himself does not actually write in Polish anymore. He's writing his new novel in German only. He told Wańkowicz about the particularly bad reception in West Germany of the new novel of Marek Hłasko *Bicze gniewu*[56] (about prostitutes and pimps in Israel). Critics named it "the worst book of 1963." They accuse Hłasko of taking some loutish situations from Europe and from Poland and setting them (mythicized) in Israel, where everything is different, and so the result lacked sense.

2. As they talked, Tadeusz Nowakowski suggested that Wańkowicz meet Nowak—the head of the Polish section of Radio Free Europe. Wańkowicz agreed. A few hours later, Tadeusz Nowakowski called Wańkowicz and said that Nowak would meet him if Wańkowicz asked for a meeting. Wańkowicz said then that he had no business there and that he wouldn't ask Nowak to meet him. So, a meeting never developed.

Before the war, "Kazik" (Kazimierz) Koźniewski was a friend of Wańkowicz's daughters. He told me that between October 1939 and middle of January 1940, he had been employed by Zofia Wańkowicz to work as "Rój's" storeman, and that "Krysia [Krystyna] had buried my underground archives in their garden but two days before the Uprising. . . . I remember being in their 'Dear Home' in Spring 1945. I was given a few copies of nicely bound *Sztafeta* from under the ruins."

Wańkowicz also wrote in his *Pitaval*: "K. Koźniewski, a friend of my house from before the war, maintained friendly relationships with me. Those relationships allowed him, back before we parted, to benefit by joining me in my car trip to Vienna."

During the trial of the author of *Bitwa o Monte Cassino*, Zofia Wańkowicz saw Koźniewski. She trusted him, and came to see him as a friend of the family. Meanwhile, "Kazik" promptly informed about their meeting. In his report, he positively "suggested monitoring" the phone call to the United States he had advised Zofia to make. To quote,

Work file No. 16039/I
Work file of Confidential Collaborator (volume I)
Note from meeting with K. pseud. "33" on 3 XI [November] 1964
(Majchrowski)

In the meeting, "33" informed me he'd had a talk with Mrs. Zofia Wańkowicz, who complained about how the authorities were treating her husband, and asked for some articles and publications she needed for her husband's defense.

"33" gave her the articles and suggested she telephone the United States and establish whether the letter written by Melchior actually made it there. As he informed me about it, he suggested monitoring that call.

In today's meeting he told me he had been summoned to the trial against Wańkowicz as a witness for the defense, and he asked for advice on how to act.

In that connection—in accordance with the order of Col. Filipiak—I alluded to the previous meetings and indicated his ambiguous stand in the case.

I led him to understand that his conduct worried us, because similar advice could cost us dearly. Moreover, his involvement in the case was politically harmful—since he was representing not only himself, but also the party officials, and that could be cleverly used in the long term. I mentioned that such attempts were already taking place.

My statement had a huge impact on "33." He declared himself ready to condemn Wańkowicz for his involvement in contacting hostile centers—that they had reportedly always been a controversy between them. He also stated that in the hearing, he would state his protest in that respect.

I told him that he should answer precisely the questions asked in the court, but that he had to speak objectively—say what he knew, regardless of whether or not it was beneficial for Wańkowicz. Principally, he should speak about Wańkowicz's contacts with Tadeusz Nowakowski, Czapski, about his publications in *Kultura*, and not about matters unrelated to the trial.

(Accepted by Borowczak)

Below another report from the same period:

Warsaw 13th October 1964

On 13th October 1964, contact "33" notified me of receiving mysterious phone calls. Unidentified callers phoned him at home at night, asking about Wańkowicz, and then connected him with some major located in Kraków.

Alarmed by the calls, "33" filed a report on the case (I sent it to Col. Pawłowicz) and asked for intervention.

In that connection, I suggest tapping his phone to establish the above-stated and possible calls.

He informed not only on Zofia, but he also wrote reports on the daughter of Wańkowicz, his friend and his love interest since youth—Marta Wańkowicz Erdman. He spoke to me about their meetings when she was in Poland, suggesting that Marta trusted him. He told me: "After the trial Marta came to Warsaw, called me, we arranged to meet in the 'Świezianka' café." Similarly, he casually mentioned that when after some years he met Zofia, they "greeted each other warmly."

Meanwhile, he wrote a report also about the meeting with the "trusting Marta," and a note was made:

> Erdman phoned, asking to meet on neutral ground.
>
> They met on 27th this month in the "Świezianka" café. The conversation gradually grew friendly, despite the initial reservations of Marta Wańkowicz Erdman, who said she "will talk frankly, but not about everything."
>
> In the beginning, she was clearly trying to convince Koźniewski that he must have known about her being in Poland, and yet he hadn't contacted her. She also said that Wańkowicz was feeling quite well as concerned his health, in contrast to Zofia Wańkowicz, who was constantly in a sickened state. Wańkowicz could not forgive Koźniewski for having revealed in court what Wańkowicz had been talking about with Tadeusz Nowakowski [he wrote a report earlier—as quoted above—AZB] when they'd met in Vienna. He held no other grudge against him.
>
> Further, Marta Wańkowicz convinced him that the case of Wańkowicz's letter, on which the trial was based, remained unclear for her and for many others. Wańkowicz had written the letter in three copies, of which she got one, and two were at home. She gave the letter to no one, and Wańkowicz showed it to a few close friends in Poland to read. In that case, how did it get abroad? Moreover, she said that Cibor, who was a witness in the case, had indeed worked as Second Secretary of the Polish Embassy in the U.S.A., but he'd left to Poland on 15th June 1964, i.e., before Wańkowicz sent the letter.
>
> Asked by Koźniewski, she explained that Wańkowicz wasn't going to appeal, but he would endeavor to establish the truth.

A thought came to my mind, how the writer's daughter, knowing from her father about Koźniewski's role in the trial, could go on meeting him and talk to him about her father's trial. And she also met him a few times later, when she came to Poland. She still saw him as her friend—despite her father's unpleasant experience, despite his *Pitaval*, where he wrote what he thought of the "Creep," or "Snitch," Koźniewski.

Many years later, already after the death of Wańkowicz, Anna[57] and Tadeusz Walendowski[58] invited Koźniewski to their flat (which used to belong to Wańkowicz) at 10 Puławska Street, to a meeting of the Flying University.[59] Of course, Koźniewski immediately wrote a report on the meeting.

Those were special meetings "with writers in disgrace with the authorities," as was clearly stated by Anna Erdman, Walendowski's wife, in her letter to Adam Janiszewski in Lublin (the letter is stored in IPN files—in Walendowski's file):[60]

27 I [January] 1978 Dear Adam [. . .] For over a year I've been organizing literary evenings in my flat. Starting September, they take place regularly each Wednesday. The participants are writers and poets currently in disgrace with the authorities (e.g., Marek Nowakowski, Tadeusz Konwicki, Stefan Kisielewski). [. . .] Anna

And so, although Kazimierz Koźniewski denounced Melchior Wańkowicz, the latter's granddaughter Anna and her husband magnanimously invited him to their salon, to an evening dedicated to the underground *Zapis*.[61] The wolf let into the fold wrote, as usual, a report of a dozen pages, where he even noted the casualness at the meeting: "They talked as they were sitting or lying down on the carpet, and the only snacks were cheese sandwiches." He listed the names of guests and discussants, for example, Lesław Maleszka. The latter, according to Walendowski's dossier, also wrote a report from the meeting, under the pseudonym "Return."

And thus all of them, Mrs. Zofia Wańkowicz, Marta Wańkowicz Erdman, the Walendowskis, all had good relationships with the man who had betrayed Wańkowicz (and despite the fact that the writer had seen through him, and revealed his role in the trial)! Indeed, the very fact of them maintaining contact with Kazimierz Koźniewski after 1964 is appalling.

In 2007, I spent long hours in the IPN reading room in Towarowa Street, going through five giant volumes of agent "33's" work. He interested me mainly as the man who informed on Wańkowicz, but I have found there a lot of different materials. Those are denunciations by an agent who for over fifty years filed multi-page reports on nearly any topic that appeared around him. I assume that he sat down to the typewriter every day to write them. "Opportunism and extremely eager collaboration," wrote Krzysztof Masłoń.[62]

In Koźniewski's files, there are handwritten reports, although there are mainly typed ones with corrections and supplementary notes, re-typed by the Secret Service and kept in two copies. Thus, in the draft it was stated, for example, "Koźniewski talked to Kisiel,"[63] and in the clean copy: "'33' talked to Kisiel."

Agent "33" was defined as "remaining in active network" still in the 1980s, and later. In his files there is a note:

Warsaw, 31st January 1985
Deputy Head of Section 4 of 3rd Dept. of Min. of Domestic Affairs
Captain A. Minkowicz

Please find attached the work file of contact pseud. "33," 307 pages, to be placed in the depository of operational materials of Bureau C of the Ministry. Please do not give out the work file to any operational units of your services, as contact "33" remains in active network.

Koźniewski was active and eager. His thorough and detailed denunciations usually amounted to a dozen, if not several dozen pages. He always found material to report.

A story about Koźniewski could be entitled "Agent '33' Reports on Own and Strangers" about a man who reported on those close to him and on total strangers. How disturbing! I was actually surprised, because—I don't know why—I thought an agent would spare his friends or colleagues. Yet Koźniewski, meticulously and without any qualms, exposed the communities close to him, and people close to him.

And he had such a good past—as you would say about someone with a similar life history.

"He had a nice history from the time of the occupation," wrote Krzysztof Masłoń. He co-created the underground Polish People's Independence Action.[64] He was a courier of the Government in London, and member of the headquarters of "Szare Szeregi" (the Grey Ranks) organization.[65] After the war, he became a journalist. He had worked as one back before 1939, publishing his work in *Kuźnia Młodych* and *Orka na Ugorze*.[66, 67]

His files[68] provide basic information:

> Kazimierz Koźniewski "33." Son of Wacław. Mother: Wiktoria Majkowska. Incomplete higher education—3 years of Polish Philology.
>
> During occupation, head of the Publishing Dept. at the "Szare Szeregi" ZHP Headquarters, pseud. "Cietrzew," "Jeż." Arrested in Kraków on 9 XI [November] 1945—suspected of WIN[69] membership. Charges not proven. Decision to release—17 XI [November] 1945. Released on 26 XI [November] 1945.
>
> (Lt. Col. St. Borowczak Senior Insp., 3rd Dept.)

Koźniewski thus wrote about himself in a handwritten resumé (fragments quoted below):[70]

> Resumé
>
> I was born on 26 7 [July] 1919 in Warsaw. [. . .] I was in the scouts. [. . .] When the war broke out, I was deputy scoutmaster of the scouts' medical rescue of the city of Warsaw. On 6th September 1939 I went to enlist together with the other scouts. I was not taken to the army, so from Chełmno I returned to Warsaw. I arrived there in the first days in October. In mid-October 1939, I and my friends from *Orka na ugorze* established an underground organization named PLAN [Polish People's Independence Action]. In January 1940, due to a leak, I had to escape. At that time my father was arrested, and then shot in June 1940 in Palmiry [a village near Warsaw]. In February 1940, I escaped abroad, first to Budapest, then from Budapest to France. In France, I joined the Polish Army. After France capitulated, I came with the whole army to Britain,

and remained a soldier there. On behalf of the minister of domestic affairs of the Government in Exile in London, Professor Kot, I was sent in March 1941 as a scout leader to Poland to reorganize the command of the Scouting Association. [. . .] In Poland, after terminating the contact with ZHP (Szare Szeregi), I became the head of the publishing department in the scouts' main headquarters and remained at that post until the Uprising. I didn't take part in the Uprising.

On the tenth day of the Uprising, I was evacuated from the Ochota district to the town of Pruszków. From there I escaped and went to Kraków in November 1944. In December 1944, I became scoutmaster of "Szare Szeregi" group and started collaboration with the Scouting Association. In August, I reported to Col. Narbut stating that I wished to take part in a convention of former armed struggle participants. I had participated in them as a "Szare Szeregi" representative. In October, I decided to move to Warsaw for academic and scouting reasons. Since July, I have been working with *Odrodzenie* and *Przekrój*.[71]

Reports filed by Koźniewski concern, for example, "the story of disbanding the 'Szare Szeregi'"; notes on today's youth; Catholic spheres and the pope's letter; *Tygodnik Powszechny*;[72] reaction to the signing of the agreement between the government and the episcopate; Edmund Rudnicki; meeting with Kętrzyński; situation in *Tygodnik Powszechny*; Meysztowicz; Polish Writers' Association; Kurzyna; description of two ZLP communities; meeting with Maciej Czerwiński; names in the "Szare Szeregi"; report from trip to France; and the story of "Szare Szeregi" disbanding and people from the underground scout organization joining the Polish Scouting Association[73] established after the war. He wrote reports on eminent writers: Aleksander Kamiński, Stanisław Broniewski, and Mieczysław Kurzyna.

He thus wrote of the book that has been and still is particularly valuable and significant to many people—*Kamienie na szaniec*:[74] "It is alarming how greatly popular this book is, and in particular among young people. There is a fear that it may possibly be another source of fire to fuel the post-occupation smoke."

On Kamiński, he wrote, for example, "Definitely hostile toward the new system and the Soviet Union."

"It was funny," wrote Krzysztof Masłoń,[75] "that this "state follower," scout activist (party member since 1955), author of many studies on the Polish Scouting Association, although he usually signed his reports to the Ministry of Domestic Affairs as "33"—that he sometimes signed them "Harcmistrz"—"Scoutmaster."

He decoded the pseudonym under which Stanisław "Cat" Mackiewicz published his articles in Paris *Kultura*. He later filed reports,[76] for example, on the writers J. J. Lipski, J. Kisielewski, A. Kijowski, A. Mięrzyrzecki, and L. Tyrmand. He provided information concerning the brothers K. and M. Brandys, A. Lisiecka, T. Konwicki, and L. Unger (Mathieu Le Soir, "Brukselczyk"), as well as J. Giedroyc.

In his report from the trip to France he wrote:

> From 22nd March to 28th April 1954 I was in France, in Paris. [. . .]
> I renewed the acquaintance with Tadeusz Łada from Lille. The contacts
> thus made establishing further ones easier. Łada introduced me to his emigrant
> friends—Szyndler, an intelligence and counter-intelligence agent, former atta-
> ché militaire or employee of the said attaché's office in Moscow (1935–1938),
> and former Home Army soldier, Engineer Sawicki. The meetings were very
> interesting as concerns getting to know a certain emigrant community in its
> wide political and material scope. Drzewiecka introduced me (out of her own
> initiative, that I eagerly accepted) to Józef Czapski and Jerzy Giedroyc, and
> through them, I met Giedroyc's brother [Henryk] and Mr. and Mrs. Hertz.
> Conversations with those people were extremely interesting and I think they
> may be useful in practice.

From 14 June 1970 there is a request for permission to give some foreign
currency of the Third Department of the Ministry—fifty dollars—to "33" in
connection with his trip to France. Colonel J. Pielasa, deputy director of the
Third Department, wrote about Koźniewski: "In France, contact '33' will be
performing operational tasks."

Years passed, and he was still reporting. He wrote about meetings of the
Writer's Association, discussed the "ideological and political" situation in
ZLP in Warsaw, and informed about his colleagues from the weekly *Polityka*. He reported what Radgowski said "behind the scenes," and reported on
his colleagues from editorial meetings. He was a member of the editorial
board from 1957 to 1982, and he wrote reports almost until his death (he died
in 2005). He wrote, for example, "On Monday, 9 December 1974 at the
Polityka editorial meeting MFR had a long and very sharp speech listing the
deficiencies and failings of editorial work—he meant the lack of materials
that were needed to adequately discuss economic, social, or other achievements in the paper." He quoted Rakowski's statement for the paper's employees to "write and give him reports on their contacts with foreigners."

He even wrote about the visit of Pope John Paul II.

> 26th May 1976, the Pope' visit
>
> Kisielewski spoke of the Pope in the highest terms. But he said that as a
> cardinal, Wojtyła had shown no political brilliance whatsoever; rather he had
> been somewhat vague, as if removed from directly political matters, sort of
> "wishy-washy." He laughed that this was the reason Wojtyła had been earlier
> selected by Kliszko as the least politically distinctive among several candi-
> dates to the Kraków archbishop's throne.

(Accepted by Borowczak)

In the files containing Koźniewski's reports—as I have already written—I sought mainly those concerning Wańkowicz. He filed reports on the writer even before the latter returned to Poland permanently in 1958. Below are some fragments from the reports I selected.

Info on meeting of Warsaw Branch of ZLP 7.02.77
14 09 77
30th April 1950

Opinions in the Team of *Dziś i Jutro*[77] on Melchior Wańkowicz's stand as revealed in the brochure *Klub trzeciego miejsca* are interesting. Dobraczyński believes Wańkowicz's stand to be right, and almost identifies herself with that stand. Furious at Wańkowicz are Lichniak and Kętrzyński—they believe the idea of isolating oneself from current matters to be plain ridiculous. I don't know the opinions of Jasienica, Horodyński, and others yet.

Reports, 25th August 1958

Right upon coming, Wańkowicz was accosted by various people. Mostly private ones. [. . .] He was invited by Bolesław Piasecki to dinner—and refused. He does not want to join PAX.[78] However, he seeks contact with people from the ruling camp. He seeks—as he says—Communists, although he asserts that he is not a Communist himself. He claims that communism has not proven itself as a welfare organization system, that capitalism gives far wider prosperity.

23rd January 1959
Report cont. Source "33"

Melchior Wańkowicz as a person is a very interesting problem, which has so far not been solved properly. As a result, a very interesting man is somehow wasted. What is his stand? He came to Poland in a blaze of glory from the Monte Cassino epic—strongly promoted rather by the Catholic camp. This is happening although, still back when he first came (fall 1956) to Poland, he stressed emphatically that he wanted to enter Poland on a broad front, and not just on one—Catholic—horse. Hence he wrote to *Przekrój*, to *Przegląd Kulturalny*, to *Tygodnik Kulturalny*, to *Tygodnik Powszechny*, to *Świat*, to *Kierunki*[79]—everywhere. [. . .] [once] this writer's features appeared in papers of extreme directions, of ideological stands plainly hostile against one another, and he was, and still is, proud of that fact. When he prepared the promotion of his book *W kościołach Meksyku*, he chose both praises and attacks from any possible side. MW likes to shock people in that way so as to tease his admirers. When the emigration named him their hero as the author of *Monte Cassino*—he presented *Kundlizm* to them, refused to sign the resolution of the Writers' Union, and as a result fell out with the whole community.

In 1960, Koźniewski provided a detailed report on Wańkowicz's plans of his trip to the States. He likely asked around about the writer, who still didn't trust him then.

> 17th December 1960. Note by "33" (accepted by Borowczak):
> Melchior Wańkowicz's Journey Plan
> Take-off—Warsaw, morning of 13 XII [December]. Two days in Paris. He'll stay in a hotel.
> Wańkowicz announced his coming to the Romanowiczs, saying, "I am not going to visit anyone, but whoever wants to see me, I'll gladly receive them in the hotel."
> He refers mainly to *Kultura* and Giedroyc, hoping for the latter's visit.
> 16 XII [December]—leaves Paris to London by plane for four days. Also no visits planned there. He only threatened that he'd go to the "veterans" and we'd see what would happen. In fact, he was gearing himself up for some squabble with the emigrants. He is to give a lecture (he didn't know the room or any details yet) organized by Taborski. He wanted to say "Moja droga do Polski" ["My Way to Poland"], to repeat the lecture he held in Poland and to show what can be said here. Of course, discussion will be most important.
> He'd like to make it to Washington for Christmas, stopping on his way in New York for a day or two. On 4th January, he flies to California for 4 months, hoping to prolong the stay. Generally, he wants to stay in the States for about a year.

On 23 November 1970 he reported: "Andrzejewski says he can't tolerate Wańkowicz."

Eight days after the author of *Monte Cassino* died, Koźniewski wrote a lengthy report, where he (writing about himself in the third person, as usual) recalled the *Pitaval* concerning him. He also filed a report concerning the writer's archive, and reported—as he wrote—conversations with his colleague from *Polityka*, Michał Radgowski.

After Wańkowicz's death, he reacted with envy to how much space was dedicated to the writer in Warsaw *Kultura*,[80] a paper edited then by Dominik Horodyński. He thus wrote:

> Generally surprised with this issue of *Kultura*. Tatarkiewiczowa, Drewnowski, Krzemiński, Koźniewski, Iłowiecki, etc., all think that Horodyński must have gone mad. This is tasteless. That someone should have stopped this, limited it top-down to one position, and not make an article which will only cause a lot of bad blood. This festival of Wańkowicz must be regulated, not cut through so mechanically. This issue of *Kultura* is something highly irresponsible—such is my opinion. ("33")

And so after the writer's death, Koźniewski still wrote reports on him—annoyed that "too much" place had been dedicated to the author of *Bitwa o Monte Cassino* in a literary weekly.[81] He would have rather seen, I believe, a note saying in small font that Melchior Wańkowicz had died, period. Meanwhile, various reporters, such as Kapuściński and others, quoted fragments of his books that they particularly valued. Ryszard Kapuściński chose a fragment from a book he valued particularly, as he wrote, from *Sztafeta*.

On 7 February 1990, sixteen years after Wańkowicz's death, I saw Kazimierz Koźniewski for the first time in my life as I visited him in his home. I was collecting materials for the book and had some questions for him in connection with the trial of 1964, as thirty-six years had passed since that date.

I was looking at an elderly gentleman, quite pleased with himself, a man who from a witness for the defense had turned into one for the prosecution, a man who had betrayed the writer and his family—whom he'd been friends with since his youth. And now he was telling me: "Wańkowicz felt some resentment, but the literary community had no grudge against me . . . I repeat—if the situation were repeated, I would have acted the very same."

At that time, I didn't know about the IPN files, about the fact that as a confidential collaborator he had written reports on dozens of people. I didn't know about either the files on Wańkowicz kept in IPN, or my own file. I didn't know he had written reports on me, as well.

His reports mentioning my name are found in the file containing materials against Wańkowicz, and in a more extensive version, in the file of materials collected against me.

Not until sixteen years after my meeting with Koźniewski did I learn that I had my "own file," and that the so-called threat description (with me posing the threat) had been given personally by my interlocutor.

NOTES

1. Communist leader of Poland from 1945 to 1948, and again from 1956 to 1970. General secretary of the Polish United Workers' Party and practically leader of the state in 1956–1970.

2. PZPR—Polish United Workers' Party (translator's note).

3. Twelfth Plenary Session of the Central Committee, J. Putrament, stenographic record, p. 76

4. Ibid., p. 92

5. Zenon Kliszko (1908–1989)—politician and leader of the Communist Polish United Worker's Party.

6. Jan Józef Lipski (1926–1991)—Polish critic, literature historian, and politician.

7. Maria Dąbrowska (1889–1965)—Polish writer, novelist, and author of the family saga *Noce i dnie* (*Nights and Days*).

8. M. Dąbrowska, *Dzienniki* (*Journals* (Warsaw: Czytelnik, 1988), vol. 5. Introduction, selection, and notes by Tadeusz Drewnowski

9. *Creativity*, or *Creative Output*—a Polish monthly literary journal, first published in 1945 (translator's note).

10. *Pins*—illustrated leftist satirical paper established in 1935 (translator's note).

11. Catholic daily (1947–1997), not acknowledged by the church authorities. The paper promoted cooperation of Catholics with the authorities of the People's Republic of Poland (translator's note).

12. *Kierunki*, "Tygodnik społeczno-kulturalny katolików" (*Directions*, "Social and Cultural Weekly for Catholics")—a socialism-friendly weekly established in 1956 (translator's note).

13. Polish Roman Catholic weekly magazine, focusing on social and cultural issues, established in 1945. Jerzy Turowicz was its editor-in-chief until his death in 1999 (translator's note).

14. *Life of Warsaw*—Warsaw daily (1944–2011). Next to *Trybuna Ludu* (*People's Tribune*) it was one of the two major opinion-forming dailies in Communist Poland (translator's note).

15. The smallest unit of the party—three party members were needed to establish one, but a unit could contain over one hundred members (translator's note).

16. *Życie Warszawy*, no. 112, 1964.

17. Also called Polish October or Gomułka's Thaw, the time marked a change in Poland's internal policy. Gomułka came to power and negotiated wider autonomy for the Polish government. For ordinary citizens, this meant liberalization of life in Poland, though only temporarily (translator's note).

18. Mel, Melo—diminutive of Melchior (Wańkowicz)

19. *People's Tribune* (1948–1990)—one of the largest newspapers in Communist Poland. It was the official media outlet of the Polish United Workers' Party and one of its main propaganda means (translator's note).

20. *Lekarz z Westerplatte. Major Mieczysław Słaby 1905–1948* (*Doctor from Westerplatte. Major Mieczysław Słaby 1905–1948*) (Rzeszów: GRFE Consulting, 2008).

21. Krzysztof Zajączkowski, "Wrześniowe archiwum Melchiora Wańkowicza" ("September Archive of Melchior Wańkowicz"), Gdańsk, *Pomerania*, no. 9 (401), 2007, pp. 29–32.

22. IPN O192/72 vol. 3.

23. Police in the People's Republic of Poland.

24. Op cit.

25. Maria Dąbrowska heard about it directly from Kliszko, as she wrote in her *Journals* under the date of 24 October.

26. Actually *Abecadło Kisiela* (*Kisiel's Alphabet*), a set of anecdotes about people Kisielewski (or "Kisiel") knew. In the same book, the author thus writes about Wańkowicz: "They locked him up for some time, threatened with a trial, but he got out of it somehow. He was a unique specimen, because he renounced the American citizenship. Americans really don't like that. What's more, Minister Moczar advised him against that. He said: 'Why do that. You're safe here in Warsaw.' But no, he renounced it." That wasn't true. Wańkowicz didn't "get out of the trial." I'd also like to make clear that he kept the American passport until his death.

27. Actually, Wańkowicz was seventy-two then.

28. Then Polish-Lithuanian Commonwealth, since 1939 USSR.

29. *Literary Life* (1951–1991)—a weekly issued in Kraków (translator's note).

30. *Międzyepoka* (*Interperiod*)—a term introduced by Wańkowicz in his book *Polacy i Ameryka* (*Poles and America*) to denote a (current) transitory period between Western civilization and a new one to appear (translator's note).

31. The writer wrote about it in the essay "Inżynier dusz petentem" ("From Engineer of Human Souls to Supplicant"), included in the book *Przez cztery klimaty* (*Through Four Climates*).

32. Związek Autorów i Kompozytorów Scenicznych (Polish Society of Authors and Composers)—a Polish organization representing artists and composers, whose mission is to "defend their copyrights" (translator's note).

33. Związek Młodzieży Socjalistycznej (Union of Socialist Youth).

34. Intentional misspelling of the word "canary" (translator's note).

35. Intentional misspelling of the word "creep" (translator's note).

36. Krzysztof Masłoń, "Rówieśnicy" ("Peers"), *Rzeczpospolita Daily*, 10 Decmeber 2007.

37. *Dziennik Polski* (*Polish Daily*, Britain's only Polish-language daily, started in 1940), London, 21 XII [December] 1964

38. *Law and Life*, a weekly concerned with legal and judiciary issues, started 1956 (translator's note).

39. See *Polska z oddali* (*Poland from Afar*) (London, 1988).

40. In the quoted book, *Polska z oddali*, J. Nowak writes: "While writing my memoirs I learned that Wańkowicz repaid Gomułka for the reprieve by sending out a letter of commendation." I have found no trace of such a letter, and none of my interviewees has heard of it.

41. Wańkowicz didn't officially renounce U.S. citizenship, which would require following a certain procedure. Neither did he return his U.S. passport to the American embassy in any symbolic gesture. He retained the American passport until his death.

42. After his meeting with Gomułka, Wańkowicz's works were published again, but he was still under surveillance. IPN files hold, for example, reports of 1966 from the golden wedding anniversary of Zofia and Melchior Wańkowicz, including the list of participants, and so forth. Further reports were written, among others by agents "33" or "Ewa."

43. Literally *A Polish Review*—supplement to *Nowy Dziennik* (*Polish Daily News*), New York, 22 October 2004.

44. Mel—short for Melchior.

45. That is not true. In IPN files I read in 2007 there are numerous reports on Wańkowicz by Koźniewski. There are particularly many from 1964. He wrote reports right before leaving with Wańkowicz to Vienna, and then almost immediately on his return he wrote another one. (I write more on the matter in the next chapter.)

46. Sanacja—from Latin *sanatio*—to heal, cure—was a popular name given to Pilsudski and his closest collaborators' program, after his coup of May 1925, of "healing" the multiparty, unstable, Polish political system which had produced short-lived coalition governments. Unfortunately, it led to the growing power of Pilsudski and, after his death, of his trusted officers.

47. In the Brest trials (26 October 1931 to 13 January 1932), leaders of the political opposition, a "center-left" anti-Sanation-government movement, were accused of plotting a political coup, tried, and sentenced to up to three years of imprisonment. The name came from the Brest (Brześć) Fortress (currently in Belarus) where the arrested leaders were kept. The trials were among the most famous and controversial ones in inter-war Poland (translator's note).

48. The Polish 1968 political crisis—a major student and intellectual protest action against the government of the People's Republic of Poland. It was followed by a wave of repressions (translator's note).

49. According to a journalist of the weekly *Polityka* (*Politics*), Michał Radgowski, Melchior Wańkowicz, interested in Kazimierz Koźniewski's reaction, asked Radgowski to show the lampoon's text to the latter. It happened while Wańkowicz was still alive.

50. Michał Radgowski (born 1930)—journalist and author, for many years deputy editor-in-chief of the weekly respected magazine *Polityka*.

51. K. Koźniewski signed his reports as TW (Confidential Collaborator) "Szcz," "Szczotka," "Harcmistrz," consultant "33," "KK," "K.Koź," and "Kazik."

52. Aleksandra Ziółkowska, *Proces Melchiora Wańkowicza*, 1964 roku, chapter: Pitaval IX, Katon K. Koźniewski (*The Trial of Melchior Wańkowicz of 1964*, chapter: "Pitaval IX, Cato K. Koźniewski"), Nowe Wydawnictwo Polskie, Warsaw 1990, p. 195.

53. Interview with Kazimierz Koźniewski conducted on 7 February 1990 (see section C: Reactions to the Trial).

54. *Politics* (*Polityka*)—Poland's biggest selling weekly, with a center-left and (now) intellectual, social liberal profile (translator's note).

55. The Zaolzie region was created in 1920, when Cieszyn Silesia was divided between Czechoslovakia and Poland—the Zaolzie part was in Czechoslovakia. The division did not satisfy either side, and the continuing conflict over the region finally led to its annexation by Poland in October 1938. After the war, Zaolzie returned to Czechoslovakia (translator's note).

56. Actually, *Bicz gniewu Twego* (*Your Anger's Scourge*), published finally as *Brudne czyny* (*Dirty Deeds*) (translator's note).

57. Anna Erdman (1945–2004)—granddaughter of Melchior Wańkowicz, born in the United States.

58. Tadeusz Walendowski (1944–2004)—journalist and filmmaker.

59. In Polish, Uniwersytet Latający—Underground educational enterprise that operated 1885 to 1905, revived between 1977 and 1981 in the People's Republic of Poland to counteract the party's control and censorship of education. Participants of that second flying university encountered much abuse and harassment from the authorities (translator's note).

60. File no. 7, IPN BU 0247/575.
61. *Notation* or *Record*—a literary paper issued since 1977, at first irregularly, and distributed in a clandestine manner (translator's note).
62. Krzysztof Masłoń, "Rówieśnicy" ("Peers"), *Rzeczpospolita Daily*, 10 December 2007.
63. Kisiel—Stefan Kisielewski (1911–1991), journalist, author.
64. Polska Ludowa Akcja Niepodległościowa, PLAN—underground leftist organization striving for independence (translator's note).
65. Szare Szeregi (Grey Ranks)—name of the underground Polish Scouting Association (Związek Harcerstwa Polskiego—ZHP) during World War II. It actively resisted and fought German occupation in Warsaw from September 1939 until 18 January 1945 (translator's note).
66. *Kuźnia Młodych. Czasopismo Młodzieży Szkolnej* (student newspaper) (1931–1936)—a monthly and then weekly edited by Warsaw high school students; *Orka na Ugorze* (*Ploughing the Fallow*)—a weekly of leftist and democratic orientation (translator's note).
67. Krzysztof Masłoń, "Rówieśnicy" ("Peers"), *Rzeczpospolita Daily*, 10 December 2007.
68. IPN BU 002082/387/vol. 1/CD.
69. Zrzeszenie Wolność i Niezawisłość (Freedom and Independence)—Polish underground anti-Communist organization, active 1945 to 1952 (translator's note).
70. IPN BU III 35534-57/08.
71. *Odrodzenie* (*Rebirth*) (1944–1950)—a weekly, the first social and cultural periodical in post-war Poland. *Przekrój* (*Cross Section*) (1945–now)—a social and cultural weekly (translator's note).
72. *Universal Weekly*—Polish Roman Catholic weekly, focusing on social and cultural issues (translator's note).
73. Związek Harcerstwa Polskiego (ZHP)—Polish Scouting and Guiding Association (translator's note).
74. Published in English as *Stones for the Rampart* (London, 1945), the book tells the true and tragic story of three young men involved in underground fight against Nazis in occupied Warsaw (translator's note).
75. Krzysztof Masłoń, op. cit.
76. IPN 16039/I/2.
77. *Today and Tomorrow*—Catholic social weekly, issued since 1945 by Catholics supporting the activity of the Communist government (translator's note).
78. The PAX Association—cooperating with Communists, a secular Catholic organization in the People's Republic of Poland (translator's note).
79. Weeklies concerned mainly with social and cultural issues (translator's note).
80. *Culture*—Polish social and literary weekly issued in Warsaw (sometimes named *Warsaw Kultura*, as opposed to *Paris Kultura* issued by J. Giedroyc) (translator's note).
81. *Kultura*, 22 September 1974.

Chapter Three

The Writer's Stand and Generosity toward Political Opposition

In the introduction to one of the books by Wańkowicz, Aleksander Małachowski wrote:

> The reader never encounters any lies or distortions of historical truth. Wańkowicz never twisted the truth to fit the needs of the high and mighty. [. . .] Not only did solid professionalism guard his credibility. He had no stains on his writer's honor. He never lied to the nation, didn't hide the truth about Katyń, or about deportations to Siberia. He also wrote about Poland, about partisans, and about the underground. He never strayed from the truth. The audience of readers has come to love Wańkowicz in a way that is difficult to describe today. He felt resentment, like we all did, toward the authorities, plus his own particular grudge. [. . .] "And generally they are rotten, don't ever forget that." He talked then of rottenness with his closest friends, often, long and judiciously. [1]

In February 1974, in Wańkowicz's home in Studencka Street, there was talk about possibly creating a movement, an organization that would group brave people who would strive to make changes in Poland. There was no such organization in Poland back in 1974 (the Workers' Defense Committee [KOR][2] was established in June 1976). Wańkowicz was worried about the country's future, as he put it, that "Poland is flooded by Eurasian sand." The writer offered his home for a meeting place. He spoke of draining Polish culture, and of the need to act. He gave the example of forest fires in America. There are a few small fires, they spread, and finally the fire engulfs the whole forest, huge areas.

"If only everyone here would create such small fires around themselves. I don't demand the impossible, but only for each of us to fight in his own backyard for things that can be created. Do not assume in advance that it can't be done. We must fight our own cowardice and self-censorship," he used to say.

The topic for discussion at the first meeting was Polish culture impoverishment. The discussion would emphasize the attack on Polish culture that was done not through violence, but through drainage. Names of people to invite were singled out: Aleksander Małachowski, Jan Józef Lipski, Jan Olszewski, Kazimierz Dziewanowski, Krzysztof Zanussi, Melchior Wańkowicz, Zbigniew Herbert, Marta Miklaszewska, Jakub Karpiński, Jerzy Łojek, Marian Brandys, Andrzej Wielowieyski, and Władysław Bartoszewski. The participants agreed that such meetings were very necessary, and were to occur without any strict discipline and oaths. Wańkowicz took it upon himself to invite people without the form of an organization. Yet the writer's progressing illness prevented any action.

The last book Wańkowicz read in his life was *The Gulag Archipelago* by Solzhenitsyn. He read it in the original Russian. He was greatly impressed by the book and told me much about it. He was worried, he said, for the Russian soul that was oppressed for so long. He saw no hope for great changes in that country. On reading the book *Powstanie Listopadowe*[3] (*November Uprising*) by Jerzy Łojek, he wondered how many wise, informed, educated, upright people we might need to fill all key posts in Poland to foster a revolution. I remember well the visits of Jan Olszewski, Marta Miklaszewska, and Jan Józef Lipski. Wańkowicz gave certain sums of money to bail out students detained by the militia for participating in political movements. In the book *Opozycja polityczna w PRL 1945–1980* (*Political Opposition in the People's Republic 1945–1980*), Andrzej Friszke quotes J. J. Lipski who said that the writer had given a substantial amount of money in 1965 to the "aid fund for persecuted oppositionists and their families." During one of the last visits of Olszewski and Lipski in 1974, Wańkowicz handed them a considerable sum for those times. He wanted that money to be used after his death to support people who suffered political trouble. Jan Olszewski, the Polish prime minister in 1991–1992, earlier—in the People's Republic of Poland—was a well-known defense lawyer in political trials.[4]

When Jan Józef Lipski spoke at the writer's funeral on 14 September 1974 in the Warsaw Powązki cemetery, he said among other things:

> I would like to say a few words about one more thing. Simply because very few people know that Mr. Melchior was a man who many times hastened to help people who needed that help. Often he helped the persecuted.[5]

Few people listened to those words, and their only trace remained in IPN files, as all speeches over the writer's coffin had been recorded and then written down by a diligent officer of the Security Service. I came across them after over thirty years in a secret file on *myself*, where after the writer's death all reports on me, a then-twenty-five-year-old girl, were collected. I also found there such interesting materials as speeches over the writer's grave and reactions thereto.

As the above-quoted Małachowski wrote, Wańkowicz

> accused communism and its leaders not only of enslaving Poland, as that was obvious, but of depriving the country of material intellectual development. Under communism, everything becomes shallow, vulgar in their hands; higher civic emotions vanish. Lies and hypocrisy are burgeoning. Mr. Melchior never had those illusions that had steered many eminent Polish writers so much they were lead astray. Maybe that was why he wasn't popular in the writers' community. But he gained much respect in opposition circles, particularly among those who knew of something that no one suspected about Melchior Wańkowicz. Unsuspected was his great generosity as concerned public purposes that stemmed from age-old traditions of Eastern Poland's gentry. For public purposes, money was always available. Melchior Wańkowicz was first to establish some kind of a single-manned KOR, a Defense Committee, just not for workers but for young people, arrested and tried for political crimes. He gave money for the Taternicy Trials[6] and other needs. I was a witness to that. He handed substantial checks to Jan Józef Lipski.[7]

Krzysztof Masłoń wrote that "it was many years after the writer's death that we learned he had offered not only moral support to the democratic opposition in Poland—also financial."[8]

I wrote about the issue in my book *Ulica Żółwiego Strumienia* (*Turtle Creek Boulevard*), and after Andrzej Friszke's publication—to supplement the information about Wańkowicz's beautiful and generous gesture—I published separate statements on that subject in Paris *Kultura* (nos. 1–2, 1995) and in *Więź*[9] (no. 4, 1995). I also wrote about it in the *Rzeczpospolita Daily* in 2007.[10] I wanted to again publicly state and emphasize all of the writer's generosity. He regularly gave certain sums of money to the aid fund for the oppressed, and just before his death, in 1974, he gave to Jan Józef Lipski and Jan Olszewski another sum—one to be considered substantial in those times—for the same goal.

Twelve years after the above-quoted book was published, in another publication of his (to be precise, it was the preface to Jan Józef Lipski's book *KOR* [Warsaw, 2006]), Andrzej Friszke mentioned Wańkowicz a few times, always in a positive context. To quote a fragment:

> Those years brought Lipski and Wańkowicz closer, and after the latter's death in 1974, Lipski was the executor of his last will. The writer had bequeathed to the fund managed by Lipski a then enormous sum of eight thousand dollars. The money was allocated for granting scholarships for the repressed artists and young intellectuals, as well as creating a reserve fund "in case of emergency."

Those sums, managed in clandestine conditions, became later the basis for KOR's action.

Andrzej Friszke wrote that sentence based on archive materials, for example, the file of Jan Józef Lipski in the Institute of National Remembrance files. For anyone seeking the truth, it is worth stressing the fact that Melchior Wańkowicz, a national writer, was also a man who had for years supported oppositionists in his oppressed homeland.

Below I quote the words of Jan Olszewski from 15 June 2009, concerning Wańkowicz's trials and his generosity:[11]

The trial of Melchior Wańkowicz in 1964 was an obvious act of revenge by the authorities of the People's Republic for signing the so-called "Letter 34." The collective protest of eminent representatives of Polish science and literature was treated by Władysław Gomułka almost like a personal challenge.

Wańkowicz's name signed under the letter might have been a particularly nasty surprise for him. Since coming back to Poland, the writer had made no official statements on any political issues. At the same time, he seemed to have been granted a particular privilege of publishing books on Polish participation in World War II including the famous description of the battle of Monte Cassino. The famous battle was a topic as popular among readers as it was detested among censors. In that situation, the writer's name under a collective protest against censorship awoke understandable fury of the "people's authorities." Security bodies used the circumstances to start a coercive action against a group of writers whom they suspected of publishing their works under pseudonyms in emigration papers. Soon after Wańkowicz was arrested and sentenced, investigations started against Jan Nepomucen Miller, Stanisław "Cat" Mackiewicz, and January Grzędziński.

The trial of Wańkowicz, as the first of the intended ones, was conducted expeditiously. The only witness for the prosecution, on whose testimony the charges were based, was an officer of the Security Service. The sentence was widely publicized by printing in selected papers not so much reports as personal propaganda attacks against the accused. Of course, neither foreign press correspondents nor any people not accepted by the security service were admitted to the courtroom. A sentence of three years of imprisonment (decreased to 1.5 years based on an amnesty) was pronounced, for allegedly "spreading false information that may cause significant harm to the state's interests."

Right after the verdict, when the court rescinded the custody applied against the defendant, Wańkowicz contacted Aniela Steinsberg, a lawyer, and asked to meet defense lawyers acting in political trials. He directed his request to Steinsberg because he'd heard of her defense in the famous case of Kazimierz Moczarski. The meeting took place a few days later in Aniela Steinsberg's home, and beside me, the participants were, if I remember correctly, Andrzej Grabiński and—possibly—Stanisław Szczuka or Władysław Winawer. Wańkowicz asked us to give our opinions on the chances of an appeal against the first-instance verdict issued in his case. Our view was unanimous:

the verdict was obviously wrong, both legally and as concerned evidence, but the chances of having it revoked in the Supreme Court—due to the composition of its criminal chamber, where the appeal would be considered—were practically null. In spite of that, we thought that an appeal should be lodged, because it gave a chance to show the obvious absurdity of the accusation, and what was more, it delayed for at least some time the threat of putting the over-seventy-year-old writer in prison.

Yet Wańkowicz did not agree with our arguments. He decided that his voluntary participation in proceedings that were, of course, fictional and biased, might be misviewed. He feared public opinion would consider his agreement of a glaring wrong as an act of justice, and at the same time an agreement dictated with the fear of being put in jail. The discussion was almost stormy at times, but finally Wańkowicz refused to change his mind. He turned out to be right. With the verdict being binding, there appeared a problem of executing the pronounced punishment of 1.5 years of imprisonment. Yet no one in the Regional Court in Warsaw dared make a decision on locking a very popular writer in prison. The Ministry of Justice was assigned the case. Thence it was sent to the Central Committee of the party. Time flew, and no official or political instance dared finally solve the touchy problem. In looking for some solution, it was decided to "make Wańkowicz sick" and state that it was impossible to put him in prison due to his advanced age and poor health. Thus the writer was summoned to appear before a medical board so that he might be examined for whether or not he qualified for being put in a penal institution. A suitably selected and instructed board was to state that the writer was unable to remain in prison conditions. All attorneys advised Wańkowicz to turn up for the examination, as they believed it to be the most painless way to close the case. On the other hand, it was feared that a refusal to appear before the board might annoy the authorities and cause them to lock the willful writer in custody. I shared that view of my colleagues. Yet my situation was peculiar. The chief judge of the Fourth Penal Department of the Regional Court in Warsaw, in whose competence the matter lay, asked me—privately, as he assured me—to give my client his personal guarantee that the medical examination would be limited only to an interview concerning the writer's health. The chief judge assured me the interview would not be bothersome at all, and that at the same time it would allow him to definitively free Wańkowicz from the threat of the pronounced sentence being carried out. I could not refuse conveying his request. Wańkowicz listened to me attentively, and then said: "You have done your duty as a lawyer, and now tell me honestly, what would you do if you were me?" I replied: "I would do the same that you are planning to do. I wouldn't go there." Mr. Melchior shook my hand and ended our conversation with the statement: "That was what I expected and wanted to hear." In the end, the files of the case were locked for a few years in the safe of the chief judge and there they remained until another amnesty in 1969, which freed the Communist judiciary from such a troublesome convict.

Based upon their experiences with Wańkowicz, in the cases of other victims of the anti-literary bashing by the Security Service in 1964, the authorities of the People's Republic drew similar conclusions. In the case of J. N. Miller, a sentence of imprisonment was issued already suspended. With Stanisław "Cat" Mackiewicz they abandoned an accusation. January Grzędziński was oppressed with a several-year-long investigation, which ended only when the suspect died.

But the case of Wańkowicz did not end there. Mr. Melchior, according to the tradition binding Lithuanian nobility—from which he descended—decided that he could not leave unanswered the innuendoes and slander contained in the press publications inspired by the Security Service and the reporting of the course of the trial. For Wańkowicz, it was impossible not to answer all the lampoons of this kind. Thus, Wańkowicz chose just one, but a major author from available operational journalists. The chosen man was Kazimierz Kąkol, then editor-in-chief of the paper *Prawo i życie*, [12] and future head of the Office for Religious Denominations, who at that time was beginning his future career in the political *nomenklatura* of the People's Republic. An attempt to gain satisfaction in the usual way of suing Kąkol for defamation would in those conditions prove, at best, utter naivety of the aggrieved party. Another way was needed to seek justice. Wańkowicz found such an unconventional way, and one in keeping with the tradition of Eastern gentry. Authorized by him, I initiated and conducted those proceedings. I admit it was a unique strategy not seen in all my law practice of over thirty years. We suggested to the editor of *Prawo i życie* that the dispute on the accuracy of his report from Wańkowicz's trial, published in the said paper, be subject to arbitration proceedings. The proceedings would take place before a peer court of one of the artist societies to which both parties in the conflict belonged—Wańkowicz as a writer, Kąkol as a journalist.

Kazimierz Kąkol—once a Home Army soldier with a very good combat history from the Warsaw Uprising (which we incidentally considered a circumstance that allowed for the honorary mode of settling the dispute)—accepted the challenge.

After complicated and painstaking negotiations, the case was accepted for consideration by the Peer Court of the Polish Writers' Union. Contrary to the speedy trial in court, the case proceeded, if I remember correctly, at least for some months. I do not wish to present here its highly interesting course, as after the forty years that have passed since then, I cannot trust my memory so implicitly. All documents and files should be found in the ZLP archives. In any case, it ended with a full victory for Wańkowicz.

To end this story, I must say a few words on a matter that gentlemen usually don't talk of—money. In the Warsaw literary community, quite commonly expressed was the opinion of Wańkowicz having an allegedly particularly commercial attitude toward everything, including his own literary work. Thus I consider it my duty to speak of my own experience in the matter.

After the trial ended, Mr. Melchior asked me to give him the sum of my fees for the legal services rendered in his case. I replied that he owed me nothing, because in my practice as a lawyer I had adopted the principle of not taking remuneration for acting in a lawyer's capacity in political trials, and that was how I viewed his case. In reply, he stated that under no circumstance could he agree to that. A long and fierce dispute resulted—although one conducted in a very friendly atmosphere—in which no party showed any willingness to concede. Finally, the conflict was solved in March 1968, when the minister of justice suspended me from my practice as a lawyer. Due to that fact, my situation in life became rather difficult. Then suddenly I learned that into my bank account, the amount in which was rather meager, a payment of ten thousand zlotys was received, which in that time was quite a big sum. As it turned out, the payer was Wańkowicz. When I tried to protest against that, Mr. Melchior told me: "You have your principles; I have mine. You defend people in political trials free of charge, and I try to help as much as possible people repressed for political reasons. Let us respect each other's principles." I had to agree with that, because since the mid-1960s Wańkowicz had been giving money to aid in helping the repressed opposition people. Acting for him, the writer's contributions were enacted by Jan Józef Lipski, and I also collaborated with him on that. The writer had wished for complete and absolute secrecy in the matter. Only three people knew of the money he gave: J. J. Lipski, myself, and the former president of the "Krzywe Koło" (Crooked Circle Club), Aleksander Małachowski. All of us have strictly adhered to that confidentiality principle. Today I believe it to be my duty to reveal it.

Figure 3.1.   Wańkowicz in Nieborów Palace, 1960s.

NOTES

1. Aleksander Małachowski, "Elegia na śmierć córki" ("Elegy on Daughter's Death"), introduction to *Ziele na kraterze* (*Herbs on the Crater*) (Warsaw: PWN, 1993), pp. x–xiii.

2. Komitet Obrony Robotników—the first major anti-Communist civic group (and a successful one) in Eastern Europe and in Poland aiming to give aid to prisoners and their families after the protests in 1976 and government crackdown (translator's note).

3. *Szanse powstania listopadowego. Rozważania historyczne* (*The Chances of the November Uprising. Historical Reflection*); November Uprising (1830–1831)—armed rebellion in partitioned Poland against the Russian Empire.

4. In the 1960s he defended in political trials, for example, Melchior Wańkowicz (1964), Jacek Kuroń, Karol Modzelewski (1965), Janusz Szpotański (1968), Adam Michnik, and Jan Nepomucen Miller.

5. IPN 0204/644. The fragment is quoted in chapter 8: "After the Writer's Death."

6. In 1968 and 1969, five young people attempted to smuggle Paris *Kultura* publications into Poland across the Polish-Czechoslovakian border. When caught, they were arrested, tried, and sentenced to three to four and a half years in prison. Two of them were Tatra mountaineers (in Polish, *taternicy*), and the name stuck (translator's note).

7. Aleksander Małachowski, "Elegia na śmierć córki" ("Elegy on Daughter's Death"), introduction to *Ziele na kraterze* (*Herbs on the Crater*), pp. x–xiii.

8. Krzysztof Masłoń, "Rówieśnicy" ("Peers"), *Rzeczpospolita Daily*, 10 December 2007.

9. *Więź* (*Bond*)—Catholic social and cultural monthly issued in Warsaw (translator's note).

10. Aleksandra Ziółkowska-Boehm, "Pieniądze dla opozycji" ("Money for the Opposition"), *Rzeczpospolita Daily*, no. 181, 4–5 August 2007.

11. Jan Olszewski (born 1930)—lawyer and political figure, prime minister of the Republic of Poland from 1991 to 1992. Mr. Olszewski authorized the text and gave permission to print it in English on 30 September 2012.

12. *Prawo i życie* (*Law and Life*)—a weekly focused on legal and judiciary issues, started 1956 (translator's note).

Chapter Four

About the Correspondence of Zofia and Melchior Wańkowicz

Interest in writers' biographies is a common and natural occurrence. The greater an author's success and fame, the more interest is awakened in him or her as a person. This seems to be particularly so in the case of a writer who had transformed himself and the people close to him into literary characters, and based a family saga on his family history. With the writer subjecting his family to the law of artistic creation, "King" and "Bunny" (in Polish, Królik), that is, Melchior and Zofia Wańkowicz, were a literary pair in many books: *Ziele na kraterze, Atlantyk–Pacyfik, Królik i oceany, W pępku Ameryki*.[1] The writer's books also feature his daughters—Krystyna and Marta.

Hence biographical inquisitiveness—which undoubtedly includes publishing private correspondence—is justified in the case of Melchior Wańkowicz, as he was a writer whose life was a fascinating subject for a reportage. Wańkowicz was truly a protagonist as he recaptured the sense of human adventure.

The letters of Zofia and Melchior Wańkowicz make up several sets of various sizes, depending on the time spent apart. The first set is contained between 1921 and 1928. However, most of those letters were written in 1921 to 1923. The second set of letters was produced during the Nazi occupation time, 1939 to 1945, with particular frequency of correspondence in 1940 and few letters from the years following. And then the third set covers the years 1950 and 1955, when—twice—Melchior traveled in Canada. The correspondence ends in 1966, when Zofia Wańkowicz stayed in a hospital confined with heart failure. The last letters are small cards written to the hospital.

The fate of manuscripts from before the war is not quite known. That Zofia Wańkowicz gave some of her husband's pre-war archives to Kraków for safekeeping is known. Most likely, Melchior's letters from the occupation time did not survive in original form as they were burned with the house of the Wańkowicz family on Dziennikarska Street in the Warsaw district of Żoliborz.

In the letters, some particular people appear often. They include, of course, mainly members of Zofia's and Melchior's immediate families and their friends, but also leading figures of the contemporary cultural, political, and emigration life are frequently mentioned.

Zofia's brothers—Kazimierz and Stanisław (both were killed in the Polish-Bolshevik war 1919–1920) appear in the first batches of letters, along with her father, called "Papanek," together with his second wife, called "Mamanek" by both Zofia and Melchior.

Melchior's immediate family included Regina, his older sister, and his brother, Witold, then the daughters of Zofia and Melchior Wańkowicz: Krystyna and Marta, and then later Marta's husband, Jan Erdman, and their children, Anna and Ewa.

How can reading Wańkowicz's letters impact the way his works are understood and evaluated? Letters are usually the most easily available and most credible research material. More so, if the letters are written to a person close to you, then one does not have to pretend anything, maintain any appearances, or play any social roles. At the same time, the letters may be treated as a work of art of the man who wrote them to enrich his works with factual human content. I shall hazard the statement that the correspondence of Wańkowicz reveals to us a writer that we do not know, a man troubled with doubts and difficulties. His reflections on the very process of creation and work methods reveal the hierarchy of values in his life and the passion of creating.

"I suddenly realized how contemptuously little I take from life by way of any pleasures," disclosed the writer who embodied taking advantage of the "beauty of life" (letter of March 1955)—as this was how he presented himself in his books and his conduct.

Melancholic confessions also appeared: "I try to imagine that I am very rich and independent, and I can't see myself losing then that deepest grief eating me inside, i.e. the emptiness of ending life. You pay for the lifelong and so highly valued paganism" (12 October 1950).

The statement may be surprising, if you just compare it with his earlier letters which show not so much Wańkowicz yielding to "paganism" as mainly his submission to the discipline of work. Work was for him a medicine for everything, a discipline he'd submitted to, his escape and help in the face of failures. He wrote to his wife: "Finally, remember: a person can feel truly defeated if he does not do everything that belongs to him. The greater the failure, the more you need to cure your spirit by adding work" (2 March 1955).

That Wańkowicz increasingly valued devoting himself to his writing and to improving his technique can readily be seen. During the Nazi German occupation, Zofia asked if they would try to keep the house in Żoliborz when the war ended. He responded writing to her: "I won't have the physical strength needed for that. Even if I do, I will devote it to my profession that I found a mere four years before the war (or even earlier. My production of 1935 was amateur, and I can only consider professional our work with Marta [daughter—note by AZB])—the end of 1936—my God, I had little time to create the technique, and it developed with every month" (3 March 1955).

Wańkowicz met his future wife Zofia Małagowska (his senior by two years, born 28 May 1890 in Skierniewice),[2] in 1914 through her brothers, Stanisław and Kazimierz. Zofia studied history while Melchior was graduating from the School of Political Studies in Kraków. (The story of the Małagowski brothers and of Wańkowicz was similar in a certain period of their lives: when the Russian revolution broke out, they all joined the Dowbor-Muśnicki Corps).[3]

Wańkowicz described his fiancée in *Ziele na kraterze* as a "saint with an inkwell":

> I remember her bringing me "grub" to the Russian prison on Daniłowiczowska Street, and a colonel of the military police cautioned her: "Young ladies are so incautious. Are you really quite sure who you are engaged to? He has no passport. . . . How can you trust a man without a passport?" [. . .] I remember, as after the failed assassination attempt against General Dowbor, she brought me a small pot of soup to prison and had to listen to the doubts whether I would have the time to eat it, as the firing squad was already appointed.[4]

They married on 8 February 1916. The ceremony was quiet because of the war conditions. Father Pomirski, a friend of Melchior's father from the deportation to Siberia, placed the rings on their fingers. On 8 October 1919, Krystyna was born. The family lived in Warsaw on the third floor of a tenement house in Elektoralna Street. Their material conditions were poor. The writer later recalled: "The windows of our flat looked out to the very same filthy yard in which old foul coots croaked. That small flat on the third floor had no lift, electricity, or bathroom, but it had bugs of iron will and a ruined toilet. It was cold. We couldn't afford the fuel."[5]

And further he wrote about himself:

> A twenty-something-year-old father and head of the family was unprepared for life as well. He had been brought up in a reverent fear of successive generations of losing their possessions. One who lost his fortune went to live off the mercy of richer relatives or went into the unknown and out of his neighbors' sight, and "surely he sleeps on benches in town parks by now." And he was

one who'd lost his fortune, the surrounding world was alien, his own strength
unknown, and the faith in possibly "doing something"—very vague.[6]

Wańkowicz stayed in Warsaw completing his studies of law at the University
of Warsaw, where he'd started before the war of 1920. Meanwhile, his wife
and child (Marta, nicknamed Tili, was born 29 July 1921) stayed in Jerka—
an estate in the Poznańskie region, leased by Melchior's older brother, Witold. Maria (Marieta) and Witold Wańkowicz offered substantial support to
Zofia during that time. They provided her not only a place to stay, but also
financial help (the same kind of help was later reciprocated for many years
by Melchior for his sister-in-law, Maria, after his brother's death).

Letters of that period—early 1920s—show how difficult it was for young
Wańkowicz to persevere, even how he broke down and rebelled. (His recollections printed in the volume of *Tędy i owędy* [*This Way and That*] titled
"Zgłębianie prawa" ["Exploring the Law in Depth"] were often either
mournful or angry and aggressive.) Letters of those years make up an impressive collection among all the correspondence exchanged by the couple. They
show their mutual tenderness, the care of each of them to know as much as
possible about the other. One may follow the stages of the children's growth,
the way in which they were brought up. Zofia Wańkowicz kept a diary of
Krysia and younger daughter Marta, where she quotes the girls' sayings, and
notes the successive stages of them maturing. The children's world is both
beautifully and movingly portrayed by their mother. Zofia as a mother
evokes affection and respect. Melchior wrote: "What you write are truly
phenomenal things—like some Divine miracle, like a plant sprouting you
describe the development of a child. I think of you as a mother with deep
reverence" (20 July 1921).

Stabilization came. Having sold some of his part of the estate in Kaunas
Lithuania,[7] Wańkowicz obtained the desired financial means and built a
house in the Żoliborz district. He co-owned the publishing company "Rój,"
or "Roy." The book that brought him publicity and fame, *Na tropach Smętka*
(*On the Trail of Smętek*), was published. The work was dedicated to his wife:
"For Mama, to whom you always come back."

Earlier he wrote *Szczenięce lata* (*The Puppy Years*). The love and longing
for the past times, people, the whole aura of childhood so strongly bound
with nature and nearly pagan customs contained in it found great acclaim
with critics. The book released the writer in him. While writing, he also
worked as an advertising adviser for the Sugar Workers' Union. A letter
survives in which he wrote to his wife about wrestling with the writing
process:

> It's quiet in the house, so work goes fine—I do a lot for the sugar workers, but
> *Szczenięce lata* I can't seem to put words on paper; I turn the pen—my

thoughts are insincere. I wonder at my own self that small things can stimulate me so at times: Olchowicz came out with me being the best traveling correspondent, saying that he truly liked reading my correspondence. I feel some abilities rising in me like water boiling in a pot. What happens if I go hungry some more? Maybe then I'll manage even without the sugar? But sometimes I plain suffocate—it is so inexpressibly hard for me in the sugar industry. Kisses, Mel. (17 August 1931)

From the packet of letters from the before the war Zofia wrote: "In Melek's [Mel's] letters there is deep love for all three of us. There is truth and integrity. Moving tenderness, care, and gentleness. He guards the dignity of our lives in them."

Not many letters from the Nazi German occupation period survived—only those from 1940 and a few from 1941 and 1945. They contain extremely rich material, and document deep feelings and events. They are also valuable because of the detailed descriptions of daily life and activities they contain. Shown is the everyday life at the beginning of the war, and the drama of the war's later years. Particularly, Zofia Wańkowicz wrote much at the beginning of the occupation, when she was still with both her daughters, selling "Rój's" books, living in a rented flat in Mianowskiego Street, then moving back to the house in Dziennikarska Street:

Dearest—today we received the first card from you to Tili. We are sitting in our bedroom near the lamp, all three of us together sharing our joy for receiving your card. Tili is nearly as happy for the machine's existence, as Krysia is with the news on the riding horse. I have written many cards to you, also the one you acknowledged with Tili's signature, that she rewrote in the post office. [. . .] Together with the staff, we are living off selling books from carts, which is very popular. We heat one room now. Krysia manages the house; I go to the office in Kredytowa Street. Hanka wants to go to her husband [about the Kisters—note by AZB], but he must apply for a visa for her. She writes texts for a publisher in Stockholm. Mr. Włodarski works with me in the office. I have repaired the roof and the drainpipe on our Dear Home. Now I'll put in some windowpanes so that it doesn't snow inside. Our home stands empty, and I'm trying to find a tenant, but it's difficult because of the heating fuel. Tol with his whole family and Hania with her child live at 4 Zimorowicza Street, near our flat. Krys is not there, but living close, and he's healthy. They pay me a little rent and I make ends meet. Of course I can't know how the business will succeed in the future. [. . .] In the store, Kazik Koźn. [Koźniewski] and our Romek are working—they carry the books, and beside them there is Helena, and the accountants Pola and Jadzia, like before. Hania comes for an hour or two to discuss current issues. I would like to put the business in order, furnish the Dear Home and whatever I can from our things, so I think it is better to stay at home than go off to the country to Renia. But of course, I care mainly for the children, so if there were difficulties here, I would go there or send them to you. Your papers and personal things are all right. Choroszczuk has the fur. Your things are packed. Is there a way you can get them? Tili worked for two months in a hospital. Krysia was affected by the fate of Aunt Jania and her family. I watch over them both all the time and came to the house first to arrange everything. We have gone through many ups and downs, of which we shall tell you later. I'm sending you the Christmas wafer,[8] and I'm sending my heartfelt wishes for your names day. [. . .] We speak and think of you so many times every day. I love you and I'm sending kisses from deep in my heart. Your picture in the drawer by my bed gives me strength and courage. Remember I'm writing all the time, I just don't know which letters reach you. Kisses—Your wife. (5 January 1940)

Five months later, she wrote to her husband, whom Tili had joined in the meantime (Krysia/Krystyna) stayed with their mother). Zofia Wańkowicz asked them not to separate. She was concerned for her younger daughter Marta (Tili/Tilusia). How impelling are her words:

My Dear—today your letter of 19 IV [April] (not numbered) reached me. I am glad that Tilusia is a good life companion for you. Do not separate. The issue of her education should not be theorized on too much. Since she is no more at home with me, let her not separate from you. We will not live forever, after all. And you have a lot to give her of yourself. The future course of events is also difficult to predict—do not separate from the Little One.

As to Krysia, we need to think of her education and entry into the world. Write me first, what education possibilities are open. In her nobleness, she doesn't want to leave me alone here, but I am ready at every moment—as I have always been—to do anything that will be best for each of them in the current situation. I also believe that now is the time for the girls to give each other sisterly love and mutual support, so it would be a pity to keep them apart. About Krysia, I may say that she takes upon herself the household duties bravely, which is not a light work. (5 May 1940)

Particularly dramatic are two letters from 1945: "I haven't found Krysia so far. Maybe you can look for her through the Red Cross in work camps" (3 January 1945). And another, written 17 October 1945, saying what happened to Krysia and other people close to them:

Krysia, as the nurses and friends told me, was killed on 6 August between 10–11 a.m. on Sunday, Transfiguration Day, in Wola [Warsaw district] with a whole group, killed by a grenade launcher. We are still digging in Wola and have buried many friends of hers, but haven't found her group yet. Rom was killed on 1 August at 9 p.m. in Mokotów [Warsaw district]. Bisia, seen the end of September in the Gestapo headquarters in Szucha Alley, vanished without a trace. Seeking information about the kids, Tol[9] was shot to death by the Germans near Skierniewice.

Reunited after the years of being separated by the war, then spending a few years in London, Zofia and Melchior Wańkowicz moved to the United States, where their younger daughter Tili had settled. Wańkowicz worked on a chicken farm and wrote. His books were published, among them the family saga *Ziele na kraterze*, issued in 1951 in New York.

He wrote in the preface to the Polish edition:

> The joys of growth and despair of destruction were present in every family.
>
> I wrote from the angle of what was most important to me—my own home. That home had its disadvantages in the time of peace, was not burnt down in its entirety during the occupation, and was affected no more than other homes in the time of carnage.
>
> Thus I would only wish for the readers to see in its history the histories of their own homes and families, and for the evoked memories to bring a tear or two for the moment through the unbearable dregs of life.

The book, one of the most famous among the writer's works, ends with Marta's letter from December 1945, informing about the birth of her daughter Anna Krystyna.

The surviving correspondence between Zofia and Melchior Wańkowicz contains later letters. We learn about the further lives of "King" and "Bunny," of the later life of Marta and Jan Erdman's family, staying permanently in the United States. A particularly interesting thread, which can be investigated quite thoroughly, is the couple's maturing decision to return to Poland. It can be seen in a letter from 1955, when Wańkowicz toured Canada for the second time—after five years—with lectures in Polish emigration centers and to collect materials for another book (the first one, *Tworzywo*, was published in New York in 1954) concerning Polish emigrants. The situation he found in Canada was different from before—he found neither any big response nor great interest among the Poles there concerning his writing plans. His letters-reports from meetings and talks, for instance with General Kazimierz Sosnkowski, Jerzy Giedroyc—like the description of a banquet with Marshal Piłsudski from before the war—sometimes end with the words: "Keep those notes—that helps avoid copying." Now, after the years, these are immensely valuable letters; they can be even viewed as historical documents.

As I've written, letters end at the year 1968, when Zofia Wańkowicz stayed in the hospital with heart failure.

The first letter, sent by Melchior to his fiancée in 1914, contains a fragment that reveals his pride in choosing "the right maiden": "I am seized with understandable, silly, and unnecessary pride. Looking at all those pairs engaged and paired by matchmakers in Lithuania, at all the young ladies and young men—and thinking of us, I have the impression that all this, small and mean, swarms somewhere down below our feet. The Lord is great, and the levels of human souls numerous."

It must be noted as one looks from the perspective of time, that Zofia Wańkowicz had her own beautiful page in the history of social activity.

In 1917, she organized community centers for Polish soldiers leaving the Russian Army after the revolution and the act of June 1917 directed at forming Polish armed forces in Russia and creating the Chief Polish Military Committee (Naczelny Polski Komitet Wojskowy, called "Naczpol").

After the Polish First Corps (under the command of General Józef Dowbor-Muśnicki) was disbanded, she took part in arms trafficking to Poland. She was heartbroken by the news that within three weeks of each other, her brothers Stanisław and Kazimierz Małagowski—as mentioned earlier—were killed in the Polish-Bolshevik war. Zofia never recovered from this tragedy.

During the war of 1918–1920, as a member of the Polish Women's Circle, she provided help for the fighting soldiers. In 1930, the twenty-fifth anniversary of the fight for Polish schools,[10] she participated in the work of the celebration committee and significantly contributed to collecting several thousand zlotys for an aid fund for Polish schools in Germany.

During the Nazi occupation, the Wańkowicz's home was a shelter for British and Polish escapees from POW camps.

Within so-called patronage over prisoners, Zofia Wańkowicz brought help to prisoners in the Pawiak prison and in Nazi concentration camps.

She presented a heartrending picture of women fighting with the occupants in an extensive text titled "Kombatantki" ("Female Veterans") published in *Kultura* (Paris, no. 10, 1954).

Not long after Zofia's death on 20 May 1969, Wańkowicz sent a thank-you note to their friends and acquaintances:

> I would like to give my thanks for the words of sympathy after my wife's demise to family, colleagues, friends and acquaintances, editors, publishing houses, associations, and institutions.
>
> I want to thank my readers for all their letters who understood under the lighthearted words of my books that they were about a life companion—dear, needed, essential. Their letters were so expressive as if they were writing of a person closest to their hearts.
>
> I can no more show her those letters from Poland and the world. I can no more tell her how the single, individual flowers covered the official wreaths.
>
> Only some comfort for me, are her somewhat awkward letters, those envelopes without a proper address, containing words full of goodness.
>
> I give thanks, heartfelt thanks for the "Bunny." But she's gone now.
>
> You have supported me in those heaviest days of losing the one who had accompanied me for fifty-three years, and who left me at the end of my writing.

The letters of Zofia and Melchior Wańkowicz show a unique example of a relation between two people who walked through life together. "I am your closest friend, who is so closely, so deeply, so personally concerned with the issues of your work and everything," Zofia wrote in 1921.

In the writer's archives, there is a ten-page file note written in 1945. Wańkowicz was waiting to be reunited with his wife after almost six years of separation due to World War II. In that note, Wańkowicz writes bitterly about a difficult time in the late 1920s, when they separated. Zofia had left him to be with his best friend, but a few months later she returned. Subsequently, they were able to put their marriage back together.

The great writer decided to be quiet about this event, and wrote his beautiful book about the childhood of their daughters and a loving family. His choice was more wishful thinking than reality, but he wanted it that way. As he commented—the painting of the sunset can be shown only in bright pink colors, and the whole palette does not have to be shown.

When writing the book *Herbs at the Crater* in early 1950, he showed how the whole world broke apart. He had lost his older daughter; the house in Warsaw was in ruins as the whole city had been leveled by the Germans during the Warsaw Uprising of 1944. The recollection of the children's childhood and the whole atmosphere is serene and beautiful. Wańkowicz's choice and his decision was to present the family that way. The book *Herbs at the Crater* is a beloved book to thousands of readers who take inspiration from the "beautiful loving family."

Figure 4.1.   **Wańkowicz as a young man.**

Figure 4.2. Zofia Małagowska, later Wańkowicz.

Figure 4.3. Melchior and Zofia Wańkowicz, Sopot 1958.

NOTES

1. *Herbs at the Crater, Atlantic-Pacific, Bunny and Oceans,* and *In the Midst of America.*

2. Daughter of Zofia née Langie and Kazimierz Małagowski.

3. Actually I Korpus Polski w Rosji "Polish First Corps in Russia," a Polish military formation formed in Belarus in 1917 after the Russian Revolution of 1917, from soldiers of Polish origin serving in the Russian Army. Its goal was to defend Poles inhabiting parts of partitioned Poland under Russian rule and support the formation of an independent Poland. It was commanded by General Józef Dowbor-Muśnicki (translator's note).

4. *Ziele na kraterze* (*Herbs at the Crater*) (Warsaw, 1976), p. 50.

5. *Ziele na kraterze*, p. 10.

6. *Ziele na kraterze*, p. 12.

7. Litwa Kowieńska, casual name for the First Republic of Lithuania (1918–1939), with its temporary capital in Kaunas (Kowno), as Vilnius remained under Polish administration (translator's note).

8. A host-like kind of wafer traditionally shared by Poles on Christmas Eve (translator's note).

9. Tol, Witold Wańkowicz, Melchior's older brother.

10. Following the revolution in Russia in January 1905, on 3 February 1905 Polish male and female students in Kielce took strike action, demanding to have classes in Polish (the town was at the time under Russian occupation). Due to severe social unrest, the tsar granted them what they asked for (translator's note).

Chapter Five

Unhealed Wounds

In a letter of 20 July 1921 to his wife, Melchior Wańkowicz wrote about his daughter Krystyna who was born on 8 October 1919, so she was almost two then:

> These are downright phenomenal things that you write me—like some Divine miracle, like a plant sprouting, the development of a child. I think of you as a mother with deep reverence. The little soul of our little animal thing transforms under your hand into a sensitive soul of a little human—a little girl. Sometimes there's fear for the little one, how she will come out in life . . . whether a joy to everyone or not, but let it be: let us develop in her a love for people, and only strengthen her physically and mentally, then she will cope with that, too. So good that you are showing her fields and meadows, the beauty of God's world. I believe that it does not go to waste, and I am convinced that Krysia will have her ideas as broad, her mind as thriving, and her love as much all-encompassing in her life, as much as her sweet sky-blue eyes manage to take in within her first six years. Those early years are the strongest, fundamental, and most educational, i.e., your own experiences. Then, together with the alphabet, everything mixes with the substitutes of foreign thought. The dust of general achievements and redefinitions from the broad high road will go through the child's soul. If you want to make our daughter an autonomous person—take care of her first six years.
>
> That is why I am so pleased whenever I hear that the little one feels fulfilled and happy when standing by the carved saint out in the fields in the evening. God bless you for that, Mother Dear.

The daughters of Melchior Wańkowicz, Krysia and Tili (Marta)—described in *Herbs at the Crater* (*Ziele na kraterze*)—are characters popularized by the writer. To what extent is the picture true, and how far did the father create a myth, moved by recollections of days past? He wrote *Ziele na kraterze* in New York, having stayed abroad for ten years. By then the old times were gone never to return. Their Dear Home was destroyed during air strikes on Warsaw. Also, his older daughter Krystyna was no more among the living, and he didn't even know where she finally rested in peace.

Wańkowicz recalls when he brought his young wife the news of her brother's death in 1919 (her other brother died some three weeks later).

> She was seven months pregnant with Krysia. She collapsed on the carpet, doubled in pain: wrestling with herself. The husband tried to lovingly take her hands from her face; he recalled someone saying to be careful when bringing news of death, because the unborn child would have a flame[1] on its face from that touch.
>
> The child was born without a flame on her face, but the fire was somewhere deep within.[2]

Among the pictures in the first editions of *Ziele na kraterze*, not many pictures of Wańkowicz's older daughter are found. Also, more pages are devoted in the book to the younger one, Tili. The younger daughter is a character of Wańkowicz's most popular book before the war, *Na tropach Smętka* (*On the Trail of Smętek*).

One may ponder, was the father biased in favor of one daughter? Can that be written after many years, when neither the father, nor wife, nor daughters are alive? We can draw on the printed word, the written word, on the accounts. Will they be true to life? We shall see.

From Mexico City, Wańkowicz wrote in 1927 to his daughters, who were staying in Poland—six-year-old Tili and nine-year-old Krysia:

> Dudududududunies . . .
>
> Daddy's writing to you "du-du-du . . . with longing, thinking he's going du-du with a choo-choo," and meanwhile—"no go," as Tili would say.
>
> "When you are sitting by the table on Christmas Eve, pull out fortune blades[3] from under the tablecloth for your Dad. Let Tili draw first, as she's the youngest—the drawn grass blade will show Daddy's life—long or short; have Krysia draw another—to tell if my baby girls will soon live with their Daddy again—the shorter the blade, the quicker this comes. (18 December 1927)

The love for his daughters would accompany him for the rest of his life. In *Ziele na kraterze,* he painted their portrait—one of talented, bright, intelligent girls of high ambitions and a pragmatic approach to life. As a matter of fact, Wańkowicz as a father played a decisive part in shaping his daughters' personalities. The remarkable symbiosis of father and daughters inspires awe and envy. Scenes from the childhood or adolescence of both girls described in the book had impact on many readers, who sent letters, often so very personal in their tone. Files containing letters documenting that book's success are the most voluminous of all. The writer's archives hold a vast collection of the readers' direct reactions, sent to the writer after they'd read *Ziele*.

Tili and Krysia were characters with whom many young people identified, whose story aroused emotions that were expressed in various forms.

What was Marta "Tili" Wańkowicz like? Called "agreeable one" by her father due to her easy and cooperative character, she was a merry, witty, independent follower of her father's motto: "not to have a boring life." Wańkowicz willingly compared her to himself, called her his beloved baby girl, of character features similar to him, and of a similar outlook on life.

He wrote to Krysia during the German occupation: "Mom used to say that it was never boring with me, as there was always something going on. That same sort of whirl was made by Tilusia [Tili]" (15 July 1940).

Encouraged by her father, the talented girl tried her hand at writing, presenting her first literary attempts. Her enthusiasm for everything and her ambition convinced everyone that her career as a young writer looked exceptionally positive. Great plans were born in Wańkowicz's head. He began with a trip over the Masurian lakes in a "Kuwaka" canoe together with his daughter. The trip gave rise to the book *Na tropach Smętka*. The war stopped his future writing plans. He now transposed them onto his daughter, in whom he confided by letter that he was sorry to see the four years of work over the book on Kresy[4] go to waste. He promised her that they would write it together one day, and that it would be an "epochal" book. In the letter, he also divulged his hopes and faith that the war would end and Marta would return home richer with knowledge of another continent, richer with new education, and therefore—how very valuable for the new Poland.

> When the situation settles in those territories—and I am in no doubt that it will be completely different—if I cannot, you will go over the area with the "Leica" and a notebook. You will see what happened to each of the people we described. You will learn of their fates and deaths, and if they are alive, you will write what abode each of those Krzywce[5] found. You will prepare the third epoch in the book. You will look at it—from the level of the other hemisphere, your experiences, the analogies you have accumulated. We will then publish the book as Marta and Melchior Wańkowicz. It will nicely crown the cooperation started in "Kuwaka," and be a good start for you. An idea runs in my head to put everything you would have written in a different type, and so several coordinate trends would run along in the book. If that happens in a good few years—when the situation in the area is completely different, and you will already have not only completed your studies, but you will also have actually worked and lived in the U.S.—then it shall simply be an epoch-making book. And it will immediately put you on top of the writing world. (4 November 1941)

In the same letter, Wańkowicz clearly states his stand concerning the future of his daughter, first sent to Switzerland, then to America to study.

Since we are talking of duties, I believe it to be your duty to come to Poland as normal as possible—to the country where so much abnormal pomposity and hypocrisy will be spawned.

The situation in "those territories" was settled in a completely different manner. Both the daughter and the father chose to remain in exile. The difference was that the father finally returned home—the daughter remained an emigrant in America.

The writer's archives hold a letter to Marta and Jan Erdman, written two years after the writer returned to Poland permanently. On behalf of himself and his wife, the writer asked his daughter for a long visit—of three months. He asked her not to wait until one of her parents fell ill, but to come then, when they were all still in good health, and give them some of her time. Wańkowicz desired that she come to her parents, without her husband or daughters—so that the parents could enjoy her stay in full. In the letter, you can see her father's tremendous hope that after such a stay, without Jan Erdman's immediate impact on her opinion, his daughter would decide to return to Poland. Wańkowicz started the letter "Dear Janeks"[6] and wrote among other things:

We'd very much like to ask Marta to come visit us for three months at the beginning of summer. We'll pay for the return ticket and for her whole stay, with all its costs and pleasures. She will have the car at her disposal (she ought to acquire an international driving license) and will stay in the best possible boarding houses as long as she wants. The main thing is—she will have no duties on her shoulders and will have twenty years' worth of lying on the beach. She will have her fill of herself alone, herself and mom, herself, mom, and me. She can go with me on some tours with lectures; she'll have the occasion to meet Janeks' siblings. She will have an occasion, if she only wants it, to meet the most eminent people in Poland. All that will depend utterly and completely on her choice. We want nothing from her—we just want her to have a thorough rest and relaxation from stress. I think she will need much rest and relaxation with regard to nerves, and a store of healthy and understanding love for the girls' growing time. And fatigue does not aid understanding love. I believe it will be a blessing for all your family. But I do not want to falsify the letter by stressing your needs. But this here is our need, and very strong. If you have the last issue (illustrated—now there is another issue coming, of 20,000 books) of *Ziele na kraterze*, please, Tili, read your letter to me on page 452. My God! . . .—I don't want to remind her of her words as a child. But maybe she'll feel good with us.

The girls? . . . Yes, we do keep the girls in mind. If you remember, last year I offered an extensive proposition—refused, without even much of a comment. The girls—we keep them in mind, and there will be time for them. But we would very much like to have Tili all to ourselves now. I do not think you could refuse that suggestion. And, to be quite honest, I cannot imagine what our relationship could look like later if you refuse. Oh, this is no threat of severing ties, which could never happen. I just cannot see for now what our relationship would feed upon then. (27 February 1960)

Wańkowicz claimed he had made a good decision when returning. He claimed he gained readers, which was more important for the writer than any political differences. With the return, he saw his literary future. He was also counting on Marta to come sooner or later to a similar decision. How much was it his "wanting" her return? How much was it his real desire? These questions are difficult to answer. He was still counting on his daughter's return. He was hoping that at least when she retired, Marta Erdman born Wańkowicz would move back to Poland. He spoke of that, although it is difficult to guess what his hopes were based on.

The conversations with her parents about returning to Poland must have had an impact on Marta, as their traces are to be found in her printed work.

In the story "Obojnaki" ("Hyphenated People"), she quoted her mother's arguments that "people did not die in the Warsaw Uprising to have their children lose their national identity now." The protagonist grimaced on hearing that, and claimed that "a person grows like a beanstalk, from the soil on which fate had thrown them." The thesis—echo of her father's convictions that "you cannot raise your children in a vacuum"—she refuted with the belief that how you lived depended on the person, and not on latitude. Still, her father claimed you could not raise your child to be someone you are not. You could not then give them what each American mother or father automatically gave their children. "You will impoverish your children if you don't raise them to be Poles, to be who you are."

What is the answer of the story's protagonist? Her stance is clearly negative. The author seems to have consumed her own reflections by mouth and considered them her personal problem. At the same time, she was aware, and knew, that the blow was too painful for her parents, and was unable to deliver it to them personally. She spoke her mind only indirectly. The reply of the literary character created by Marta in her story sounds sharp and cruel:

> But I am not Polish anymore. I am not an American just because of the passport, only for convenience. I love that country. I miss it when I leave. I am angry with what is wrong in it. I have lived here for most of my life. Here I have studied. Here I have fallen in love and married. Here I have worked. Here I have had my children. Here I have a home. It is my country.

But even at moments of greatest irritation, she hesitated to use a coup de grace, to say simply, calmly, reasonably: "My dear, you are wrong in the very assumption. I am not Polish anymore."

Yet life showed that it was still too painful a blow to deliver, even if veiled with a literary character. After the story was published in the Paris *Kultura* (*Culture*) monthly, which occurred soon after her visit to Poland in

1960, Marta waited for her father's response and for him to judge the text. He always did that; he was glad with every printed word of hers, and commented on each. Now there was complete silence.

After Wańkowicz's death, Marta asked me if I knew anything about it, as she didn't dare inquire earlier of her father. I remember the writer had showed me Marta's story. He knew its content, but—as he put it—he was not capable of any comment. He chose silence.

He treated the literary form as a camouflage for his daughter's attitude toward Poland and was astonished with her confession. Any other woman could do that, but not her—the daughter of such a father, raised in a house of rich Polish traditions, coming from a family with a highly developed sense of national identity.

How different were those words uttered by Marta in the mouth of the story's protagonist, from the ones she'd written in a letter to her father (just before she left Poland) about their last meeting with Krysia? She had written, "I knew that on leaving I would leave behind something that no other country and no other life could give me."

So what was Marta the exile like, really? In how far was she still that same ambitious daughter of her father, the same girl who offered so much promise in her early youth?

The answer to that question may be found in a book I was sent by Jan Erdman, Marta's husband, after her death. The posthumous volume is entitled *W oboim żywiole* (*In the Dual Element*).[7] The copies are numbered, with the words "Private printed material not meant for trade" printed on each.

The book starts with a motto which at the same time explains the title. It is a quote from Adam Mickiewicz's ode "Do samotności" ("To Loneliness") of 1832.

> *I bez oddechu w górze, bez ciepła na dole,*
> *równie jestem wygnańcem w oboim żywiole.*

> (No breath up high, down low no warmth, I lament,
> Equal exile I am in the dual element.)

In the introduction to the book, Marta's husband thus wrote about her decision to stay in exile:

> The decision didn't come easy. The transplantation from a very Polish, very patriotic, even nationalistic home atmosphere to the American soil did not go painlessly. It was a shock, the repercussion of which she suffered through decades. We all pay the transplant costs, we all stay "in the dual element," but Marta felt it more intensively. She was more sensitive.

The fact that she felt it acutely, that constantly she wrestled with the—in the words of the Canadian poet and academic, Danuta Bieńkowska—"exile hump," that it became one of her complexes, a painful subject constantly re-considered and experienced anew, is proven emphatically by her own book. The preface says that the volume includes all her texts scattered over various papers, and that the selection was done at the author's request when still alive. She wished for it to be sent to her friends and family.

The dominating theme of the book is staying in exile and the relationship of homeland-exile. In nearly every text, the author seems to have to prove to herself again and anew that the decision she had taken was right.

Two stories are particularly important for deciphering Marta's Polish-American complications. One is the above-quoted "Obojnaki," the other, "Popatrzcie, proszę, na Barbarę" ("Please Look at Barbara").

The latter shows two friends, emigrants, living in Washington, DC, for over twenty years. Both carry their load, mental wounds from the past, but they are also joined with a similar story and similar existence. One of them, Barbara, earning her living as a manicurist, suddenly decides to visit her homeland. She prepares carefully for her two-month journey, with much sacrifice, saving the money she would need. At first her friend is not happy to observe it, but slowly she is drawn into the events. She helps Barbara in everything, and sees her off at the airport.

Two months later, she is waiting for her friend to return. Barbara returns different, strange, bitter. She says, "All that," pointing at the parkway, cars, the spire of Washington's monument, the Capitol's white dome,

all that seems strangely foreign to me. You need different lungs to breathe this air. Flying over the Atlantic, I thought all the time that there was no place for me in this world anymore. And it seemed to horrible to me that I swore to myself to hide it like leprosy. [. . .] All that looks so different from Poland, somehow ridiculous. We all, we are actually helpless puppets that dangle in a vacuum. We think that we are wearing an armor—and we are naked. We stand at a post that is there no more. We stubbornly defend what we remember, and not what there really is. We are such wretched generous-at-someone-else's-expense Joes, ready for sacrifice but not ours, generous at someone else's cost, strictly judging others, miserable savers for new fridges, as no one collects "gold for the Homeland" anymore. The Homeland is over, and all Ordon's Redoubts[8] are no more ours. We walk around like bleak Half-Lordlings[9] overblown with platitudes which are supposed to save us, and we stop believing even what each such platitude really used to once be. We wake each morning with the distaste of guilt towards that former home and towards what some lunatics among us call their "new home." A new homeland, what is that strange creature? Today learned doctors can slit the human chest open and insert a machine to aid the patient's heart. But they cannot exchange the heart. You walk about in the world seemingly the same, and yet there are moments that you have a battery in your chest, not your own living heart. That saves your life and is considered a great achievement of science. But no one has come up with a new heart.

The words are singular, so sharp, so unfair, perhaps, and how true at the same time. One may surmise that just like her protagonist, Marta—despite other comments scattered in the book—is still unsure of her stand, one "neither-fish-nor-fowl." She defined herself clearly: "We are incurably hyphenated people." She does not consider the fact of possibly having "two homelands" as a great luck or wealth—she sees it as great poverty.

At the end of the story, the narrator—Barbara's friend—notices the handful of earth brought by her friend from Poland in a small bag.

> The earth in the triangular cornet was dry, grey, barren. Nothing could grow out of it. There was no resemblance to that warm, juicy, black soil that she used to let run through her fingers, unthinkingly. It was sad, the saddest thing on Earth, like withered flowers, like empty eye sockets, like a barren woman.

The protagonist wants to touch, to feel the warmth of that "land back there" in her hand. Kneeling, she gathers "grey dust." There was only a handful of it.

Next to those fragments, which move the reader with the yearning for the home soil, the home country, the childhood, Marta Erdman puts others, contrary ones—not so much to be contrary, but to show co-existing feelings.

And thus, Krystyna, the protagonist of "Obojnaki," returns to the United States after a few years and looks at the Statue of Liberty with the greatest "intense shiver of emotion," and names New York's panorama of skyscrapers "the most poetic sight on Earth." To a friend who was beset with doubts whether she could give her children what she should as a mother, she wrote in a letter:

> It is not about giving your children a vast love of Poland—it is about developing in them a predisposition to love. Love is an amazingly all-encompassing virtue, and from that virtue there later grow attachment, courage, willingness to make sacrifices, honest judgment. I think that if you encourage musical talents in your child, and facilitate the talent's growth, it doesn't really matter later if the child plays Bach, or Beethoven. Further I think, quite heretically, that if you arouse a religious spirit in your child, then, as a matter of fact, it does not matter if the child is a good Quaker, Catholic, or Protestant. And actually, it does not matter to me much whether my children are good Americans, or good Poles. I think that both here and there, the required psychological predisposition is the same, and it is that predisposition that matters, and you surely cannot achieve it with abstracts. The only part of the world to which I can attach my children in reality, not in abstract, is America. And thus this is what I am trying to do.

Krystyna—who can to some extent be viewed as Marta's reflection—happily ended her visit in the country. There she had "solved the complex of longing in herself," and with joy boarded the ship to America—this time by her own choice, not by coincidence and not forced to do so by the war.

Marta herself visited Poland many times. Altogether there were eleven such visits, starting with her first coming after the war. About her last visit, which was in the fall of 1980, and which was actually her farewell to Poland, as Marta was already ill with the same illness as her father had, she wrote a story that ends the sad book. In the story, she showed the significance of those visits for herself. Her visits to Poland taught her mainly humility and tolerance. Humility, as everyone told her, that she wouldn't understand the country anyway, wouldn't understand its surrealism. That she had alienated herself living on a different continent. She also found tolerance in herself— she thought—higher than the tolerance of people staying there in Poland. She admitted that it came easy to her to be intolerant toward others when she had an American passport and a return ticket to the United States in her pocket. Marta was constantly perplexed with the thought that there was no way of knowing what she might do in someone else's place.

Marta Erdman already had her place, her spot in the world, chosen for living and for the future of her children. By then she was far from the doubts that accompanied her during her first visit to the country, at which she was looking through the eyes of her daughters. She tried to imagine them walking next to her through the streets of her childhood, staying with people whom she knew and who were still close to her. And it happened to her then that it seemed her children could not belong to any other place in the world.

Yet right after that, she called her emotions "the recollection of past emotions, wilted like reheated supper."

Thus, she is full of contradictions—thoughts, emotions, recollection, freed and then promptly smothered within her. The exile is for Marta a constant problem, a subject she is grappling with, one that overcomes her, plagues her, sweeps her whole, and subordinates her to itself. Her exile is a fate that seems to have squashed all the others, and foremost, it didn't bring anything great. Marta wrote a few stories, some reportages, but if you look at her life's work collected in the posthumous volume *W oboim żywiole*, the slimness of the volume, the modest scale of interests amazes and puzzles one. At first, very promising as a writer, the young Marta Wańkowicz essentially did not produce any great work, nor did she really make any attempt to—she didn't do much to change anything. What did it stem from that she was only able to reflect the years-long topic of the transplant?

In a letter to his daughter (19 August 1944), Wańkowicz complained that Marta had

> lowered the atmosphere of her spiritual life. She was beautiful in Switzerland and in September in Poland during her first year at college, but at the second year, something started to deteriorate and went down after attending the PIC

[Polish Information Center, where Marta worked in the lecture department—note by AZB]. You are a beautiful, plastic, sensitive material—but sensitive to everything that life brings—the good and the bad. That same little girl would have been different breathing the pure air of Monte Cassino, and completely different breathing the air of PIC.

Why didn't the daughter of Wańkowicz—after her studies in Switzerland and in America, with fluent English, after the war ended—try her hand at any ambitious venture? Why did she instead, on marrying, settle with her husband on a farm and spend a few years of her life raising chickens? After the war, emigrants with complexes who lacked sufficient knowledge of English, set up such farms. Hence, Wańkowicz was so pleased later, when Marta worked for a few years as a researcher for *Time* magazine.

He wrote her in 1941:

> I think that it is not the mystery of life to drudge too much, but to live intensively. I mean with it, to have much pleasure, but for each pleasure to be a conquest, experience, relaxation. The motto: not to have a boring life! And here I am not afraid for you. If you ever tell yourself that you owe something to me, maybe it will be this. (4 November 1941)

But didn't he miscalculate in assuming that his daughter would be ambitious enough to be an achiever and climb the ladder of success, like he'd taught her?

Wańkowicz was aware of the fact that Marta did not entirely meet his expectations and the hopes he'd placed in her. To him, the explanation was clear. First of all, he knew that the decision to stay in exile permanently and definitely did clip Tili's wings, and also—a thing he mentioned rarely and reluctantly—he decided that the cause lay with his daughter's marriage. The deep regret he felt on learning about Marta marrying Jan Erdman, stayed with him for the rest of his life. Erdman was not the husband he'd imagined for his child, and he was surprised with Marta's sudden decision. More so, he regretted having been omitted when the decision was made. Earlier, his daughter sent him letters that described her friendship and then engagement to a young boy, her age, by the name of Paweł, and Wańkowicz actually had no reservations about him. He still controlled the situation, advising his daughter a practical approach to the matter, and also approving of her choice. Zofia Wańkowicz was also acquainted with the issue—so far that when she learned of her daughter being married, she wrote to ask, "Paweł, how is Tili's husband?"

Wańkowicz had known his son-in-law, Jan Erdman, earlier as a good sports reporter, but certainly he wasn't thinking of him as a husband for his beloved younger daughter. Years later, he spoke with reluctance about Erdman's "doctrinarism," saying he had imposed his vision of the world on

Marta, and she, being a "conjugal" type—in the words of Wańkowicz—adapted quite obediently to her role as a wife.

Also, Erdman showed no great liking for Wańkowicz. He had to realize his father-in-law was being rather unfriendly to him. In the introduction to Marta's book, Erdman wrote openly of Tili's father's reaction to the letter that informed him of her decision to marry.

> When we set the date, the younger daughter informed Melchior Wańkowicz of the joyous event, the writer then fighting with the 2nd Corps somewhere on the Italian peninsula. Meanwhile, instead of a blessing, a telegram came suggesting that we postpone the wedding until peace is restored, or in other words, without the diplomatic dodging—to break off our relationship. Fortunately, the telegram came 14 days after the unbreakable marriage oath was taken. Wańkowicz's telegram had been delayed by the army censorship.

Lack of any greater enthusiasm in the relations of Erdman and Wańkowicz can be seen in later, enigmatic, and sometimes scathing comments made by the author of *Monte Cassino*. His son-in-law returned the favor with similar ones. In his book (a very interesting one) *Droga do Ostrej Bramy* (*The Road to the Gate of Dawn*),[10] when writing about Major Hubal's unit, Jan Erdman quoted Wańkowicz many times, and at the same time did not fail to quote—with a certain satisfaction and spite—a misprint which had crept into the first issue of the book on Hubal's soldiers. His disdain ignored how publishing the book in exile soon after the war's end might not incur a sloppy revision.

Jan Erdman was Marta's senior by fifteen years. In a letter to Erdman (of 23 September 1944), Wańkowicz explained he had been afraid that the man had been "too far formed in spirit not to affect Marta, who was just developing to life."

Yet was it only her husband who had stifled in her the ambitions of achievement in writing, her own aspirations? And to what extent did her popular father impact Marta's inability to create herself fully, to express herself fully? How extensively did she not want to, or wasn't able to match him as a writer?

Anyway, she changed her life philosophy rather quickly, the philosophy that she had developed for years in her home, had announced it to everyone and had done so everywhere she could. Much must have changed in that nineteen-year-old girl, so self-confident, since her arrival in America, that is, since 1940, when only four years later she wrote to her future husband how she would like to spend her life, how she imagined it to be. The young girl explained her ambitions and plans for life—so different from those she declared four years earlier:

So far I had little occasion to test my life philosophy. But the basic premise is thus: I like belonging to one world, and if everyone makes one world, then I like to feel that I belong to one place in that world.

And so I am not rejecting homeland or state. Quite the contrary: during the war I'd like to contribute, be it in a boring way, to regain that own place of mine. In the time of peace, I would like to furnish it on my own, like my own home, sweep out the dust, wash the curtains and make chicken for Sunday dinner. Maybe it's not a mission, but that is how I would like to live.

I don't reject family, as my own family was such that I didn't have to bend to it, such that I could belong there by my own choice, with a clean conscience and my entire love.

I do not reject family also because I would like to have children myself, at least two. If I had them, I would like to give them as much love, understanding, and interest in life as I was given. And the same deep breathing with the world. They will have their own yard to which they will not be chained, which they will be free to leave, but which they won't wish to leave, as they will remember various things that don't have much meaning. They will recall events like the ones I remember: a fresh morning as you sat on a plow in the farmyard, as you drilled a hole with your bare heel in the damp black earth, a sudden awareness of an amazingly strong growing and maturing of the ears of grain in the field or the berries in the wood, some harm that you wanted to redress but not the injustice to the international proletariat, retaliation for that smallest "snotty" hurt from some backyard confrontation in Nalewki district harvest festival, Our Lady of Herbs in a sweaty wooden church. Such various little things, everything around you to be observed.[11]

Marta died from the same illness as her father did, eight years after him. Thus passed away the last of the four protagonists of *Ziele na kraterze*, a book telling the story of one family. The first to go was Krystyna, Wańkowicz's older daughter, participant of the Warsaw Uprising. In 1969, Zofia Wańkowicz died, and five years later, Melchior.

How can it be said—or can it be said at all—that the father was biased in favor of one of his daughters?

By the end of his life, the writer spoke of his relationship with the two daughters. It was with great pain that he spoke of Krysia, with whom he hadn't had such an easy contact as with the younger Tili. Krysia—according to him—was a difficult child, haughty, tenacious. She stayed with her mother and took care of her. When remembering Krysia, and comparing her to Tili, Wańkowicz claimed that had she survived the war, she would have stayed in Poland, as she was extremely attached to Polishness, to the Polish land. She wanted to study agriculture.

"I focused on Tili," he said, "as she seemed easier, simpler, she seemed to be more promising, but I think I underestimated the other one. She wrote better, and had an undeniable talent for writing."

He wrote to Tili during the occupation of Poland:

Krysia—she is my greatest wound. The girl has a talent for writing of which she doesn't know, and very poor makings of a farmer. Maybe there will come a time that you will help her get better. Let's hope it doesn't come too late. (26 August 1940)

In Krysia's letters which can be found in the writer's archive, one can see undoubted ability, great sensitivity, an insightful look at people and herself, and the ability to precisely define her own feelings. Krysia emerges there as a noble, deep girl.

Wańkowicz said that in everyday life Krysia was difficult, but after years he noted she had the makings of an interesting person. He regretted not having understood that in their early period. He resented his sharp conflicts with his adolescent daughter. Neither did he ever forget that they had separated in such a difficult time of tensions—as it turned out—forever.

He recorded the scene in *Ziele na kraterze*:

> On the third day of the war, when the trains still ran fairly regularly, Dad brought her to the train station to send her to Kamienna Góra village. She took many university course books with her. The patriotically demonstrating crowds filled her with aversion. It was her father's wish to keep her safe in the country in that troubled time, but he was surprised that she agreed, while the other, younger daughter was fighting her way through Scandinavia to the burning Poland. When the train was about to go, the father incautiously voiced his doubts.
>
> "Should I stay?" she asked.
>
> "Oh, no, not at all. . . . All that you can do now, is learn," he lied. [. . .]
>
> When a week later they were walking through a meadow, an enemy pilot came shooting at the shepherds. As she watched the aircraft disappear, Krysia said: "It unsettles me that I cannot hate." The words held contrariness against the crowds shaking in the shelters and loudly voicing their hatred. She wanted to live a free, unhindered spiritual life, independent of any events. When the Serebryszcze village was bombed, she was the only one not to go down to the cellar, and chose this particular time to do her manicure. She read books. She opted for much sleep. She wanted to live—at all costs—her former life, a life of her own choices, independent of any necessity. She rebelled against events or people—friends or strangers—imposing any constraints on her. [. . .]
>
> When later there began the whispers and spreading bulletins, conspiracies, and conversations, listening to the radio in secret—she took no part in that.[12]

Krysia—with her seemingly cold approach to life.

"At school and at the university she was asocial. She had no best friends or any rank in the students' council. She mocked at the secret conspiracies in 'Thirteenth May,'[13] Wańkowicz wrote in *Ziele na kraterze* (p. 353). Later she had a turning point in her patriotic awareness. She then took the portrait of her uncle, killed in the Polish-Bolshevik war of 1920, down from the attic, and hung it up in her room. As Wańkowicz put it, "The flames have come."

In letters to her sister, you can hear a tone of some exceptional maturity, a note of maternal feelings. She wrote of her peers, of boys staying in camps or those who even when they seemed crushed with the situation did not lose their dignity and the will to learn. Also, her peer Jan Strzelecki drew my attention to that protectiveness toward boys of her generation. He said among other things, "Krysia is one of those few people from back then whom I'd keep with me." He thought that after Tili left, Krysia gained some new colors, new expression. He visited their "Dear Home," working long hours in the library. He admired Krysia's friendliness, the ability to understand, her sense of the atmosphere, her calm when it was needed.

Zofia Wańkowicz wrote to her husband and daughter:

> Melek, Tili—you ought to be told of Krystyna, and foremost, Krystyna deserves that from me. When you were leaving, she was but a girl yet. Now she is a human.
>
> Most of all, she has integrity. She hates lies and weakness of character and protests against compromises. Another feature of her is searching: she searches for the truth and great causes. She knows that of herself. She once wrote a humorous announcement: "I am seeking ready-made worldviews." She could be rough with the pain of searching, but when she sometimes—oh, how seldom—talked of her inner issues, she was charming and sweet. She was often deep in thought, and sad. A third feature of hers is great girlish purity. And Krystyna does not plan her future with anyone. She is self-contained with her life. She hates grand words and gestures. She loves life; she likes life. You can feel the store of cheerfulness in her. Once she said that she would have liked to sing at home. She loves beauty with a genuine and heartfelt feeling; she avidly revels in the beauty of nature, and her sense of beauty in domestic matters is unerring. She delights in clean and beautiful surroundings. She is happy with the Dear Home that she manages by herself, purposefully and skillfully. Lately she wants to have some fun, dance; she enjoys her dresses, invites friends, reacts to the human race and the merits of social life. She misses you, but never speaks of it. When she makes some decision about her education, or later when she made her military decision, she would say: "Right now, when I need my father, he is not here." She never complains about any practical matters. When I told her that after the war she would go abroad, would travel, she didn't reply. She wanted it very much.
>
> She is healthy, strong and emphatically says: "I've got so much strength; I am so healthy and strong." She develops physical courage (do you remember the "Cossack spirit"?) and spiritual fortitude in herself. She develops responsibility for the undertaken obligations in herself. What she undertakes, she does perfectly, systematically, and patiently (managing the house, the lot, the garden). She is diligent in learning. Her intelligence develops, and her abilities are somehow charming, graceful. She is very anxious and concerned what her father will say about her when he returns. And she is so alike Melek in her character, mind, and reactions in life. And yet she is "her own," unique. You can feel so much spiritual virtue in her, still unrevealed, of which she is still unaware herself (the letter bears no date).

During the occupation, Krysia missed her father greatly. She confided it to her younger sister, who was staying an ocean away—the missing of her father, her reflections on the times that she happened to be living in, when "fathers are so necessary."

In June 1941 she wrote to Tili:

> I keep thinking of father. I was just bringing order to the storeroom, and among other stuff, found packages with his things and papers. As I organized the particular files, prints, loose pages, books, stands, maps, films—I was overcome with a strange feeling. I had the feeling of recalling and putting away all his life piece by piece, with his work, with his passions, starting with the final school examination, with the student's volume of his *Bez przyłbicy* (*Openly*). I think that I only now realized many things about Father. I miss him so inexpressibly much. I think of our meeting with mixed feelings: for between 19 and 21 a person changes completely and becomes someone else altogether. So did I. And it is difficult for people to meet if they were completely different on parting. He surely imagined that I would do more for myself, that I would live up to his aspirations. When I think of that, I sometimes get up at night and grab another dose of English, for what else can I do! Nothing, nothing, nothing! The war is nasty. It robs daughters of fathers when they need them most.

Krystyna was aware that she had changed, that the times were different, and that now her relationship with her father could have had a completely different character from when they were parting. She knew his ambitions for her and wanted to live up to them. She confided in him her plans, her activities, the successive household courses she completed, and which were so very useful in life under the German occupation. She also waited greedily for his letters. The letters weren't frequent. Zofia Wańkowicz asked her husband to reply to Krysia's letters and to treat her gently. She was worried for her daughter:

> Krystyna is not in a good spiritual condition: she feels much emptiness and is very resentful, I must say, also against herself. I take care that there doesn't appear an inferiority complex mixed with youthful conceit. She is oftentimes in such a mocking, dismissive mood, and then again, how to name it, in the style of the literature which I didn't accept with our partners. She is very noble and bravely struggles by my side to survive. (Zofia Wańkowicz to Melchior, 6 June 1940)

Krysia wrote to her father:

> Your letters support us, stimulate us to work, to prove the love that helps us live. Despite all those sharp words towards me, after which I cried day and night (awful frog, you had to put a sting in almost every letter!), I don't know how to thank you for those letters of yours, where every single sign swells with your heart. (2 July 1940)

In fact, her father *was* that "awful frog that stings" in many of his letters. He made fun of her household duties, her gardening work, raising chickens. He suggested that she also raise *rabbits*!

> Would it be very unreasonable to buy a pair of bunnies? Then you would have three, one to raise for a skin for Pusio after its longest life, and the bought pair—for breeding. Rabbit fricassee with rice—scrumptious. Or maybe you'll treat yourself to a goat? Huh? . . . Since I'm not there, you should be the one to take some initiatives, so that "Bunny" doesn't have a boring life. . . . (15 July 1940)

Reportedly, Krysia cried after reading that letter, feeling humiliated. Wańkowicz's letters to the older daughter are different from those to the younger one, in whom he confided his writing plans and ambitions, and whom he treated like a partner of equal standing. Krystyna knew she wasn't distinguished that way. She complained, "Now that you are so far away— there are so many things I would like to tell you, ask you, seek your advice. I so awfully regret that you cannot remember me fondly. My dearest!" The next sentence is crossed out, but you can still read it: "Recall from time to time that you have an elder daughter."

It would seem that Krystyna suffered from a sense of inferiority toward her talented younger sister, her successes, her America. She wrote of her days in Warsaw anxious that, as compared to Tili's correspondence, her own letters were wan, uninteresting, that they couldn't please her father, that they didn't match her sister's letters.

> I am ashamed to compare my letters to Tiluszek's [Tili's], for of what signifi- cance may any cooking, typing, or driving course I completed be as compared to what she has given forth from herself. Her competition is a too strong for me in the pursuit of your highest, fatherly favor. I hope you won't put that last sentence down to envy or bitterness. It only speaks of my admiration and esteem for the younger button. (2 February 1941)

Krystyna was full of admiration for her sister, and she often wrote about it to her father. She was able to maintain an objective view on Marta. She wrote again about Tili's letters in the same, above-quoted letter:

> They are so righteous and cordially judicious, and they show such wonderful attitude, and such integrity. And you can see how many values she managed to meticulously collect for her 19 years of age. Nothing is wasted with her; she turns everything for the good. I believe you can be pleased.

Yet she openly acknowledged—regardless of her awe and love for Tili— being envious of her father's feelings. She was deeply affected by her sister's leaving: "To be honest, I was seething with envy as Tili was leaving, and her trip was a bad moment in my life, but naturally I never held a grudge against you for that. Now I am glad it all happened as it happened." (25 April 1940).

Still, she admitted it was hard for her when her friends asked outright: "Do you envy Tili that she's in America?" She tried to avoid people, because when constantly compared to her sister and questioned about her, she could not find the immunity in her then.

Yet I think she believed her place was in Poland, as "we must sit here, for although the heart is reaching from here to you, I think this is where our place is" (12 January 1940).

When Krystyna asked Marta in a letter about a possible trip abroad, Tili wrote her in all honesty about her feelings, so hard when finding herself in the new country. She judged her sister to be more difficult, "headstrong," and thus expected it would be worse for Krystyna. She actually doubted if Krysia could leave Poland at all:

> I simply wanted to tell you how infinitely hard it turned out to be, and completely unexpectedly for me, the rolling stone, to be among strangers, completely unknown people. And hence this part of my reflections "Krystyna abroad" was that you would feel at least like I do, and likely even worse, as you are more "headstrong" than I and less compliant. You would probably never leave at all. And the "new chapter" is—how would you settle your life and conditions here? Would you be able to cope with those people, or rather not with them, but with yourself in relation to them? (27 August 1940)

A certain contrast to Krystyna's longing for a different life, to living abroad, which sometimes appeared, can be found in a moving letter from Kamienna Góra. The young girl revealed in it both her no mean gift for observation in the beautiful description of nature, and at the same time a reconciliation with everything, with herself. Her words are worth quoting here:

> Dear Papa—yesterday "Bunny" saw me off to the train. I was alone in the compartment, so I had much time for reflection. The more so, as just before setting off to catch the train we received Tili's letter, with a picture of her on it cut out of some paper. It seems she has absorbed there with all her ability to assimilate in foreign environments. Yesterday was sunny, and I amused myself by watching the boring, flat fields, which I know so well, bleached with ripening rye, the thin paths, worn out in the white sandy soil, the kids wrestling with some meager bovine creatures in the ditches by the railway tracks. I would not like to leave that behind not even for the price of America. Let Tiluchna [Tili] gather knowledge across the world, and let her come back to those sandy soils with a suitably packed braincase. I write as if I had at least a hundred alternatives to choose from, but it is always easier if you persuade yourself that you are doing something out of one's own free will. (13 June 1940)

Krystyna, in whom Wańkowicz finally noticed, albeit too late, undoubted writing talent, wrote to her sister rather infrequently, but those were always mature letters, moving and expressive. She knew how to write, and she knew how to feel.

Her untimely death in the Uprising prevented anyone from verifying their opinion of what kind of writer Krystyna would be—had she become one. A small proof of her sensitivity can now be found only in her letters—for instance the following one written to Tili:

> New Year's Day 1941
>
> Sometimes there comes over you such sharp awareness of each moment being irrecoverable, the awareness that each day you've lived through becomes a number under "credit" or "debit" in the balance of life, a number which can never (a dreadful word!) be wiped out and which must impact the final recapitulation. At such moments, when certain trite clichés come alive and palpable, you even cannot find words to define them different than the ones used for centuries ("lost moment," "irrecoverable days," "passing youth" etc.). Then you focus, terrified, on the time that has flown and is still flying; you repent of your sins and swear to remedy your ways.

On the day she became of age, she wrote: "I try to sometimes penetrate the future with the thought, and imagine our meeting. When? Where? How?—I cannot. How will we celebrate it when you come of age? I do hope that day will be less bitter than mine. God willing!"

She confided in her sister her thoughts on the war and, as always, missing her father:

> I used to believe that the war was a free game of powers—a great whirl that rejected the weaker human element, and chose the bravest. Now I know that it destroys those most brave. Around us it gets more and more empty; it is a more and more barren desert, across which you trudge with this mortal sorrow in the heart, which cannot be effaced anymore by any changes that will come or by the youth which hasn't passed yet. I'm thinking of Father. Never before have I felt so lonely. And never before have I needed him so much!

Her longing for her father burst out many times with great force, for instance after she returned from the country:

> I dreamt in Kamienna Góra of seeing Father tired and sick. And the whole dream had such a terrible hue that I woke with my pillow moist with tears, and for many hours, until morning, I lay there sleepless, which for me is a weighty phenomenon. I never thought you could get so dreadfully worn and tired in your sleep. I miss Father so terribly.

Zofia Wańkowicz wrote to her husband about Krysia (Kraków, January 1945):

> She went to the storm unit having made a final decision, self-knowledge and will. She had no combat preparation; she had no sense of danger. She was cheerful. She flew there like a bird. You understand: freedom, Homeland (and liberation from the petty everyday life). But naturally, she never said any of those words. She wanted no part of auxiliary service. With disgust, she rejected any sanitary services, educational, inns, or social welfare (she completed a training course for education instructors, and had the right to the rank of second or first lieutenant). She wanted to fight for her Homeland in a storm unit, protesting against the war with all her might, all her soul.
>
> She took nothing: not the emerald ring which she was so happy to receive (for her coming of age), not the coins sewn into a small cushion, not the chain bracelet "for a rainy day," nor the worst frocks from her clothes. She prepared her sports equipment carefully, and with love. She lost those things twice in the first days of combat. She went just like that, in the navy blue pleated skirt, in casual shoes (without her beloved boots) and a white blouse. Rafał's liaison. Four of them went together. Krystyna was cheerful. The bondage was choking her, but now—she believed—the Uprising had to be successful. She had no sense of danger: she was Krystyna and nothing could harm her (I don't know what it was like on the Uprising days, but she often used to tell me: "Remember, no harm will come to me").
>
> On the 1st August she went to her duties on the same bike, her dream bike, the one from the trip across Belgium and France. Oh, Tilusia! Her rain cape was blowing, and her hair flowing: "See you, Mother Dear!" We were to meet later that day. I never saw her again.
>
> They said they went in twos. Krystyna at the forefront, carrying her nurse's bag, acting as liaison. Cheerful, joyful. Like a bird. They were singing. A shell hit.
>
> The wound was large, in her chest, just near the throat.

Krystyna Wańkowicz, pseudonym "Anna," a liaison officer of the scouts' battalion "Parasol," was killed on the sixth day of the Warsaw Uprising, during fights in the Protestant cemetery in Młynarska Street. The body wasn't found. Her mother dug through the Wola district for a year, starting with the Calvinist cemetery, and helped move the exhumed bodies from there to the Powązki cemetery. She never found her daughter's body.

The parts of *Ziele na kraterze* which speak of the search for Krysia's body and Zofia Wańkowicz being there when the successive graves were dug out, the bodies examined, make up one of the most heartrending images of human suffering.

> In February, when she started to dig, the temperature was below zero; she thought she would still be able to make out some remnants of the face features. If it was later, maybe she would recognize the pleated skirt. But in spring, the

ground was soggy, so maybe just the braids . . . the combat jacket . . . the cross from "Śmiały's" crew.[14]

Those words were written by a man who didn't experience it himself, who was at that time far away from his country. Why is it then that the book emanates the truth so beautifully? Was the description the writer obtained from his wife so extremely vivid? Or was it so that the father felt her story so much, because he'd lost a child who for him was a "huge, unhealed wound," and overcome with the pain wanted to help himself with writing about her?

As a father, Wańkowicz—the great writer—as he bitterly admitted a number of times—did not succeed in such a dimension as he had wished. He lost his elder daughter at a moment when he could and already started to have a closer psychological relationship with her, when she was ready to open to him, and he possibly to her, ready for mutual love and friendship. Maybe it wasn't Marta, in whom he'd invested so much, but Krystyna, who would have fulfilled his dreams, his hopes?

He lost the younger one, as well, imagining that he would raise her for himself, according to his own plans, such as he wanted her to be. He was disappointed. She did not meet, or could not cope with, or live up to his ambitions and expectations.

At the end, the terminally ill writer summed up his life and clearly saw and defined all that. The writer's personal drama, shown by the daughters' letters and conversations with their father, the complicated fate of his fatherly ambitions for the lives of both his daughters, based on the sources left, completes not only the book *Ziele na kraterze*, but it also complements the writer's profile. It penetrates—to some extent—one of the many secrets he left behind. An interesting man, a monumental writer—so popular, and so little known and understood.

Figure 5.1.　Wańkowicz with his daughter Marta, Bucharest 1940.

NOTES

1. Nevus flammeus, or port-wine stain (translator's note).

2. *Ziele na kraterze*, p. 361.

3. One of the traditions of Christmas Eve is to put hay under the tablecloth for Christmas Eve supper; a once common old custom has young women pull a blade of that hay from under the cloth, or from under a plate, to show (usually) whether they would marry, and how soon (translator's note).

4. Kresy—"Eastern Borderlands," or "Borderlands," a former territory of the eastern provinces of Poland. These territories today lie in western Ukraine, western Belarus, and eastern Lithuania, with such major cities, as Lwów, Wilno (Vilnius), and Grodno.

5. Meaning people from Krzywiec, a village in the Mazury (Masuria) region (translator's note).

6. For Mr. and Mrs. Jan Erdman, but on first-name terms (translator's note).

7. Sigma Press, Albany, NY, 1983.

8. "Reduta Ordona" ("Ordon's Redoubt")—a poem by Adam Mickiewicz describing the defense of Warsaw from the Russian Army, in the Polish November Uprising against the Russians (1830–1831). Juliusz Konstanty Ordon was the commander of one of the redoubts during the storm of Warsaw. In the last moments of its defense, the redoubt was blown up by one of the defenders. In the poem, Mickiewicz has Ordon blown up himself and the redoubt in a heroic act. Ordon actually died a suicidal death in Florence in 1887 (translator's note).

9. In Polish, Półpanek—a gentleman of average standing who pretends to be a great lord (translator's note).

10. Operation Ostra Brama (literally Operation Gate of Dawn) was an armed conflict during World War II between the Polish Home Army and the Nazi Germany occupiers of Vilnius (Polish: Wilno). It began on 7 July 1944, as part of a Polish national uprising, Operation Tempest, and lasted until 14 July 1944. Though the Germans were defeated, the following day the Soviet Red Army entered the city and the Soviet NKVD proceeded to intern Polish soldiers and to arrest their officers. Several days later, the remains of the Polish Home Army retreated into the forests and the Soviets were in control of the city.

11. *W oboim żywiole*, p. 6.

12. *Ziele na kraterze*, pp. 353–54.

13. "Club of the Thirteenth of May" was a small, illegal organization of Warsaw high school students (translator's note).

14. *Ziele na kraterze*, p. 391.

Chapter Six

The Last Days of Krystyna Wańkowicz

"Gryf's" Story

Ziele na kraterze (*Herbs at the Crater*), a book about the Wańkowicz family, was published in New York in 1951, had sixteen editions in Poland, and became one of the great writer's most popular books. The book became compulsory literature for high school students in schools and a beloved book for many Poles.

Living with his wife in the United States since 1949, where his younger daughter Marta had settled, Melchior Wańkowicz wrote a book on what had passed away never to return, on his daughters' childhood and their adolescence. The book described the German occupation and the Warsaw Uprising and the tragic death of his older daughter, Krystyna, on the sixth day of the Uprising.

Many years later he wrote

> I dislike people who hate a nation. When in the September days I was walking through a field with my daughter and a German pilot came shooting at the defenseless shepherds from the sky, my daughter told me: "It unsettles me that I cannot hate the Germans." I then felt rewarded for the years dedicated to her nurturing.[1]

In *Ziele*, he wrote that "the maturing process with Krystyna was extremely slow. At school and at the university she was asocial."[2]

He wrote, based on what her mother recalled, how Krystyna was changing during the occupation. One day she said:

> How could I have lived like that! With that learning. That household work! How foolish I was . . .

145

The mother listened meekly. The fires have come . . .
The flame was coming—unstoppable.[3]

In the Warsaw Uprising, Krystyna, pseudonym "Anna," daughter of Zofia and Melchior Wańkowicz, was the liaison officer for Lieutenant Stanisław Leopold, pseudonym "Rafał," commander of the first company in the "Parasol" battalion. "Rafał" was a first cousin of Captain Andrzej Romocki, pseudonym "Morro."

At her own request, she joined the storm troops unit of over forty people, commanded by "Gryf," that is, Janusz Brochwicz Lewiński. The group commanded the units that were retreating from the Wola district. They fought at the corner of Żytnia and Młynarska streets. On 6 August 1944, the group started to retreat along Żytnia to the Calvinist cemetery. After the briefing, at about 5 to 6 a.m., seven people, Krystyna among them, went through a hole in the cemetery's wall and moved along the path by the fence. There they were raked by German mortar fire.

The fragments of the book that describe the mother searching for the grave of Krystyna in spring and summer of 1945 are among the most heart-rending ones and move each reader. Let me recall a fragment:

> In one of the nearby cellars she found the words "Parasol soldiers" written on the wall. A passing worker told her seven bodies had been buried there. Zula said she'd heard that seven were killed on that path by the cemetery where Krysia's protecting unit was retreating.
>
> They found a collective grave and the place in it where those seven were buried.
>
> She patched together seven coffins. Managed to get two sheets to wrap Krysia's body. She would know it. In February, when she started to dig, the temperature was below zero; she would still be able to make out some remnants of the face features. If it was later, maybe she would recognize the pleated skirt. But in spring the ground was boggy, so maybe just the braids . . . the combat jacket . . . the cross from "Śmiały's" crew.
>
> In the grave there were six boys and a girl. Krysia was the only woman in the unit. So—it was over. . . . She could be sure.
>
> She bent over the decaying remnants. She knew unerringly—that wasn't Krysia. That wasn't how her hands would lie, that wasn't Krysia (the body was then identified as a nurse named Irena, from the "Józek" group, also from "Parasol")."[4]

Now, after so many years have passed I think . . . could it be that the mother did not recognize the body of who at the moment of death did not have plaited hair and wore a uniform and not a pleated skirt?

At the end of the book, Wańkowicz writes that his wife Zofia came from Poland for Christmas 1945. The couple hadn't seen each other since September 1939.

She had a bundle with her. Inside there was a spare shirt and stockings, my fur cap, found in the ruins of the burnt house, and testimony of a nurse and liaison, Zofia.

A fragment of what the liaison officer "Zofia" related:

They were lying in a row, one next to the other, seven bodies, from the side of Żytnia Street. All had wounds of the necks or heads. The first was a beautiful young man with fair hair, next an older man with a roughly-hewn face. . . . Farther lay "Anna."

I sneaked my hand under the combat jacket: there was no heartbeat.

Her eyes were half-closed, the lips slightly parted. Blood was flowing from her mouth. Just a tiny trickle by then.[5]

Account of the liaison officer "Lena":

On the sixth I was at the Calvinist cemetery with my medical point of "Rafał's" first company. I saw "Gryf's" group run down Żytnia [Street]. I peeked through the gate: it was quiet, they formed twos. I saw them go through the hole in the fence, singing "Parasol's" song: "Pałacyk Michla."[6] "Rafał's" liaison, "Anna," went with them. I saw her laugh at something.

It was then that the shell hit. Many fell. "Anna" was closest.

I ran to her, grabbed her hand, called her by her true name.

"Krystyna! . . . Krystyna! . . ."

She didn't answer. There was no pulse, no breathing. She was dead.

For two days we couldn't get to them due to the fire. Finally "Rafał," "Gryf," and some others crept up to bury them.

Later "Rafał" brought me "Anna's" watch with the engraved inscription from her mother, to take it back to her family.

When I was badly injured in Czerniaków,[7] I gave the watch to Bożena, "Szary's" sister. Bożena was killed in Powiśle.[8] "Rafał" was killed before the Krasiński Palace, defending the Old Town. "Gryf" hasn't been found so far.

It is all I know.[9]

That account and the sentence: "'Gryf' hasn't been found so far" end the book *Ziele na kraterze*.

Then there is the epilogue and the prologue, for example, "Father's Letter to Krysia" (diminutive of Krystyna).

The writer tried to contact "Gryf," that is, Janusz Brochwicz Lewiński. At the end of 1948, living with his wife in England (they left for the States in 1949), Wańkowicz wrote a letter:

15th November 1948
To the Office of Officers' Records in Witley

I enclose a pre-paid postcard with address and would kindly request information on the place of stay of

Lt. Janusz Brochwicz Lewiński

The officer, demobilized from the Polish Resettlement Corps on 16 IX [September] 1948, is the only witness of my daughter's death in the Uprising and the information he has is crucial for finding her body.

M. Wańkowicz

As it turned out much later, "Gryf"—Janusz Brochwicz Lewiński—could not be contacted for many years.

In late fall of 2010, during my six-week stay in Poland, I learned that "Gryf" was in Warsaw. Thanks to Anna Komorowska-Sławiec and Agnieszka Bogucka (we were all friends with the late Zofia Korbońska), I met "Gryf."

The now General Janusz Brochwicz Lewiński knew we would be talking about the liaison officer "Anna" and he was prepared. We talked for several hours, in his Warsaw flat, with Anna and Agnieszka also present.

We later met in the Warsaw Castle on 13 November at a concert which was part of the celebration of Chopin's two hundredth birthday. My husband and I were sitting next to the general. During the intermission, I asked the general more questions, which occurred to me after our previous meeting. He had a playful look in his eye as he said in English: "Your wife is constantly making some notes."

"She often does that," Norman answered.

That first meeting, on 9 November 2010, was very moving. "Gryf" spoke of Krysia with emotion. He said she had made a great impression on him as a brave and righteous person. He was her commander. He was with her in the last days of her life. He saw her dead and buried her. He said he had been deeply affected by her death.

Both the general and I realize that this text is the last link concerning the reminiscences on Krysia Wańkowicz.

Below is "Gryf's" authorized story, written down by me on 9 November 2010.

Earlier, before the start of the Uprising, on 10 July, I carried out an assault on Wende's Pharmacy at 55 Krakowskie Przedmieście, where we gained surgical instruments, operating tables, and large amounts of medications.

We started the Uprising with the feeling that we were going to fight the German occupier, that we would "free our Homeland." In the first two days, there was little combat and the time was used to build barricades. Our battalion, "Parasol," that I belonged to since February 1944, consisted of academic youth and pupils of secondary schools. Their age ranged from sixteen to twenty-five.

The concentration of the battalion's forces was set in the Old People's Home in Karolkowa Street. While on patrol on 3 August, I found a house at 40 Wolska Street. It was a stout villa, which we boldly named a palace, built at the end of the previous century. It had a strong iron gate, and was a good place for an ambush. The fight in Michler's "palace" was the biggest one in the Wola district. We repelled five assaults, during which units of an SS armored division, German tanks, tried to fight their way to the barricades in Wolska Street to break them.

The Germans didn't know I was staying in that house. First I ordered my young soldiers to have the attics and the cellars checked for anyone hiding there, for the so-called pigeon snipers. The snipers were well trained, and they could stay two to three days in hiding. They sat there and waited for their prey.

The house was clean, no snipers or explosives, that the Germans often put under stairs or by an entrance.

In the evening of 4 August, it was quiet and we organized a small evening get-together. We invited a few people from the neighboring units, we had some wine, some food, and the girls prepared snacks. There were about forty of us, and the atmosphere was unique. We were singing. It was there and then that our song was created:

Pałacyk Michla, Żytnia, Wola . . .
Bronią jej chłopcy od "Parasola."[10]

Ziutek Szczepański, a talented musician and composer, wrote the song. It was that day, at 9 to 9:30 p.m., that we all first sang it.

I met Krystyna Wańkowicz on 3 August, in the afternoon. She came with a report from "Rafał," then went back to him. Earlier, "Rafał" had been wounded in the back in an action he carried out in Kraków, and for several days was hiding in their "Dear Home"[11] in Dziennikarska Street in the district of Żoliborz, in the house of the Wańkowicz family. He had a problem with a wound that didn't want to heal. Wańkowicz writes in *Ziele na kraterze* that when the maid saw the bloodied sheets, she asked what had happened.

Krystyna was also there at the get-together in Michler's "palace." She was a well-built girl with beautiful, fluffy, shoulder-length, dark blond hair. She wore a blouse and a pleated skirt, and a wide leather belt.

She gave the impression of being somewhat distant. She seemed slightly shy, focused, and serious. I saw her make some notes in a notebook she had.

After the get-together, four girls went to the bathroom and changed into uniforms. Those were uniforms captured in Stawki Street by the battalion "Zośka."[12] Two battalions were uniformed that way, and we obtained some. On the right arm our soldiers wore the insurrectionist armband. So Krysia wasn't wearing the pleated skirt anymore, but a uniform.

During the get-together Krystyna asked "Rafał" to transfer her to my unit. She was then assigned to education; she was to run the canteen, and take care of the wounded there. But now she chose a front task.

As "Rafał's" liaison she had quite difficult tasks. She had to carry reports, but it was safer than what she was to do while in my storm group.

Krystyna didn't have to be in the front line. She was assigned to the rear, and she would have probably been fine there.

She was determined to stay with us—and so she stayed. I agreed only with reluctance, because I knew she wouldn't be safe.

What encouraged her? . . . Maybe she wanted to be with us in the front line of combat to have materials for her notes? As a writer's daughter, maybe she wanted and decided to witness and describe everything? . . .

She was a very brave girl, very heroic. From that time on, she was always with me, in all five assaults I carried out, in all actions she was with me. I have a combat logbook where she is mentioned.

It was an awful fight, five assaults. Many were killed on both sides, and many injured. Forty to fifty Germans were killed; then by radio they drafted their tanks to come. The tanks stopped 300 meters from our house and opened fire with their main cannon having a caliber of 88 mm, and beside that, each tank had three machine guns.

The German crews were soldiers from the very elite Hermann Goering formation, an armor-parachute division with great combat experience gained in Italy and Africa. Hitler transferred them to Warsaw to fight us. The crews were accustomed to working in radio contact with the tanks and directing their gunfire.

After the fifth assault, the tanks wrecked our gate; then systematically all floors and the attics were destroyed, in succession.

There was terrible gunfire. We destroyed one tank; another was damaged and retreated. I set up a barrier with smoke bombs—the Germans didn't figure that out, and they began to use bigger armor units.

We didn't have much ammunition. Each bullet was worth its weight in gold. The end of ammunition meant the end of combat, and I was almost out of it.

I received an order from the battalion commander to leave Michler's "palace" and move to neighboring houses.

I was moving with my soldiers, with the storm group I was commanding. I came to Żytnia Street. The Germans were on one side, we on the other.

Krystyna was with me, in both the houses and on Żytnia.

Through two successive houses, we went toward the barricade in Wolska Street, which was damaged but still held on. It was solid and strong, built of streetcars and old cars, and around it there were flagstones, sandbags, and lots of barrels.

But the Germans had cannons—150-mm caliber. One shell was enough to tear apart a whole streetcar.

It was a very difficult fight. On 6 August, about 7 to 8 a.m., we destroyed one tank and killed about twenty German infantry soldiers.

Earlier, at night, it was calm. The house I occupied with about twenty of my soldiers was a building at the corner of Żytnia and Młynarska. The windows looked out on the cemetery. The building was partially demolished; we entered it climbing a ladder. The staircase was slowly smoldering (now the house stands no more).

I remember well the night of 5 to 6 August. A cold wind was blowing from the female cemetery. In my small room, there were some chairs and armchairs. Krysia was very tired. I told her to sit down in one of the armchairs and rest. She covered her legs with a coverlet and started a conversation. Earlier there was no occasion for much talking.

She spoke of "Rafał," how she hid him in the "Dear Home," about her house and parents. She told me, for instance, that after leaving home and just before the Uprising she had cut her braids. She also told me she was a little afraid. . . .

I think we talked for some two to three hours. Our conversation made me worry; I felt responsible for her life. I saw her constantly making some notes.

About 2 to 3 a.m. a female liaison came from "Jeremi" (Jerzy Eugeniusz Zborowski), who was second in command of the battalion, and she gave me a written order to retreat. Soon, another order came.

Then I sent the men—to go to the evangelical cemetery nearby. I didn't want to go to the cemetery, but such was the order.

Six men went, and Krystyna went with them. She had volunteered.

I wished for them to reach the cemetery without trouble and wait for us somewhere in the thickets.

They went out the back.

It was 4 to 5 a.m.

She shook my hand in good-bye and laughed.

They were singing "Pałacyk Michla, Żytnia, Wola." . . .

Half an hour later they were all dead.

What happened? . . .

An observer from the German artillery sat in his hiding place with binoculars and saw my seven soldiers. He was about 500 meters away from a grenade launchers' battery, and passed the information through the radio to the battery crew. As a result, the grenade launchers' battery began heavy artillery fire—with 81 mm caliber mortars. It was a lethal series from mortars—the shells fell 1–2–3–4–5–6. . . .

Together, all my seven soldiers were killed by those shells.

This happened 50 meters away from my position.

We crawled there with "Rafał." I saw bodies torn apart. I knew Krystyna also had to be there, so I kept looking around.

Her left arm was ripped, and there was a watch on the other wrist. "Rafał" took it off; it had some engraving. She had a wound near her throat and in her chest. I took off my combat jacket and covered her body.

I felt Krysia's death very deeply. I saw my soldiers, liaisons, nurses die, but Krystyna's death affected me so tragically.

There were seven bodies including Krysia's, and they had to be buried. The ground was difficult with pavement everywhere.

Some hour or hour and a half later the shooting had ceased. I buried them then. "Rafał" was with me.

We dug a shallow grave, maybe 40 cm [about 16 inches] deep. It was long like a gutter. We buried them together, Krysia and the six men she was with. We covered the makeshift grave with boards, bricks, whatever we had. We tied two pieces of wood with a string and put our improvised cross on top.

The combat continued. Two days later, on 8 August, there was some shooting in the cemetery and I was hit in the jaw. Only a movement of mine made the bullet exit through the side and not the back of the head. They took me to Jan Boży Hospital. I had half of my face shattered, and I kept losing consciousness.

"Rafał" visited me and cried as he looked at me.

He also said: "What am I going to say to Mrs. Wańkowicz . . . how do I tell her that her daughter is dead."

He wasn't given the time to say anything to Zofia Wańkowicz. "Rafał," that is, Stanisław Leopold, died on the twenty-fifth day of the Uprising defending the Old Town—in the area of Reduta Banku Polskiego (Bank of Poland Redoubt), at 2 Bielańskiej Street.

The commander of Krystyna Wańkowicz, Sergeant Cadet Officer Janusz Brochwicz Lewinski, "Gryf," awarded with the Virtuti Militari order and promoted to the rank of a second lieutenant by the order of 13 August, stayed for some time in the Jan Boży Hospital. He had a festering jaw and his tongue was burned. He was then sent to a temporary hospital in Freta Street, which he left guided by others through the sewers. It took twenty hours. He remembers cries, remembers the rats running about. The bodies left there had to be drawn aside. There were places where you had to crawl. He says he owes his life to the soldiers and the nurse who were leading him. He never knew their pseudonyms or names.

In September, he was conveyed to a hospital in 111 Marszałkowska Street, where he stayed until the end of the Uprising. He was placed successively in a transitional camp of Lamsdorf (Łambinowice), then in a POW camp in Murnau. After the camp was liberated by the Americans, he spent the time from April 1945 to February 1946 in a hospital in Scotland, near Edinburgh. He underwent a range of complicated bone transplant surgeries. Once healed, he continued his service in the First Independent Parachute Brigade with General Stanisław Franciszek Sosabowski. In October 1947, he joined the Third Royal Regiment of Hussars. He worked as a British intelligence agent, active among others in Palestine and in Sudan. On ending service in the regular army, for fifteen years he was a quartermaster and administrative officer in the English Military College "Windsor School" in Germany. Since 2004, "Gryf" has been living in Poland.

In July 2007, he became an honorary citizen of Warsaw. On 24 April 2008, President Lech Kaczyński promoted "Gryf" to brigadier general. On 17 June 2009, he became a member of the chapter of the Virtuti Militari Order Committee.

NOTES

1. M.Wańkowicz, *Rozmowy w ciemnościach* (*Talks in the Darkness*), the writer's archive.
2. M. Wankowicz, *Ziele na kraterze* (Warsaw, 2009), p. 391
3. *Ziele,* p. 398
4. *Ziele*, p. 422
5. *Ziele*, p. 425
6. Michler's "palace."
7. A region in the southern Warsaw district on the left bank of the river Vistula.
8. A region in the center of Warsaw.
9. *Ziele*, pp. 425–26.
10. Michler's "palace," Żytnia (street), Wola (district), defended by the boys from "Parasol."

11. Domeczek, the house of the Wańkowicz family in Warsaw.

12. Scouting battalion of the Polish resistance movement—Home Army AK—Armia Krajowa during World War II. As part of Radosław Group the battalion played a major role in the Warsaw Uprising of 1944. "Zośka" was named after Tadeusz Zawadzki, who used it as his pseudonym during the AK's early days. "Zośka" was killed in the Warsaw Uprising.

Figure 6.1.   Krystyna Wańkowicz

Figure 6.2.   Janusz Brochwicz Lewiński, "Gryf"

Chapter Seven

His Version, Her Version

Zofia Romanowiczowa (née Górska, 1922–2010) was an accomplished author of novels and short stories, like *Baśka i Barbara*, *Przejście przez Morze Czerwone*, *Szklana kula*, *Łagodne oko błękitu*, and *Skrytki*.[1]

In 1974, Romanowiczowa sent her new book *Groby Napoleona* (*Napoleon's Graves*) to Wańkowicz.

The writer told me her moving story many times: she was a liaison officer for the Union of Armed Struggle,[2] she participated in the resistance movement, 1942 to 1945, and she was a prisoner in German concentration camps. They met after the war in Italy and became friends.

He recalled meeting in Italy a young girl, fearful, a former concentration camp prisoner. She lived in a temporary shelter in one of the Roman monasteries.

He told me:

> Many people showed interest in her, talked to her, but then they returned to their own lives. My daughters were her age and I thought I knew what she might dream of, what she should be doing.
>
> I went with her for some ice cream, took her shopping, and bought her a new dress. I asked if she had any place, any friends. She was lonely and helpless.
>
> I bought her a typewriter and told her to write, told her that I believed in her. I took care of her, employed her as my secretary while writing *Monte Cassino*. With my help, she had a debut in 1945 with a story titled "Tomuś" ("Tommy"), published in *Orzeł Biały*, a weekly of the Second Corps.
>
> We spent a lot of time together. I took Zofia to restaurants, suggested interesting books to read. She was immensely thankful, followed me like a faithful puppy, quiet, attentive, a constant observer. I took her with me to Germany; sensitive and vulnerable she was a like a litmus paper to me.

Zofia had been eighteen when she'd been tortured for distributing illegal brochures. She was sentenced to four years in Ravensbrück.[3] Wańkowicz memorized one scene that he used in his book *Karafka La Fontaine'a*. He and Zofia were in Dachau.[4]

> Once she found out that among the war criminals imprisoned, the infamous Ravensbrück commandant, named Mandel, was included, she asked me with high emotion, "May I report to her: *Häftling Nummer . . . meldet sich an Stelle?*"[5]
>
> [. . .] The young and beautiful Mandel rode her bicycle along the line of nine thousand women. Such a ride was sure to bring someone disaster; hence many of the prisoners whispered prayers. If Mandel saw someone's lips moving, she would lash that prisoner's face with her whip as she rode.
>
> I looked at Zofia, all afire with emotion. When asking my advice, she surely thought of friends tortured to death, of her own father, beaten to death in the cellar of Gestapo headquarters in Radom, of the co-prisoners—tortured "guinea pigs."
>
> "Better not, Zofia" I said.
>
> The girl was wearing a uniform with the Polish eagle, with all her decorations. The situation would have been reversed completely. Such a triumph over Mandel seemed too easy to me.
>
> I am not sure if I did the right thing.[6]

Some other memories apparently disturbed him, a different kind than shown above. He shared them with me:

> I'll tell you about one day, a situation that often came back to me. I gave it much thought. . . .
>
> Once, as we were traveling, we spent a night in a small wooden hotel on a creek. Only one room was available, so they put a camp bed for her in my room.
>
> In the morning she came to my bed. It was cold; she said she wanted to get warmer. She lay next to me, saying something. . . . I was just over fifty years old. . . . I felt a rush of desire for her. . . . She was thirty years my junior, a delicate, sensitive girl, full of complexes from her war experiences. . . . I was ashamed of my thoughts. . . . I'd treated her like a daughter, she trusted me fully and submitted to me, and now suddenly I was about to smash all of her enthusiasm, all her faith in me. Roughly, fiercely, I ordered her out of the bed, saying it was soon time to go, that I wanted to sleep—I do not remember what I said. I cannot recall a scene of similar tinge at any later time.
>
> I found her a place at a school, sent her to Paris, established and funded a scholarship. Somehow, I felt responsible for her.
>
> For years we exchanged letters; I visited her a few times. I saw she was doing fine; she literally soaked up learning.
>
> Zofia had a normal life. She graduated from the Roman Philology at the Sorbonne University, married, settled in Paris, had a daughter. She and her husband, Kazimierz Romanowicz, founded a publishing company "Libella." I remember she sent me her first book, asking for my opinion. I thought her

talented. I'd encouraged her to write before, was the "godfather" of her first story.

She sent me more books as she wrote them.

In the 1960s she came to Warsaw. We saw each other for the first time after many years. She was an adult and a beautiful woman. I took her to dinner and we talked long hours. And then I said, "Zofia, I would like to ask you something. . . . Do you remember one morning in Italy when we spent the night in one room, you came to me . . . to my bed, to warm up, and I threw you out."

"Yes, I remember that well," she answered.

"Do you think that it could have come to something between us then?"

"So what?" she challenged me.

. . . I was astonished. She did remember. Practically, she told me that no harm would have been done. I didn't understand, but I asked no more about it.

I am telling you that now, because that situation still rankles me. . . . Maybe all my fears for that girl, what she would think, and so forth, were unjustified, and everything could have been different, could have gone in a completely different way.

A few years after Wańkowicz's death, the same story reappeared to me in a different form, now told by writer Zofia Romanowiczowa.

In 1979, Marta Erdman visiting from the States brought me Zofia Romanowiczowa's book *Sono felice*.[7]

She told me,

You know, the book is about my father. He bears a different name, but it is about him. There are clear references—to Monte Cassino and so on. I think that Zofia paid a debt she definitely had toward him similar to a longtime overdue bill. You will see for yourself, anyway.

Wańkowicz's words that were in my memory were now brought from a different perspective and told by Romanowiczowa in her book.

The story's protagonist was Teresa, a young, married woman. She was living in the suburbs of Paris, in a modest flat on the seventh floor, with a view of house roofs and chimneys. She earned her living as a typist. It was morning; her husband had just left to work. Teresa was cleaning the house, when the phone rang.

As she remembered his words: "I am passing through Paris; let's meet."

It was Szymon on the phone, a friend of hers, once very close to her. He invited her to dinner at an expensive restaurant on the Seine.

Teresa abandoned the cleaning, had a bath, took out the hidden money she'd been saving for a special occasion, maybe for holidays. She went to a fashion house and chose a dress—red, low-cut, stunning. She also bought a new coat and shoes. The old things—bought together with her husband, practical, "suitable," durable—she took to the storeroom at the railway station.

Teresa recollected. She had been a young girl, a former concentration camp prisoner, staying in a convent in Rome. She had been lonely, with no plans for the future. Then she'd met Szymon.

She was pulled out of the convent by some phone call the nuns told her of—some compatriot had remembered she existed. The nuns wrote in printed letters—just in case—which streetcar to take, where to get on, where to get off. And on that very first expedition of hers, she met Szymon. He immediately took her life in his hands, starting with the dress store and all the way to the school and Paris. They'd known each other barely five minutes when he pulled her into the best store in the district. She trusted him immediately as all fears and doubts left her. He asked about nothing, and knew everything. He could do anything. Unthought-of miracles opened at his bidding. Throughout that period back then she timidly shuffled in his shadow, careful only not to stay behind.

As she remembered about him, you never knew if he was serious or joking, and how far he would go for a laugh. He took her to restaurants and chose the food. She didn't hold her liquor well, and at that first formal dinner together she got tipsy. She did remember! She suddenly realized that she recalled even what they had eaten, how the table was set, what trouble she had using lobster tongs, and how truly funny that was for Szymon. Later he saw her off to the convent. She held on to his arm, her legs slightly unsteady, and that was hardly due to the new pumps. With Szymon you walked at a stroll; he puffed a little, and she was probably humming to herself. Yet she was a bit worried: Would the nuns see she had been drinking? And anyway, why was she back so late? They might not open the gate for her.

Szymon rang the bell without much ado, as if he was ringing the bell for a servant. Then he talked to the white-coiffed figure in the tone of a kindly joshing bishop, making the coiffed one all gooey at once. And so Teresa got away with that first return at night, nay, almost in the morning.

Still, the nuns were watching her with some distrust noting for instance that sudden change of clothing. She went out a strangely attired creature, and came back all elegant. Quite understandably, the nuns wondered. They knew she was penniless; after all they'd offered her a place for free, out of Christian mercy. She did not attempt to explain; anyway, her Italian was mostly limited to gestures. Teresa was absent more and more frequently, and returned at ever later times. Szymon joked about it, but for Teresa it was a true ordeal. What if they decided to throw her out of the convent? It was thus a great relief for her when finally she accompanied him on the trip to Germany and from there directly to the school in Paris.

He took her to Germany in part because he liked her and in part due to the fact that to his inquisitive eye she was a kind of litmus paper. How would she react? She disappointed him, as she showed little reaction. What was happening there was it so much the times long past, some two months or two centuries ago? The past was over. Anyway, when she was with Szymon, could there be anything like taking the route back to hell at all? Nothing could harm her when with him, even memories.

He called her Little One. Never used her first name. When he met her for the first time, he asked her name. "Teresa." She reacted as if she'd just been called to the board. He could not introduce her with the camp prisoner number burnt on her arm. "But the Little or the Great one? The Little One! But of course!" Szymon stated playfully. And so she remained the Little One, without the Teresa. He liked it that she had immediately grasped the question for her patron saint: whether it is the great one from Avila, or the Little Flower from Lisieux. His "of course" said that her lame-duckling image didn't quite fit the great patron saint.

Teresa now went to the beauty salon and the hairdresser. She still had the time to drop by a café—she chose an expensive one, beautifully located. In any other situation she would have chosen the first best one, as long as it was cheap. But today, the new face, clothes, the new look were obligatory. Szymon would have been the best adviser which café was "the most fitting." She had time. She kept on reminiscing.

As Teresa remembered, she owed so much to Szymon. He had bought her the typewriter. A typewriter! She didn't believe it. He could have just as well bought a piano all of a sudden and told her to play. He bought her a typewriter and told her to write. He trusted her immediately, too. What was more, he immediately believed in her.

As she recalled Szymon's words: "This is your tool of trade. You, Little One, don't know that yet, but you already know how to do it. This typewriter will serve you to create yourself. To create what you were made for. I am telling you that."

With his instruction, she started making notes on everything, the travels, her thoughts. Then, his glasses perched on his forehead he read her first stories with the close attention of a teacher. She typed them painstakingly on the brand-new typewriter exclusively for the reason that he not be disappointed. He was reading them as if the stories could severely impact world literature in general, and Polish literature in particular. As if Cervantes himself, freshly released, had handed them to Szymon. He was merciless. The copies of her stories came back to her littered with pencil markings; mocking notes danced in the margins. But when he hunted down something that he thought indicated she had struck the right tone or found the perfect word, he beamed, and treated her to some ice cream. Or *caffe con panna*[8] (or a delicious dinner)!

As she remembered, she'd had no other paradise in her life, no other childhood, but the one Szymon had given her for one summer and half the fall.

He sent her to school. Sometimes he called on her, took her to dinner or sometimes just for cake or ice cream as a reward "for good grades." The time spent with him was never wasted for her. She viewed it as time gained. They spoke of everything including things outside of the agenda, not on topic, beside any topic. He opened limiting brackets, broadened her horizons. The school library never imagined having the books he provided her with, or indicated to her.

When she cried on parting, he mocked her, like he did in other situations. As Teresa recalled, he spoke on a serious note:

Take you and me. We've met by the greatest chance in the world. Just think: to have that, we needed the war—another one for me, and the first one for you— to break out! And since then, we walked some part of our way together. You're crying because I am going to see you off to school in a moment and leave you there. You think it some terrible separation, abandonment. But before that, do you think we are equal together? How do you know that tomorrow, when some severe teacher orders you to the board, I won't be with you more than I am now? That at that point, some book, some quotation of mine won't aid you? Will one of my little mockeries? And how do you know that tomorrow you won't be closer to me than when you were really sitting next to me, and I was thinking about my own matters, which neither concerned nor involved you?

That was earlier. Now—according to Teresa's words—she was afraid of that meeting. She was afraid that he'd sense she'd almost turned back into that Cinderella state out of which he had pulled her several years ago. "Just no pity!" She shuddered at the thought of anyone pitying her, the more if it were Szymon's pity. Her defeat would have been completed. Szymon was so sure that she'd made it, that she was happy. So she would be. For him and with him. Today.

She finished her coffee. It was time to go. The café they were to meet in was not very far. She entered the café, and Szymon was already waiting for her.

He hadn't changed at all. Neither aged nor fatter, the years had left no trace on him. Only later, when he took the embossed paper of the menu, did she notice that his hand was shaking. When he stood up to say hello to her, she had no problems recognizing him. Szymon. The same. So very much the same.

He, on the other hand, was openly looking over her face, hairdo, and clothes. He commented on any changes. Even told her to turn around and walk a few steps, to make sure she had finally learned to walk on high heels. And all of that was done in fun, half-fatherly, half-friendly, no traps, no hidden meanings.

As she recalled his words:

So, would I recognize you or not? . . . Not on the street, I think. Not at once. Now you've got something. . . . Let's face it, you are a woman now. Back then you were a lame duckling that could fledge either into a swan or a hen. See, I knew the swan in you even then!

She was moved when he frowned his bushy eyebrows, considered what to order, inquired if she still liked this or that, or maybe her taste had changed? The menu in his hands trembled slightly, his glasses dropped to his nose, and he perched them higher on his head with an impatient gesture, like he did earlier. An innocent ritual, in which she took part like she used to do before— like when they had their first culinary celebration of her first story, saved by Szymon from the rubbish pile. As she recalled Szymon words, "You can do better," he'd said, but he'd beamed at her. "But this here is not all that bad."

They talked, they laughed, and they reminisced. They jumped from one mood to another. Szymon was looking at her all the time in a funny way, and although they jumped from topic to topic, she had the impression that he had some question, something important, just on the tip of his tongue, something he was postponing, but still heading there. Then she voiced his words, "You know, I haven't told you the most important thing yet. I mean, I haven't asked about the important thing. You really think I would look you up and phone you in a selfless gesture? It doesn't work like that, just any old way in the street."

They went to another café. Teresa was relaxed now. To her, Szymon was just as old and just as young as he used to be.

He gave her jocular, mocking, friendly looks. His huge body was still in balance with life. He still liked and knew how to eat and drink, watch and listen. No, she wasn't as timid as she once was. Today they were peers. He got no older while she did; she had to take special care to look younger, to dress up for tonight. He talked and listened. He talked of her and of himself.

According to Teresa's recollections he was saying:

I don't know how it is with your writing now. You haven't made a name for yourself yet. I think, I would have heard of it. But you've got time. Remember? *Et quand á ecrire ne sois pas trop presse?*[9] Who said that? You don't know again? Then what are you staying in Paris for? I told you that once, and I am telling you now. I used to urge you, true, but it was just to prepare you for the start, to make you believe that you could do it if you wanted to. You are still young. There's time; there's no urgency. Only for happiness there's not a moment to lose. One moment and it may be too late. You know, just between you and me, all that literature.

According to the writer's story, Teresa—the main character in the book—was stunned. Analyzing, she wondered, what did he mean, "Just between you and me"? What did he mean with "all that literature"? Who gave her a typewriter? Who sent her to school to learn more? Who imposed volumes of additional literature? Who corrected her sentences, and instructed her in the mysterious art of paragraphs and punch lines? Who set his own diligence as an example? Who would stay up at nights, typing away?

Szymon explained:

I write, I do, even though she did not voice the question. I write out of momentum. Out of habit. I won't change jobs in old age. . . . But what once seemed to me urgent and necessary to report, immediately on happening, seems urgent or a necessity no more. I did not describe the creation of the world; I was not there. A few times I thought I was reporting its end. Nothing has ended. A few little worlds, yes, they ended as I looked. In my time, but for the real end, I will surely not be appointed a special correspondent. I do not even care anymore.

According to Teresa's recollections, she wanted to go back. But somehow she felt that it was not Teresa, but the Little One that he'd wanted to meet in Paris. That his thoughts were elsewhere, that he wanted to ask her something. That thought lasted for a while; actually, since the first moment they'd met. He spoke up.

As she recalled Szymon's words:

I have a certain issue, important to me, a question which got stuck like a bone in my throat back then, when we said good-bye to each other on that boat, or more precisely, during our trip to Germany. I want that bone out. . . . If you do not tell me here and now, I'll die not knowing the answer. We don't have much time. There's no other way, I have to ask that question even though you're on your last leg. You just tell me: yes or no.

Teresa observed Szymon—he glanced at his watch again, as if the rushing sweep hand spurred him on. She made a sudden decision to say yes. Whatever the question, she'd say yes, yes, yes, if that was so important to him. No more screaming "No!" either in her dreams or in real life. By the trembling of his hand, spilling ash on the carpet, she saw how very difficult it was for Szymon to ask.

Do you remember one part of it, near the border? When we had to sleep in one room? In the morning I said: Come! You jumped into my bed without much thinking. Like a child. Like a puppy. I . . . I wasn't as old then as I am now. If . . . back then. . . . Damn it, why I am playing so coy, you're grown up now. You're married. We are friends! So, if I had acted differently toward you than I did, would you . . .

"Yes," she said, seeing him in torment.

"Do I take it you took it into account then?"

"Yes."

That second "yes" sounded weaker, but it also sounded true. She even met his eye. But he didn't meet hers.

As she remembers, Szymon commanded, "Well, time to go. The taxi is waiting outside. Come on, Teresa."

She was surprised that he used her name Teresa. What happened to her nickname Little One?

She continued her recollections: "No!" She should have said, "No!" That was the truth. That was the only real truth of that morning back then. Even if for some reason Szymon would have liked to hear a "yes" today, she had not the right to deceive him.

Did he want it? She was lost in all that and in herself.

She remembered very well what it was like, that morning; she'd even dreamt about it just recently. The walls smelled of wood. The creek rumbled. They were supposed to hurry, but Szymon was kind of lazy. She wasn't surprised; he'd been driving the whole day before, and it had been so hot. He said, "Come!" So she came. She was a bit cold in the narrow camp bed, anyway; the cover had slipped to the floor somehow during the night. She was even pleased that she'd warm up. Sharing a bed with friends was nothing new to her. In the camp, you slept cuddled in four on the bunks, and thanks to that, thanks to the warmth shared between you, you could survive freezing nights.

But no, no, no! There had been no such thought; there couldn't be. She had no idea that Szymon could think anything like it. Nor was there a trace of thought of accepting or refusing. No, no, and no! Even today, she would have bet her bottom dollar that no such thought could have come to Szymon then, because and if? Since he came here after all these years actually just to verify that? Ask that question? Impossible? No, no, no! There had been different ties between them then, more significant, stronger, better. And he'd never let her feel how he'd felt. A caring, normal hug, a cuddle. To warm up. He'd even said, "Goodness, you're an icicle, Little One! What is wrong with your covers?"

And then suddenly he'd said roughly, "Enough of that cuddling! Get up. Get ready. We're having coffee and off." True, he first said, "Come!" And then, "Go!"

But he didn't think to ask about anything. Then.

And now she'd answered yes. To a question not asked back then. He also remembered that morning. Since this moment, he would view the memory quite differently. He would think, or maybe he already had, that she'd lied then, acted the innocent. Not Little One anymore, but Teresa. The truth was, she'd lied today. Today Teresa lied for the Little One, denied her own self.

Why did he ask? Now she had a right to ask him, "What about you?" It would be even more a duty than a right, to ask, "Were you thinking of it then, when you said: 'Come? Yes or no?'"

A rift then, a rift now, lies linked between the present and the past. A discordance, a note from out of the melody that had been playing between them for so long, the melody that they had picked up so easy, so spontaneously after all those years. The one in which they'd recognized and found each other. Because, if he had thought at least that one time . . .

And now? Did he regret an opportunity he'd let pass? Or maybe he regretted having been so thoroughly mistaken about her?

Going in the same taxi, they were both silent. He was deep in thought, far away, remote. He told the driver to stop at the airport. She was going farther. A farewell.

As she remembers his last words, "Thank you. My regards to your husband. I hope he won't be angry I'd swept you away for that one evening. A pity, though."

"Pity what?"

"My pity, not yours. Don't worry about me. Thank you. Wish you all the best. Have fun."

Teresa recalls she went on in the taxi. Alone. Just a moment ago, they'd been together. Suddenly she felt regret and pity. To pity Szymon! Why hadn't she taken his hand in the taxi? Stupid shame, stupid fear. He would have had a different flight now in his aerial boat.

Charon's boat. Yes. She was sure all of a sudden that they would not see each other anymore. And sure that he would have pushed her hand away.

Romanowiczowa's book has other threads, as well. Many good scenes. I do like her writing style. Her protagonist Teresa's thoughts include other people, from the present, not the past. But the point of the book is that scene of returning—both by protagonists and their memories. In particular, one memory—that one meeting, that one question asked by Wańkowicz, which later came back to me in the story of the protagonist of *Sono felice*.[10]

NOTES

1. *Baśka and Barbara* (Baśka is a diminutive form of Barbara), *Passage through the Red Sea, Crystal Ball, Gentle Eye of the Blue, Hiding Places* (translator's note).

2. ZWZ—Związek Walki Zbrojnej, a Polish resistance organization (translator's note).

3. Ravensbrück was a Nazi concentration camp for women, near the village of Ravensbrück, 90 km (56 miles) north of Berlin. It was particularly notorious for the medical experiments conducted there, without consent, on the prisoners. The experiments tested the efficacy of sulfonamide drugs. By deliberately cutting into and infecting leg bones and muscles with virulent bacteria, cutting nerves, introducing substances like pieces of wood or glass into tissues, and fracturing bones, they served to study bone, muscle, and nerve regeneration and the possibility of transplanting bones from one person to another. Some of the *Króliki* (Polish), *Kaninchen* (German), or "rabbits/guinea pigs" died; others survived with permanent physical damage (translator's note).

4. The Dachau concentration camp was the first of the Nazi concentration camps. It is located near the town of Dachau, about 16 km, or 9.9 miles, away from Munich, Bavaria (translator's note).

5. German for "Prisoner number . . . reporting" (translator's note).

6. *Karafka La Fontaine'a* (*La Fontaine's Carafe*), vol. 2, pp. 94–95.

7. Zofia Romanowiczowa, *Sono felice* (London: Polska Fundacja Kulturalna), 1977.

8. *Caffe con panna* (Italian)—coffee with cream.

9. (French)—When writing do not be in a rush.

10. *Sono felice* (Italian)—I am happy.

Chapter Eight

After the Writer's Death

Wańkowicz died on 10 September 1974. As they were taking him to the hospital, he told me: "I'll come back here."

Two days later, the casket was brought into the house in 50 Studencka Street in the Warsaw district of Mokotów.

He had lived in the house for only a year.

His daughter, Marta Erdman, came from the United States for her father's funeral, and stayed in Poland for over a month. Together we settled many issues. Our conversations then were special, held long at night, after the writer's body was brought in the covered, simple, light-colored, wooden casket. The drawing room was filled with gladiolas, long sword lilies, the flowers he liked in particular and which bloomed in September. Candles were lighted, as well as side lamps. The light refracted, casting golden shadows.

People came from early morning, such as were known and unknown by the writer. There was no obituary in the press yet, but they already knew and came to Studencka Street. The press informed people of his death, and then about the funeral. The Writers' Union's delegation of several people[1] came to talk about the funeral. Marta was asked if she agreed to a state funeral, with the casket lying in state in the Primate's Palace in Senatorska Street. After some consideration, she refused. She said her father would have surely liked a more private ceremony. People who were to speak at the cemetery—Mieczysław Kurzyna, Aleksander Małachowski, Lesław Bartelski, and Jan Józef Lipski—came to the writer's home.

On the day of the funeral—14 September—the casket was brought to St. John's Cathedral, and after the Mass, at 3 p.m., it was to be taken from there to the Powązki cemetery. Marta and I came to the cathedral around noon; we sat down in the pews. In the middle of the cathedral stood the casket, and former soldiers from Monte Cassino and from Major Hubal's partisans took turns standing guard over it. With his books, the writer had greatly contributed to the legend of Monte Cassino and of Major Hubal. People came up to the casket and put flowers on it. Soon the casket was all but covered with small bouquets. Beside it there stood stately wreaths; constantly new ones were brought in, from organizations, associations, groupings, officials. At some point, I went to the casket to rearrange some flowers. I left my handbag in the pew, next to Marta. When I came back, she whispered to me that a woman had approached her, saying: "Please watch Tili's handbag, so that she doesn't lose it." As mentioned earlier, Tili was Marta's nickname, given to her by her father, and recorded thus in the books he wrote about his family, about his daughters' childhood. Marta was clearly amused with that remark and with people taking me for Tili. She said that readers of Wańkowicz's books wanted to see her still as a young girl, such as she was in her father's books. Even on the day of his funeral, readers did not want to accept the passing of time, even though I was younger than his granddaughters, but I was at the age of his daughters when he wrote about them.

The cathedral and streets leading to the Old Town's Market Square were filled with people. The Mass was celebrated by Bishop Zbigniew Kraszewski. The fact that a bishop said the Mass himself was rather surprising. Probably the Church decided so out of regard for a great writer, although he didn't attend church and privately called himself an agnostic. He was very attached to tradition. Brought up as a Catholic, he passed the faith to his daughters. He said that nothing could equal the beauty of a traditional, Polish, Catholic funeral. That was how he buried his wife, and asked for such a funeral for himself. Mieczysław Kurzyna, the writer's biographer, told me that Wańkowicz asked him to cross out a sentence in the book on himself which defined him as an "atheist." He changed it to "agnostic." "I do know that God exists," he said. He liked looking up fragments in the Bible and translating them for himself. "Do you believe that angels came down to earth?" he reportedly asked Kurzyna. Marta believed, in turn, that her father was not lucky enough to meet a partner in religious matters in his life. She gave the example of the great theologian, Father Jan Zieja, an exceptional man. Reportedly he told her he had been told to go to Wańkowicz when the latter fell ill. Father Jan replied that when a man suffers, a priest's coming is not human, so it is not divine. He was not a priest who "went for the soul while armed with a spear." He waited hoping that maybe Wańkowicz himself would ask him to come.

Many years later, I was embarrassed to hear a remark by an employee of the Museum of Literature. The employee was showing the writer's study to a group of young people and indicated the kneeler that bore clear signs of wear as an example that the author of *Szczenięce lata* prayed on his knees. Actually, Wańkowicz kept that kneeler next to his armchair and used it as a footstool.

After the requiem Mass, in a large crowd and with some difficulty, the casket was placed in the bus provided for family and friends. Wańkowicz was to be buried in his family grave in the Powązki cemetery, where for over five years the body of Zofia Wańkowicz lay, along with her two brothers—Stanisław and Kazimierz Małagowski, Polish Army officers (as mentioned earlier) killed in 1919 within three weeks of each other. The grave had a low relief on it that had been pierced by a bullet during the Uprising in 1944. The writer had asked not to repair it.

From the gate, the casket was borne by, among others, Krzysztof Kąkolewski and Jan Józef Lipski. At the head of the funeral procession walked Bishop Kraszewski, priests, and a Dominican father representing the parish church in Dominikańska Street. State television, which transmitted the funeral, took great pains to avoid showing the priests.

The bishop said the prayers, and then speeches began. Jan Józef Lipski spoke, an academic, writer, leading anti-Communist, and human rights advocate—reading the text he had shown us earlier, in a trembling, quiet voice.

On behalf of the Writers' Union, the writer Lesław Bartelski spoke first, then Mieczysław Kurzyna, a journalist. Then we heard a cry of anguish. A grave beside us collapsed and some people fell into the hole. (Marta paid later to have the damage repaired.) At the end, standing over our heads on the base of one of the gravestones, Aleksander Małachowski spoke, a journalist and politician, in a sonorous voice. On behalf of the late writer's family, he thanked Bishop Kraszewski for coming to the funeral.

Małachowski's speech caused much misunderstanding and distortion later. Reportedly, the authorities imputed to Małachowski that he had not thanked everyone, meaning the distinguished officials who'd come, among them the minister of culture or the American ambassador. Next day, the daily press printed notes that carefully listed the names of the officials who'd been to the funeral.

Before the grave was covered, a new voice was heard. A man, standing near the grave, read a few sentences written down on a sheet of paper. He said that we should all remember Katyń and observe its anniversary. Later on, Marta and I learned that the man was Wojciech Ziembiński, an anti-Communist activist, who later was to be a member of KOR.[2]

Descriptions of both the funeral and the atmosphere before and after it are found in a few books, as well as in IPN files.

In his book on Wańkowicz, published in 1975 a year after the latter's death, Mieczysław Kurzyna wrote:

> The days about the funeral became an occasion for wide circles of readers to express their feelings. As was the old Polish custom, the casket was lying in

repose in the house in Studencka Street, and from early morning to late evening there moved through a procession of people who wanted to personally pay their last respects to the late writer. There came the young and the old, bringing rich, gorgeous bouquets, and single, modest flowers. They were friends, acquaintances, and common book lovers. Candles were lighted behind the casket, and on top of it there lay a cross made from shrapnel of a shell which had exploded near the writer during the battle of Monte Cassino. Most visitors said prayers; some stood in sad silence.

On Sunday 14th September, Bishop Zbigniew Kraszewski said the Mass in the Warsaw Cathedral. He also led the procession up to the family grave. The crowds that came to say farewell to the writer included representatives of the highest authorities of Poland, writers, people of culture, academics, and masses of readers. The crowds filled the Cathedral, and the fourth gate of the Powązki Cemetery looked as if it was All Souls' Day.

The writer's daughter, Marta Erdman, who'd come from the United States, wanted to have nothing of a stiff, ritual, official character in the ceremony. She wanted a family atmosphere, and old-Polish tradition, just like her father had wished. And so it was. Neither the funeral speeches nor the presence of the most famous, or the special radio and TV broadcasts could change that character. Melchior Wańkowicz left surrounded by people close to him, without show or pompous grandeur, but surrounded by those to whom he was truly dear.[3]

Nineteen years later Aleksander Małachowski wrote:

As soon as she got off the plane from the U.S., Marta Erdman, Melchior's daughter, was offered a splendid funeral for her father, paid for by the state. I objected to this. A few days earlier, Melchior kept my wife and me at his hospital bedside until three o'clock in the morning. He made us swear that we would not allow the state to organize an official, government-sponsored funeral, for "they'd certainly like to be photographed over my coffin." [. . .] The coffin—at my request—was not placed in some dreary morgue, but according to old customs, it was placed in the beautiful salon of the new house on Studencka Street. [. . .] Melchior's funeral, according to his will, was a religious affair, with the costs borne by his family.[4]

In the files of IPN—the Institute of National Remembrance[5]—there are numerous materials concerning that funeral. A document containing fragments of speeches is quoted below:[6]

Ministry of Domestic Affairs
Department 3
Warsaw, 20th September 1974
Information about speeches at the funeral of Melchior Wańkowicz
Confidential

On 14th September this year, the funeral of Melchior Wańkowicz took place in Warsaw. At 11 a.m. the body was escorted out of the villa at 50

Studencka Street to the Cathedral, where the requiem Mass was said at 3 p.m. by Bishop Zbigniew Kraszewski. About 5,000 people were gathered in the Cathedral and around it.

At the funeral ceremony in the municipal cemetery of Powązki at 4:30 p.m. to 6 p.m., about 1,500 people were present, including among others: the U.S. ambassador, some writers and journalists—J. Iwaszkiewicz, J. Andrzejewski, A. Słonimski, W. Bartoszewski, Al. Małachowski, L. M. Bartelski, M. Kurzyna, M. Radgowski, E. Bryll.

Speeches were given by:

Lesław M. Bartelski—president of the Warsaw Branch of the Polish Writers' Union—said among other things that "the works of M. Wańkowicz won over readers with the magnificence of their language. To the ever more impoverished modern language, littered since long ago with many terms of foreign provenance and with the bureaucratic jargon, Melchior imposed live language . . . of typical Eastern border syntax."

Melchior took from gentry-type storytelling the earthy expressions, humor and flow, and abandoned talkativeness and shallowness. . . . He was to be a war correspondent in Colonel Rowecki's brigade. His daughter Krystyna was killed in the Warsaw Uprising as a liaison of Colonel Radosław's units. He left us, still unnoticed.

Jan Józef Lipski—employee of the Institute of Literary Research of the Polish Academy of Sciences[7]—said among other things that "M. Wańkowicz was also a realist. He knew it is not sometimes but very often that we have to compromise in our lives to protect what we consider the most important. We all know how dangerous that can be.

"He did not belong to writers who could ever resign themselves to writing words that would not be published. But with the natural logic of those matters, it happened most often to him and people like him, to put ready work away unpublished. We are not aware how many books we, Polish readers, are unable to read, as they have never been published . . .

" . . . More than once, Melchior indicated his so far unpublished manuscripts in a broad gesture, saying 'My Powązki.' He meant the books being buried then, but—let us hope—not forever . . .

"A man who was able to pay such a price for it that he ended up charged and tried . . ." "much has changed. Fortunately, people learned to show respect for Melchior.

" . . . And Melchior valued it. Yet there remained the daily troubles, worries, everyday fight for yet another article, for printing it whole, for one more chapter in a book which should survive as a whole. But that was something else, something different. That is the daily life of almost each Polish writer.

" . . . I would like to say a few words about one more thing. Simply because very few people know that Melchior was a man who many times hastened to help people who needed that help. Often he helped the persecuted.

" . . . We promise to do everything to perform the duties which fell upon that group of friends I'd mentioned, according to his intentions."

Mieczysław Kurzyna—a journalist, member of the presidium of the PAX Association, said among other things that " . . . M. Wańkowicz was persecuted for his activity. He could fight for the truth along with a small circle of friends, with whom he met in his home, he fought for purity of Polish culture."

A Hubal soldier, speaking "on behalf of the soldiers of Her Majesty Poland," said he was speaking of a bard of great deeds, who awoke consciousness in people. He recalled their last meeting with M. Wańkowicz at a service for the late Paweł Jasienica, and that they were to meet again in three days at a service to commemorate General Olszyna-Wilczyński.

On behalf of the writer's daughter, Marta Erdman, his family, and closest friends, Aleksander Małachowski—editor of the Polish Radio—thanked Bishop Kraszewski for participating in the funeral and the requiem Mass. He thanked his colleagues for the speeches, thanked scouts and people who stood honor guard. Małachowski stressed that the late writer had been closely bound to his nation. "M. Wańkowicz spent his whole life paying tribute to the Polish nation for its fight for independence. I would like to say 'God bless' to all readers and friends of Melchior, on his behalf. So many people gathering here at the cemetery is a tribute to the writer. Melchior Wańkowicz grew together with his readers' esteem and served Poland well."

Despite representatives of the Communist Party and the government being present at the funeral, Aleksander Małachowski did not extend any words of thanks to them, passing over the fact in silence. Neither did he mention the U.S. ambassador taking part in the ceremony.

We have information that the writer's family is not agreeing to a state-organized funeral resulted from Jan Józef Lipski influencing the daughter of M. Wańkowicz—Marta Erdman.

In artists' communities and among people close to M. Wańkowicz, opinions are formed on the funeral. Jan Józef Lipski, Jan Olszewski (lawyer), Mieczysław Kurzyna, Marta Erdman, and others are pleased with the Catholic funeral and passing over the participation of the authorities. But another group of people from the journalist community, e.g., Michał Radgowski from *Polityka's*[8] editor's office and Krzysztof Kąkolewski from *Kultura*[9] believe that the facts of M. Wańkowicz's family refusing a state funeral and Al. Małachowski not thanking the authorities for participating in the funeral, resulted in the regulation in the censors' office to stop all publications concerning M. Wańkowicz in the mass media. It has created a bad atmosphere in part of the artistic community.

Director of Department 3
(Col. A. Krzysztoporski)

Soon after the writer's death a censorship regulation was made (mentioned in the above report). From that moment on, no texts could be printed about the late writer (*Polityka* managed to print a short text by Michał Radgowski just before the regulation was enacted). My long-accepted text to be printed in *Literatura*[10] was withdrawn. Western papers, for example, *Time*, published comments and notes, always stressing that Wańkowicz had been subjected to a political trial in 1964. A great Polish writer died, and Polish literary papers weren't allowed to print any occasional texts. They couldn't use words like "great writer, brave man." You could write about him, but sparingly and with restraint. After many years, I found the actual text of the regulation: "Any publications concerning the person and works of Melchior Wańkowicz that go beyond the sphere of technique and literature issues (naming him a man of great courage, politician, activist, national hero, etc.) must be stopped and signaled to the management of GUKPPiW"[11] (13 September 1974).

In 1993, I wrote about the period in a biographical book[12] and soon after the funeral there also appeared some incredible news concerning the writer's last will. Presumably, the writer had given a substantial sum of money to the Katyń case. The news was even repeated, reportedly, by the Paris *Kultura* stating he had left money to have a Mass said for him on every 17 August. There was also much speculation about the writer's possible wealth and its division. Marta Erdman, who stayed with me for nearly a month, heard that news with much surprise. At the same time, we saw astounding things. The house in Studencka Street was watched day and night by two cars parked nearby, mysterious men sitting inside. One day I was asked to come and see the vice minister of culture, Aleksander Syczewski. During the meeting in his office, Syczewski told me that many people were "concerned" about the security of the writer's archives. He suggested placing the more valuable documents in the ministry's building, where "they would be safe." I replied that I did not intend to hand the archives over to anyone. The writer had bequeathed them to me, and I was their lawful owner. I was writing a doctoral thesis and intended to use the materials in my research. I remember that Aleksander Syczewski did not insist, and in general, he was friendly toward the writer's case. The minister of culture, Józef Tejchma, had earlier shown his goodwill toward the writer, as he intervened when the publication of *Opierzona rewolucja* (*The Fledging Revolution*) was hindered. After the writer's death, he complied with the family's request not to have an autopsy done (Wańkowicz did not want one). After we talked in the Ministry of Culture, Andrzej Kurz, director of the Literary Publishing House (Wydawnictwo Literackie) came to the house on Studencka Street. He tried to persuade Marta to convince me to agree to hand the archives over to some "safe place." Of course, Marta was against it. She thought that had her father wanted to offer his collection to some institution, he would have done so himself or left instructions to that effect. Probably the friendliness of many people made the topic of the archives finally subside. I, on the other hand, was given a real safe. Minister Tejchma gave it to me with the advice to keep in it the "most explosive" materials. He said he was afraid of other groups—Security Services—who might try to "steal" the materials.

In 2007, those issues came back to me as I was reading the reports collected in the Institute of National Remembrance (IPN).

According to the will of the author, I became the official, lawful owner of the writer's archives. Wańkowicz dedicated the second volume of *Karafka La Fontaine'a* (*La Fontaine's Carafe*) to me with appreciation for my cooperation in the project. He sent it to the Literary Publishing House asking them to add it to the manuscript—this was a most beautiful present from the writer. I highly value the enormous trust placed in me by Wańkowicz—again. The contents of the archives were a subject for speculation and conjecture, suppositions and rumors. So far, I have allowed few people access to the archives: Professor Marcin Kula, Robert Jarocki (to materials concerning Jewish issues), Kazimierz Wierzyński's letters I have shown to Paweł Kądziela, Zofia Kossak-Szczucka's correspondence to Mirosława Pałaszewska, Jarosław Iwaszkiewicz's correspondence to Radosław Romaniuk, Westerplatte-related materials[13] to a doctoral student, Krzysztof Zajączkowski, and general materials to Anna Malcer-Zakrzacka from Gdańsk, who was writing her doctoral thesis on the author of *Szczenięce lata*.

The archives were the subject of many talks and discussions. It was also the reason for the security services collecting "documentation" on me. I learned of it over thirty-three years after the writer's death.

NOTES

1. Led by Lesław Bartelski,
2. Workers' Defense Committee—(In Polish, KOR—Komitet Obrony Robotników), civil society group that emerged in 1977 under Communist rule. It was one of the movements whose activities led to the creation of Solidarity in 1981.
3. Mieczysław Kurzyna, *O Melchiorze Wańkowiczu nie wszystko* (*About Melchior Wańkowicz, but Not All*) (Warsaw: IWPax, 1975), p. 292.
4. Aleksander Małachowski, "Elegia na śmierć córki" ("Elegy on Daughter's Death"), introduction to *Ziele na kraterze* (*Herbs at the Crater*) (Warsaw: PWN, 1993), pp. xi–xii.
5. Full name: Instytut Pamięci Narodowej—Komisja Ścigania Zbrodni przeciwko Narodowi Polskiemu (IPN) (Institute of National Remembrance—Commission for the Prosecution of Crimes against the Polish Nation)—Polish research institute with prosecution powers established in 1999.
6. IPN 0204/644.
7. In Polish, Instytut Badań Literackich PAN (translator's note).
8. Center-left weekly, established 1957 (translator's note).
9. Social and literary weekly, issued in Warsaw 1963–1981 (translator's note).
10. Literary and social weekly, issued in Warsaw 1972–1981 (translator's note).
11. Główny Urząd Kontroli Prasy, Publikacji i Widowisk—Main Office for Control of the Press, Publications, and Public Performances—Polish state censorship body functioning in 1946–1990 (translator's note).
12. Aleksandra Ziółkowska-Boehm, *Ulica Żółwiego Strumienia* (*Turtle Creek Boulevard*) (Warsaw 1995, 2004), pp. 203–9.
13. The Battle of Westerplatte was the first clash between Polish and German forces during World War II (and the first battle of the war in Europe). Repeated attacks by 3,500 German soldiers were repelled by 180 Polish soldiers for seven days, stalling further German attacks along the coast (translator's note).

Chapter Nine

The Writer's Files and Operation "Teenager"

"You've certainly had an interesting life." said the young IPN[1] historian, Andrzej Boboli, when handing me my file. "I really believe that what was happening around you then, was almost like a script for a thriller centered around the main character—a young woman—along with 'operational combination' of the Security Service, confidential collaborators, dissidents, a great writer and his heritage, on which legends were already circulating."

"In those days life demanded courage and decency by you," he continued. "*Summa summarum*,[2] it is worth being simply decent in life, even if everything encircling you convinced you to act otherwise, that nothing would happen if you deceived your very own self once or twice. As Chekhov put it, 'rust eats iron, and lies eat the soul.'"[3]

When looking for materials concerning Wańkowicz in IPN files, I found a file on me.[4] My "case" was handled by then a major, later director of Department 3 of the Ministry of Domestic Affairs, General Krzysztof Majchrowski. My file is a highly peculiar thing, in places sad, in others grotesque. First let me talk about the latter, grotesque part. As it is a file on me, I quote many fragments from it, because I am able to verify many reports by myself.

"OPERATION" TEENAGER

Melchior Wańkowicz used to say that to avoid boredom, you should let your listeners or readers "have a refresh laugh" from time to time. When I looked into my two hundred–page file, I learned it had been started even before I met the writer. And the reason for starting it was purely ludicrous. In 1974, files on a case where I was the main character were transferred from Łódź to Warsaw. The case: in 1967 Section 3 of KMMO[5] in Łódź started an "operational case" on me, then a high school pupil.

To make it even weirder, I described the issue in 1993 in my autobiographical book *Ulica Żółwiego Strumienia,* and I remember Jan Nowak Jeziorański, a director for many years of Radio Free Europe, commenting on that fragment. I wrote then about being summoned to KMMO in Łódź in the last one of my high school classes, and since I was a minor at that time, my father was summoned with me. As it turned out, they had intercepted cards I'd sent to the "Rendezvous at 6:10" broadcast of Radio Free Europe (RFE). My brothers and I would listen to that broadcast when doing homework. These daily broadcasts were great! The 1960s were the time of the Beatles, Paul Anka, Ricky Nelson, and many others. The hourlong program ended with "listeners' choice"—they played recordings as requested by their listeners. Again and again, they gave new addresses to which you could send cards, and stressed that if you sent them at once, they would reach them. After a few days, it was said, such an address was intercepted and the mail was confiscated. Jan Tyszkiewicz, Jan Herburt-Hewell, Barbara Nawratowicz, and sometimes Tadeusz Olsztyński (Nowakowski) hosted the program. Some of my letters reached their addressees, and I was so glad to listen to a recording played for me, at my request. I knew I shouldn't use my first or last name, so I signed those cards with the name Magdalena, as I particularly liked it at that time. Some of them—three, I think—were intercepted.

After the years—when I found the file on me—it turned out that in 1967 Section 3 of KMMO in Łódź started an "operational case" on me, codenamed "Teenager." The whole case was described very seriously in IPN documents. I would like to quote some fragments to render the character of that Aesopian speech:

> Cryptogram received KM [Municipal Headquarters] Łódź, 14th September 1974 at 2 p.m.
> Confidential
> No. 1269
> From 14th September 1974 at 12:50 p.m.
> Ldz oe-02925/74
>
> Head of Section 4 Department 3 of MSW[6] in Warsaw, Lt. Col. Komorowski
>
> Referring to the telephone conversation of 14.09.1974 with Maj. Gruchot, I am sending the information which is of interest to you.
> On 29.05.1967 Sction 3 of KMMO in Łódź has started an operational case No. 11908 crypt "Teenager." The case was started due to the "w" section intercepting documents sent to Krzysztof Staniszewski 65 rue de La Conven-

tion Paris 15—France, which address was a mailbox for Radio Free Europe. In the aforementioned document, its author, signed as "Magdalena," extolled RFE's program, praised its objectivity, and at the same time accused our media of partiality and lack of objectivity. The operations we conducted led us to establish that the author of the anonymous letter was citizen Aleksandra Ziółkowska, daughter of Henryk and Antonina. [. . .] At the time of writing the letters she was a student of 5th High School in Łódź on 5 Wspólna Street [. . .] her brother Henryk was a student of the Łódź Polytechnic Institute, her brother Krzysztof was a pupil. [. . .] Based on the expertise performed by local Criminology Laboratory No. zke-0206/67, it was proven that the said citizen sent three anonymous letters to the above address, and moreover, it follows from their content that she had sent other letters to the address of a Swedish mailbox of RFE. [. . .]

On 27.07.1967 talks were conducted in the headquarters building with the said citizen and her father. In the talks, the citizen fully confirmed the fact of writing the letters, explaining that she had wanted to hear her favorite melodies in "listeners' choice." She was unable to give reasons for slandering the media in Poland. [. . .] As the letters were not legalized, the citizen was registered as author of anonymous letters, and after a preventive talk on 29.07.1967 the case was placed in archives under No. 03410/2.

Deputy Head of Section 3 of KMMO in Łódź, Maj. Gruchot.
Encoded by: Miszczak on 14.09.74 at 1:40 p.m.
Decoded by: "chudy" at 1:55 p.m.

Wasn't that ridiculous? They wasted money and time on decoding anonymous cards sent by teenage girls asking to hear their favorite recorded melodies.

BALLET AROUND THE WRITER'S ARCHIVE

As Anna Bernat commented,[7] "But later, after Wańkowicz's death, when it turned out that he had appointed you the keeper of his archives, more serious things began."[8]

And as Aleksander Małachowski wrote many years later:

Right after the writer's death, the police danced a pathetic ballet around his body. The mourners were observed where they went after seeing the coffin [. . .] right the next day after the funeral—when the authorities came for the manuscripts, which possibly included dangerous descriptions of the trial and the stay in prison. Various dramatic events occurred. They threatened to search the premises and demanded the whole manuscript legacy be deposited in Wydawnictwo Literackie [Literary Publishing House]. Negotiators, Minister of Culture Józef Tejchma, and Director of Wydawnictwo Literackie Andrzej Kurz exerted some pressure, but never crossed the line of decency. The ballet ended with Aleksandra Ziółkowska, who by virtue of Wańkowicz's will being the owner of the whole manuscript legacy, obligated to accept a huge safe, where the papers were to be kept. Oleńka [Aleksandra] even kept preserves in that safe.[9]

The case of Wańkowicz's archives was a subject of many investigators. My file started to swell. This is what IPN files say:

> Operational Report Section 4 Department 3 of MSW
> Operational Inspector—Krzysztof Majchrowski
> Issue—Culture and Art
> Object—Polish Writers' Union
> Community—Artists
> Forms, means and methods of operational work used: operational questionnaire, using two operational contacts, PT "W," "B," "PP."
> Full name and numbers of the person/s registered at "C" to the given threat/fact—Aleksandra Ziółkowska

According to the files, the "threat description" was provided personally by Kazimierz Koźniewski, TW (Confidential Collaborator) "33," an enemy to Wańkowicz and informer on him (and many others).

Threat (Fact) Description

> On 18th September 1974, source "33" informed the MSW Security Services that writer Melchior Wańkowicz (deceased 10.09.1974) bequeathed to his secretary—Aleksandra Ziółkowska, resident of Warsaw, 30 Studencka St.—his political archives consisting of three parts:[10]
> "Powązki"—texts of books and articles unpublished, e.g., due to censorship reservations. The typescripts include a book on Zionism *Posłannictwo i obcość* (*Mission and Foreignness*) and text of a book in preparation on the lives of Poles after World War II—slandering the relationships in the People's Republic.
> collection of articles (including lampoons) and clippings from Polish and foreign press with his own negative comments concerning the alleged drainage and fall of Polish culture.
> political diary—covering a detailed record of political events in Poland over the last years, interwoven with descriptions of meetings and talks with former political, social, and cultural activists, as well as artists.
> Besides Aleksandra Ziółkowska, who maintains social contact with Zbigniew Racięski, RFE collaborator in Britain, it has been established that the political archive of M. Wańkowicz is freely available also to his daughter Marta Erdman. She is a U.S. citizen, a literary collaborator of the Paris *Kultura*—who is temporarily staying in Poland due to her father's funeral.
> The stand of Al. Ziółkowska and M. Erdman is adversely influenced by a circle of people known for their oppositional attitudes and connections with subversion centers. They include editor Aleksander Małachowski—employed in the Polish Radio and TV, Jan Józef Lipski, Ph.D., employee of the Institute

of Literary Research of the Polish Academy of Sciences, [11] lawyer Jan Ol-szewski, lawyer Stanisław Szczuka. Al. Małachowski and J. J. Lipski all who used the funeral ceremony for negative public speeches. Those people had been authorized by M. Wańkowicz to supervise the execution of his last will and to present issues connected with his work before Polish cultural institutions.

Left to people known for their oppositional attitudes and connections with subversion centers, the literary materials of M. Wańkowicz constitute a threat of spreading false information. Firstly, by making them known in Poland and secondly by transferring them to a foreign center acting against the political interest of the People's Republic.

(Head of Section 4)

Another report by Koźniewski:

Warsaw, 18th September 1974
Source KO [Operational Contact] "33"
Accepted by K. Majchrowski
Operational Information

Yesterday, i.e., on 17th September this year, in the editor's office of *Polityka*, I had a longer talk with Michał Radgowski concerning the "literary" legacy of Melchior Wańkowicz. Radgowski remains in good social relations with M. Wańkowicz's secretary—Aleksandra Ziółkowska-Tomczyk—and is informed by her on a current basis about the situation that has developed after the writer's death. [12] Radgowski informed me that the political archive of M. Wańkowicz consists of three parts:

a. A part called "Powązki"—texts of books and articles which have not been published due to various reasons, also censorship issues. There is a text of a book on Zionism written some years earlier. The only published text was a chapter on Hertzl. Reportedly there was a possibility to publish the text a few years ago, but someone convinced Wańkowicz not to do that. [13] It seems the person was Ms. Ziółkowska, his secretary, who is said by Radgowski to have a very philo-Semitic attitude. The book's text is rather anti-Semitic. [14]

b. A collection of articles, clippings, etc., which show the social changes, the fall, and drainage of Poland. The collection, said to have been very carefully prepared by Wańkowicz, is negative, black documentation on everything that happened in Poland after the war.

c. Various texts, often lampoons, features against various people. For a long time Wańkowicz prepared for himself (he stressed in any conversations that they were not meant to be published) such short *pitavals* features aimed against various people. A few months ago he had shown to Radgowski a feature against Kazimierz Koźniewski from *Polityka*—asking Radgowski to show the text to the man. [15] Radgowski showed the text to Koźniewski, who viewed it as very venomous, vitriolic, and extremely violent. Due to the latter's negative reportage on occupying Zaolzie[16] in 1938, Wańkowicz had been provoked to write such a text on Koźniewski.

All that archive, remaining in Wańkowicz's villa in 50 Studencka St., has been—according to Radgowski—bequeathed in its entirety to secretary Aleksandra Ziółkowska, whom Wańkowicz valued very highly. He claimed he owed the last year of his life entirely to her. Radgowski sustains the high opinion on A. Ziółkowska's intelligence. He claims that A. Ziółkowska has remained in separation from her husband Tomczyk for a long time now. [. . .]

Radgowski told me he was persuading Ziółkowska not to give access to the political archive to anyone under any circumstances, particularly not to give it to anyone from her family, but to keep it to herself. Also Wańkowicz's library, according to Radgowski's information, has been bequeathed to A. Ziółkowska, but she does not want to accept it, as she does not know what to do with it.[17]

The house was bequeathed to M. Wańkowicz's daughter, Marta Erdman, but with the reservation that Ms. Ziółkowska is to stay there as long as she does not get her own privately owned flat, for which she had already paid deposit money. According to Radgowski, Ziółkowska also has a few years' salary guaranteed from the inheritance, as the editor of his selected works and other things. Radgowski assured me that beside him, Jan Józef Lipski had enormous inspirational influence on A. Ziółkowska.

Radgowski is very critical toward the events of M. Wańkowicz's funeral. He thinks the speeches over the grave were bad. He claims that Małachowski should have thanked the Minister of Culture and the Party Secretary for coming to the funeral. He believes that Marta Erdman is very critical of the People's Republic. Getting off the plane to attend her father's funeral, she allegedly only agreed to having the body lie in state in the Primate's Palace, as the representative of the Minister of Culture suggested, because she understood the palace was really the palace of the primate. When it was explained to her that is not to be the case, she withdrew her consent.

Marta Erdman has not decided yet what to do with the house in 50 Studencka St. Her daughter, Anna Erdman, does not want to live there, as she thinks she has a better flat in 10 Puławska St., closer to Sródmieście.[18]

The censorship regulation concerning the press publications on Wańkowicz had colossal impact. A quarter of an hour after the censors called *Polityka* (*Polityka* didn't intend to publish anything more, anyway) they had a call from Ms. Ziółkowska, very upset, as both she and Marta Erdman understood (they already knew) that it applied to publishing Wańkowicz's books. Marta says she will complain to the U.S. ambassador. [. . .]

"33"

(IPN file, pp. 67–70)

Warsaw 19th September 1974
Confidential Note

M. Wańkowicz left a political archive called "Powązki" (about 35–40 binders, kept in the house in 50 Studencka St.)

- since September 1956 he kept two journals of political events in Poland and abroad, adding his own comments[19]
- the materials were typed in 4 copies and remained under the personal supervision of his secretary, A. Ziółkowska
- the information obtained indicated that copies of those materials may be found:

    a. with Jan Józef Lipski—employee of IBP PAN[20]
    b. with Mieczysław Kurzyna—PAX editor
    c. no data on other possible owners of the copies

Ziółkowska says to her friends, e.g., to Michał Radgowski from *Polityka*, that the whole "political" archive has been bequeathed to her by M. Wańkowicz. Secretary A. Ziółkowska-Tomczyk:

- Recommended for work with M. Wańkowicz by J. J. Lipski[21]
- She has prepared, cataloged, and edited all literary and political materials of M. Wańkowicz; she knows the people whom M. Wańkowicz gave some of the materials to,
- After the funeral, A. Ziółkowska secured M. Wańkowicz's political archive called "Powązki" in the house at 50 Studencka St., afraid it would be taken by people from outside.

A. Ziółkowska's personal situation:

- She is treated like a member of M. Wańkowicz's closest family, and manages all the inheritance matters on a current basis.
- She has been guaranteed that she can stay in the house at 50 Studencka St.—until she gets her own privately owned flat.
- She remains separated from her husband Wojciech Tomczyk, resident of Łódź [. . .], with whom she has a son, Tomasz, 5 years old (currently staying with her parents in Łódź).
- The writer's will guarantees to A. Ziółkowska a few months' salary as M. Wańkowicz's former secretary.[22]
- Her relations with Marta Erdman and other members of M. Wańkowicz's family are not good.[23]

A. Ziółkowska's contacts concerning the securing of the political archive:

- In a conversation with her father on 18.09.74, she informed him that there are attempts made to take the political archive by people from outside, but that she had hid (secured) the materials.
- She talked to Aleksander Małachowski from the Literary Section of the Polish Radio on possibly providing him with M. Wańkowicz's materials on journalist training.
- Michał Radgowski, journalist of *Polityka*, with whom she had a conversation on 18.09.74 between 6 p.m. to 8 p.m. in his flat, has much impact on her stand and the possible arrangements concerning the archive.

Negative influence on A. Ziółkowska is exerted by

a. Jan Józef Lipski—employee of IPL PAN
b. Aleksander Małachowski—Literary Section of the Polish Radio
c. Mieczysław Kurzyna—PAX board member
d. Father, Henryk Ziółkowski—office worker at the Design Office [. . .]

A. Ziółkowska and Marta Erdman (M. Wańkowicz's daughter) are alarmed with the ban on press and TV publications concerning the late M. Wańkowicz.

- Marta Erdman was informed of the issued censorship ban by secretary of the *Literatura* weekly, Agnieszka Andrzejewska.
- It was confirmed by Michał Radgowski from *Polityka*, who promised to intervene in the matter with the political authorities.
- M. Erdman spoke of the matter with PAX editor Mieczysław Kurzyna, who also confirmed the news to her.
- Marta Erdman and A. Ziółkowska stated that they would raise the matter of the ban on press publications on M. Wańkowicz with U.S. Embassy employees, on 18.09 this year, when returning the American passport of M. Wańkowicz (they were in the Embassy on 18.09 this year at 11.00 a.m. to 11.55 a.m.) (no signature). Typescript, same font as in K. Koźniewski's report.

Particularly interesting is the report quoted below because it cites a writer, A. Bocheński, author, for example, of *Dzieje głupoty w Polsce* (*The History of Stupidity in Poland*), who supposedly said he had "full information" that I "received the writer's villa as Wańkowicz's sweetie." (Of course, the writer's villa went to his daughter, and I must admit that the very word "sweetie" reminded me of primary school times with its so-called puppy love).

Source "Renata"/Accepted by Cz. Grobecki/ Confidential.
Report, Warsaw 20th September 1974

　　On 19th September this year, I met Aleksander Bocheński, a well-known PAX activist. During the conversation, I also raised the issue of the literary and material legacy left by Wańkowicz. Bocheński gave me—as he claims—the fullest information in the matter.
　　The only main heir of Wańkowicz is his daughter—Erdman from the U.S.A. In a special legacy, Wańkowicz also bequeathed the house, car,[24] and a range of other things to his last secretary, a student from Łódź, who—as Bocheński claims—was Wańkowicz's "sweetie." Also by virtue of Wańkowicz's special legacy, his library becomes property of Mieczysław Kurzyna from PAX. However, everything indicates that Kurzyna will not take the library, as there is already a project to set up a Wańkowicz Room in the Museum of Literature in the Old Town of Warsaw. Organizers of the event have asked Kurzyna to donate the library to equipping the room as one of the keepsakes after Wańkowicz. Reportedly, Kurzyna agreed to that.
　　"Renata"

A copy of Wańkowicz's last will appeared in the collected materials, perhaps being due to that report. They made sure that according to the writer's will, the house, copyrights, and so forth, belonged to his daughter, and the archive belonged to me. A report on the subject appeared as quickly as four days after the writer's death.

Warsaw 14th September 1974
Confidential
Note
Source "KR" states that Melchior Wańkowicz, resident of Warsaw, 50 Studencka St. (villa), left a last will which consisted of four parts:

- fiscal matters
- publishing matters
- family matters
- formal and legal matters

The last will is to be opened after the funeral. Since returning to Poland in 1956,[25] M. Wańkowicz had kept two political journals. One contains "day events" recorded on a current basis, and the other includes broader descriptions of the more interesting political conversations and events in Poland and abroad, also the writer's comments, negative in their essence. All the notes had been typed, ordered, and catalogued by his secretary, Aleksandra Ziółkowska-Tomczyk.[26]

The source judges there are about 40 to 50 ordered binders. The documentation ought to include, e.g., important Polish and foreign letters, as well as leaflets and other documents related to political events (March 1968).[27] The source is not sure whether all the aforementioned materials are currently in M. Wańkowicz's place of residence, or if they stayed in his former flat in 10 Puławska St.

Warsaw 14th September 1974
Confidential
Note
From the obtained information (source "AK,")[28] the secretary of Melchior Wańkowicz was Aleksandra Ziółkowska-Tomczyk. She is the daughter of Henryk, born 15th April 1949 in Łódź, Master of Arts in Polish Philology, married, 1 child (5 years old), non-Party member, resident of Warsaw, 50 Studencka St., using a Fiat 126p No. WR-43-01, phone 43-68-15.

The said secretary was recommended to Wańkowicz by Jan Józef Lipski. She was the "ear and eye" of the late writer, and managed all matters related to typing, cataloguing, and settling matters in publishing houses and the Ministry of Culture and Art.

The reports ascribed to me a greater role than I actually played: at twenty-four years, I didn't advise the writer on anything. He had wise and experienced people around him, but most of all, Wańkowicz knew very well himself what to do. Until the end of his life, he had a very sharp mind and was highly independent in his thinking.

FORMER JOURNALIST OF RADIO FREE EUROPE—ZBIGNIEW RACIĘSKI AND TW "MIECZYSŁAW" RYSZARD LASSOTA

My acquaintance with Zbigniew Racięski,[29] whom I'd met when I went with Wańkowicz to Britain for his surgery, clearly made the Security Service officers uneasy. Racięski, retired employee of Radio Free Europe, valued the writer highly, and maintained contact with him after Wańkowicz returned to Poland. Sometimes he called, or sent short letters. With time—but only in the later years, as I visited Britain when writing about the life of a Hubal soldier, Roman Rodziewicz—I became better friends with him and his wife Stanisława, and always I have valued that longtime friendship. I was also friends with other figures of the Polish community in London—Kamil Czarnecki and his wife Irena Delmar, who was a popular theater entertainer, the graphic artist Stanisław Gliwa and his wife Maria, and others.

But back then, in 1974, they had already exhumed the information from Łódź that I had written cards to RFE as a high school pupil, and they initiated a special operation "Teenager." This effort revealed my acquaintance with a retired RFE journalist and aroused a near alarm.

> 9th October 1974
> Handwritten note
> Comrade Bielecki [Col. Z. Bielecki]
>
> In my opinion, that report should be qualified as "01002"—an exile and refugee from Poland, employed in subversion centers, contacting a citizen of the People's Republic.
> The person of A. Ziółkowska must be recorded and entered in information No. 17. The record number will be the same, as an operational questionnaire will be established.
> If you agree with my suggestion, tell them to complete that and send it to me.
>
> (illegible signature)

They tried various strategies to take the writer's archive away from me. When I read the IPN materials, many things became clear. Various "publishers," "writers," "friends of the house" were sent to visit me, and people I hadn't known before also came. From Britain, for example, Ryszard Lassota came. He claimed he had a letter and a "small package" for me from Mr. Zbigniew Racięski. Lassota behaved and spoke in a clearly provocative manner. He suggested, for example, to have Wańkowicz's archive transferred to

London—to Racięski, who was, as Lassota put it, "suggesting" that to me. Everything he said sounded improbable, even suspicious. Once Lassota left, I called Racięski, who was surprised with such news and stated he had not suggested anything to Lassota and that he actually barely knew him. I notified Marta Miklaszewska and Jan Olszewski of that meeting and the proposal, and they warned me against Mr. Lassota. The man called me nearly every day, and I kept saying I was busy and didn't have time to meet him, which quite annoyed him. The situation of the threatened archive was difficult. Marta Erdman and I were both aware of that, and out of caution, I saw neither Lassota nor anyone else whom I didn't trust. I had serious and trusted people around me for advice—J. J. Lipski, Jan Olszewski, and Aleksander Małachowski—who were concerned that the writer's archive did not fall into the wrong hands, and they simply "stood by me" constantly in this matter.

Meanwhile, Ryszard Lassota (as it turned out years later) wrote an elaborate report on me, giving completely concocted facts, as—I repeat—I never had any conversations with him.

The case is quite well documented in my own IPN file. "Lassota's case" is exceptionally interesting. Everything started with a note from TW "Mieczysław," which was the pseudonym of Ryszard Lassota.

Confidential
Information
Talk on Ms. Aleksandra Ziółkowska

On 30.08.74 I spoke in London with Zbigniew Racięski, a former RFE employee in London, a journalist, currently correspondent of the Polish emigration press of the U.S.A. in London. He asked me to take a letter to Poland, together with a small package. At first he didn't tell me whom it was for. When I decided to take it, he explained it was for Wańkowicz's secretary—Aleksandra Ziółkowska. I asked if she was someone I could trust, and if she wouldn't blab of my contacts with Racięski. Mr. Racięski emphasized that Ms. Ziółkowska was a person who enjoyed full trust of his and of others in the West, a person who knew many interesting things about today's Poland and the behind-the-scenes intrigues in the world of culture. I understood that Ms. Ziółkowska did not keep such information only to herself when she was staying in the West, and in particular during her stay in London with Wańkowicz, when he'd gone there to undergo surgery.
"Mieczysław"
Description:
The report on the conversation and Ms. Aleksandra Ziółkowska is part of the information concerning "Mieczysław's" stay in London.
I will have the whole information by the end of the week.
Tasks will be worked on after the whole information is received.

Inspector of Section 4 Dept. 3 of MSW
Capt. B. Piekarski

Warsaw, 21st September 1974
Source: TW "Mieczysław"
Accepted by Lt. Bogdan Piekarski
Confidential
Operational Information
Talk with Al. Ziółkowska on 20th September 1974

The letter and package from Z. Racięski from London opened to me an inroad to A. Ziółkowska's trust and confidence. She shared her reflections with me from the first moment on. First she said she was being watched for some days now, and her phone was being tapped. Ziółkowska maintains that the vast material left by Wańkowicz, which exposes the process of "draining Polish culture," as well as with the presence of Mrs. Erdman, Wańkowicz's daughter, could very well lead to the daughter taking some materials of the writer over to the U.S. Embassy. [30]

The last will, as Ziółkowska says, is favorable to her. It bequeaths to her the entire private archive of the writer, called Powązki, full of virulent attacks on the People's Poland and the USSR (Katyń). [31]

Lassota successively wrote down some hearsay about the ambulance and the paramedics "not wanting to help Wańkowicz." He even wrote that Marta Miklaszewska was for her part "also" collecting materials on the case, to prove that Wańkowicz was "treated so as to speed up his death." Some snatches of such news reached Marta Erdman and me, but we didn't try to solve them, as many different rumors went around at that time, and we had no grounds for dealing with them.

TW "Mieczysław" also wrote that allegedly I told him "myself" that I was "staying under the influence of such people as J. J. Lipski or Wojciech Ziembiński" (I have never met Ziembiński in my life).

That reminds me of Graham Greene's book *Our Man in Havana*. Based on that book, a beautiful film was made in 1959 with Alec Guinness, Maureen O'Hara, and Noel Coward. The main character, a British spy, wrote fictitious reports.

To keep their jobs or earn more money, fictitious or embellished reports were also written by Security Service agents.

When now, after the years, I read the "reports" of Ryszard Lassota collected on me, I am amazed by such sentences and statements as, for instance, this one: "Wańkowicz let her [meaning me—note by AZB] give Racięski many interesting facts to uncover the inside secrets of the Warsaw regime."

From Racięski, "Ziółkowska was given a suitcase full of books, for example, on Katyń." "*The Gulag Archipelago* has numerous notes added by Wańkowicz, supplementing the records on the NKVD and KGB crime."

"Ziółkowska is angry with the 'regulation' on censorship that bans publications on Wańkowicz. She is aware that she is probably missing potential financial benefits, as now the time is good for writing about the deceased. On the other hand, she knows that the unclear situation with the 'Powązki' archive, Lipski, Ziembiński, and the writer's daughter, makes leniency of the authorities impossible."

"Moreover, I noticed that A. Ziółkowska shows much interest in men."

That last comment made me laugh. Good thing I didn't show interest in women! And just how did he get to "notice" that during one short visit?

Meanwhile, according to the IPN documents, it turns out that Lassota, who'd written the above-quoted reports on me, was in a way punished. Not immediately, it was after a year, but he "was punished."

The case of Wańkowicz's archive was further examined in every manner. I was invited to the Ministry of Culture and Art, where I met Vice Minister Aleksander Syczewski, the publisher Andrzej Kurz, and another man who didn't introduce himself. The latter man made notes diligently on the side and according to the notes he'd made and signed (which are now in my file), his name was Szapałas. The archive was discussed with me, and I was warned that "some people" might want to take it away from me. I replied that it was already happening, as a Mr. Lassota had come to me and made some (as is quoted in the IPN papers) "ambiguous and incomprehensible proposals," and that he was a liar, as Racięski had never asked him for anything in London.

A report from that meeting is there in IPN, and the most peculiar thing is a separate note saying that my behavior, as they put it, "might create conditions to expose 'Mieczysław,' particularly in the context of "tasks concerning employees of ideological subversion centers that he performed for Dept. 1 of MSW, and divulge a question as to the possibility of 'M's' further actions in the future." And that "there is a need to inform the individual of the ensuing situation."

So I exposed a conspirator! I caused his operation in Britain to become hot news! How "poor" and at the same time "unable to defend themselves" would Lassota's reports on me look like without the two documents quoted below.

11th December 1975
Note from an explanatory talk conducted on 10.12.1974 with Aleksandra Ziółkowska-Tomczyk
[. . .] She mentioned a "strange" (in her view) episode that occurred after the death of M. Wańkowicz. A man had come to her, under the name of Ryszard Lassota, a writer from Warsaw who was returning from abroad (he'd stayed, e.g., in Great Britain). He gave her Racięski's regards and a present from the man, and moreover, he made some (as she put it) "ambiguous and incomprehensible proposals" concerning possible help in keeping the materials inherited from M. Wańkowicz safe. Since she had doubts "as to Lassota's

true intentions," she informed Racięski of that fact. Racięski reportedly stated that "he gave no orders to Lassota and barely knew him." And in some trite conversation in London, he said nothing about Ziółkowska to Lassota.

In her opinion, Lassota seemed a "swindler who wanted to use her inheritance after Wańkowicz to his own purposes."

And another document followed:

NOTE

Special confidential significance

The following comments arise in connection with the operational meeting of comrade Szapałas with Aleksandra Ziółkowska-Tomczyk on 10.12.1975 (note of 11.12.75):

1. TW "Mieczysław" performed tasks in London in 1974 and 1975 resulting from operational objectives of Section 8 Dept. 1 of MSW, in consultation with Section 4 Dept. 3 of MSW. The results of the tasks performed have been assessed very positively by Dept. 1 in their report to us of 14.03.1975 No. OCE-0638/75.

2. According to the commissioned task, "Mieczysław" participated in passing a letter and package (which we controlled) from London from Racięski to A. Ziółkowska.

3. The content of the conversation "M" had with A. Ziółkowska is contained in an extensive report of 20.09.74, which gives statements by A. Ziółkowska concerning the archive in a different version than the one given in the meeting on 10.12.75.[32]

4. This year, "M" has been continuing a task from Dept. I of MSW in Great Britain and FRG. "M's" tasks and reports are judged as positive and proven by facts.

5. The operational meeting with A. Ziółkowska on 10.12.75 could create conditions for exposing "Mieczysław," particularly toward employees of ideological subversion centers, and call into question the possibility of "M's" further actions in the future.

6. Considering "Mieczysław's" journey abroad, planned for January 1976, to continue similar tasks, there is a need to inform the individual of the ensuing situation.

Senior Inspector of Section 4 Dept. 3 of MSW
Col. Jerzy Wojcieszek

I repeat, it turned out that I had exposed an agent, and it was decided to withdraw him from operation in Great Britain. So he was particularly punished for playing the same role as Alec Guinness, "our man in London."

PUBLISHER AK

Other reports in my file refer to a contact named "Editor K." I conclude that was Andrzej Kurz, director of the respectable Wydawnictwo Literackie, which did much to make Wańkowicz's books available to readers.

Both when Wańkowicz was alive and after his death, Andrzej Kurz visited the house in Studencka Street. After 10 September 1974, he talked to Marta and me as an editor who wished for the books of the author of *Bitwa o Monte Cassino* to continue being published. Particularly, he did not want to interrupt the "selected works" series that had already been started. When the writer was still alive, Andrzej Kurz published the first volume of *Karafka La Fontaine'a*—not in the series yet. Materials concerning generally understood criticism and censoring were not included in the volume, for censorship reasons. Kurz told the writer that he would try to include those materials in the second volume. Now he said to Marta and me that he was afraid that the situation about the archive could lead to suspending the publication of the writer's books.

Wishing to know exactly what her late father's archive contained, Marta Erdman spent a week looking through most of the materials and making a very general index of its contents. Andrzej Kurz asked her to give him a copy of her notes. Marta agreed. Several days later, she gave her notes to the editor at a meeting that we both attended with the vice minister of culture and art, Aleksander Syczewski. There are two contradictory reports on that meeting in the IPN files.

But most of all, there is a report detailing the plans made in order to take over the writer's archive.

> We established so far with editor "K" that when talking to M. Erdman and Al. Ziółkowska, he should suggest three possibilities of technically taking over the materials:
>
> a. bringing the packed materials to "K's" flat in Warsaw on 21st this month
> b. bringing the materials temporarily to the Min. of Culture and Art (also on 21st this month)
> c. bringing the materials directly to Wydawnictwo Literackie in Kraków, maybe accompanied by one of these people.
>
> (The talk with editor "K" was conducted by K. Majchrowski and Jan Bil)

25th October 1974
Confidential
Operational Information

> Within official duties in the case crypt. "Mewa," I spoke today with editor "K." He informed me e.g. that on 22nd October 1974, M. Wańkowicz's

daughter Marta Erdman, in the presence of his secretary Aleksandra Ziółkowska (during their meeting with the vice minister of culture, Aleksander Syczewski), handed him a detailed list of literary and political materials left by the writer and secured by M. Erdman and A. Ziółkowska in the house in 50 Studencka St.

Due to the justified need of our Service to take further interest in the case, it would be recommended to obtain a photocopy of the above-mentioned list of materials left by M. Erdman in the Ministry of Culture and Art, for the needs of MSW.

Senior Inspector of Section 4 Dept. 2 of MSW
Maj. K. Majchrowski

And further information, contradictory to the statement above:

13th November 1974
Confidential Note

On 12th November this year I had a meeting with editor "K," who showed me a binder with literary and political materials left by M. Wańkowicz on "culture drainage in Poland." The binder is titled "Cywilizacja wyjaławiania" ("Drainage Civilization"). M. Wańkowicz listed the following subheadings:

1. Envelope, the return to Poland (actually the envelope with the materials is not in the binder).
2. Role of press articles in the drainage issue, and the author's comments
3. *Karafka La Fontaine'a*—chapter on censorship

Editor "K" was provided the said binder with materials by secretary Aleksandra Ziółkowska to read and promptly return on reading.

The materials mentioned—the chapters concerning censorship and criticism—were given to the Wydawnictwo Literackie by the writer himself, as part of the first volume of *Karafka La Fontaine'a*.[33] The materials, as well as the typescript of an unpublished book *Posłannictwo i obcość*,[34] are included in the files of collected reports on Melchior Wańkowicz. The files include, for example, a copy of the letter to Artur Starewicz (in 1956–1963 the head of the Press Office of KC PZPR)[35] to not withhold the writer's subscription to the Paris *Kultura*. Starewicz probably showed the letter to various services, and hence it came to the file of reports on the writer. There is also a report (quoted fully at the end of the previous chapter) which stated among other things: "After Wańkowicz's death, part of 'Powązki' was obtained due to operational activities (these are materials and studies concerning the political situation in Poland) attachment 2. (signed): 2nd Lt. B. Pollak."

I believe it to be yet another "linguistic maneuver" of a security official or agent. Very soon after the writer's death, I had taken the most significant materials from the writer's archives to my parents' home. I did that carefully enough not to leave a trace (or note) on my action either in my file or in the file on Wańkowicz.

What else can be found in my two hundred-page file? There are statements that astonish and overwhelm me, for example, "In the fear of losing the archive, A. Ziółkowska has hidden it in her divan. She is also worried about the safety of the three-year collection of Paris *Kultura* issues, given to her by M. Wańkowicz."

Or "Marta Erdman suggested making two photocopies of the archive, wishing to take one with her to the United States but A. Ziółkowska did not allow that."

The phone calls made by me—or anyone in the house on Studencka Street—were tapped (it was called Source "Mewa"). Some of the notes were

> Warsaw, 17th September 1974
> Confidential
> (handwritten)
> Excerpt from Source "Mewa" information of 17.09.1974

> At 10:31 a.m. Aleksandra called Małachowski. She thanked him for a beautiful feature over the radio and said she would like to talk to him about the archive. [. . .] When ending, Małachowski promised once again to come to her in a few days.[36]

Many pages include pictures and biographical information on the people who visited the house on Studencka Street, and even those who just stood in front of it. Marta was closing down the house during that time, and various people came there. When I now look at the pictures and read the short notes on the people, I wrack my brain over "who might that be." I also saw a picture and note about someone whom I met in the United States twenty-five years later.

> 18th September 1974

> Findings—about the owner of a Volkswagen car, No. 60-90W0, present in the message from observation of the object crypt. "Jama" on 14.09.74.
> Based on the register of motor vehicles in the Communications Department of the District Office of Warsaw Mokotów, it was established that the owner of the aforementioned car is

> Andrzej Mirosław Jacyna
> Son of Kazimierz and Maria born Piłsudzka
> Born 28 VI [June] 1946 in Kraków
> Polish citizen, secondary education
> Occupation: technician
> Married
> Cit. Jacyna resides in Warsaw, 7 Odyńca St., flat No. 5

He came to the above address from 64 Kajki St., flat No. 1 on 24 II [February] 1964. In the application for an ID in the ID Bureau[37] of 7 VIII [August] 1974 he stated he was working in the United Business Complex "Veritas" in 31 Chłodna St.

Enclosed 1 photo

Deputy Head of Section 4
B Office, MSW
Lt. Col. Tadeusz Bartoszewski

In one picture, I recognized a journalist from the Polish community abroad, author of the book *Na pograniczu światów* (*On the Border of Two Worlds*), Andrzej Jacyna from Philadelphia. I called him from where I live in Delaware.

"Andrzej, what were you doing in 1974 in front of Wańkowicz's house?"

"I was giving a lift to Nik Rostworowski. I sat in the car waiting for him," he replied, surprised, after much thought.

What else is in the file?

Copies of the layout of the house, the rooms. My photograph, taken by a Hubal soldier by the name of Jan Sekulak. He gave me a few copies of it (I remember whom I gave two copies to, but I don't want to give names so as not to cast suspicion on anyone, as I don't know how the picture got into my file). There are photos from the funeral, and funeral speeches transcribed from recordings.

There is also a letter they intercepted, with press clippings concerning Melchior Wańkowicz, sent to me by Marta Erdman. I read her letter years later:

31st October 1974
Dear Oleńka,[38]

As promised, I am sending the clippings I received after Father's death. It is not complete, but it's all I have.

I'm waiting impatiently for news about your flat and other issues. I am sorry all that could not be settled before I left.

You said that you could use one desk from the study for Tomek.[39] I don't remember if I told you that in such case I decided to give the other to Maciek Mycielski.

It's been 6 days since I'm back home, but I'm still strangely tired, sleepy and I still have one foot back there. I only take care of the most important things, but there are a lot of them, too.

Give my love to Tomek and take care,
m.e.

The inscription written for me by Marta in the New York edition of *Ziele na kraterze* before she left Poland: "To Oleńka Ziółkowska—with whom fate has joined me in difficult times which required us to show integrity, courage, and faith—the last from the "Dear Home," Marta Erdman (25 October 1974)."

As Andrzej Boboli, the IPN historian I mentioned in the beginning, told me: "They wanted to set you and Marta Erdman at variance, and they didn't manage it."

"They" didn't manage a lot of things. When I look at the collected documentation on me after the years, I may almost say they quite become me. I didn't allow myself to be pulled into any operational action, and acted—for a twenty-five-year-old—quite cleverly. However, I was not alone, and I have to stress that. Many people favorably inclined toward the case of Wańkowicz stood by me, and I previously had many hours of earlier conversations with the writer, who besides bequeathing his archives to me also left me oral instructions concerning them.

Finally, the Security Service abandoned further invigilation. The record in the file says: "We cannot see a possibility of operational use of Aleksandra Ziółkowska, and we do not see symptoms of political threat in her current attitude and activity. We suggest abandoning further invigilation within the record questionnaire and placing the materials in Section 1 of the 'C' Office of MSW."

NOTES

1. Institute of National Remembrance.
2. Latin—all in all, sum of sum, on the whole.
3. Words of Andrzej Boboli, authorized 5 V [May] 2009.
4. IPN 0204/644.
5. Municipal Headquarters of the Citizen's Militia (police) (translator's note).
6. Ministerstwo Spraw Wewnętrznych—Ministry of Domestic Affairs.
7. Anna Bernat—journalist, author of books on Polish painting.
8. Anna Bernat, "Szelest liści i szum wiatru" ("Leaves Rustling and Wind Swooshing"), *Nowe Książki*, January 2008, pp. 4–9
9. Aleksander Małachowski, "Elegia na śmierć córki" ["Elegy on Daughter's Death"], introduction to *Ziele na kraterze* (Warsaw: PWN, 1993), pp. x–xiii.
10. The archive description and the whole document is also in the file of K. Koźniewski's reports. TW "33" wrote his reports in a few copies, and sometimes shortened the text or added to it.
11. In Polish, Instytut Badań Literackich PAN
12. Radgowski visited the writer from time to time, also when the latter was ill, and sometimes played chess with him. I didn't speak to him in private. I could not suggest anything to Wańkowicz "a few years ago," as "a few years ago" I was living in Łódź, learning in high school, and didn't know the writer yet. I became friends with Michał Radgowski and his wife Krystyna after Wańkowicz's death. They invited me to visit them, and after a while became very close to me. I write about that in my book *Ulica Żółwiego Strumienia*.
13. As above.
14. I write about the typescript below.

15. He told me in the interview of 1990, printed herein, that he had seen the *pitaval* only after the writer's death.

16. After Cieszyn Silesia was divided between Poland and Czechoslovakia in 1920, Zaolzie was the part of the region that was in Czechoslovakia. A continuing conflict over the region finally led to its annexation by Poland in October 1938. After the war, Zaolzie returned to Czechoslovakia (translator's note).

17. From the library—according to the writer's bequest—Mieczysław Kurzyna and I took about fifty titles in total. All the other books from the collection were donated to the Museum of Literature, as an integral part of Wańkowicz's study.

Also TW "Mieczysław" wrote in a report about who was getting the library (that I "didn't want it"). And TW "Renata" reported different facts (that "Mieczysław Kurzyna got it").

18. The center of Warsaw.

19. That is not true. Wańkowicz kept no journals. He allocated all his energy and time to writing books.

20. Institute of Literary Research of the Polish Academy of Sciences (translator's note).

21. I went to the writer myself. When writing a master's thesis about him, I wrote him a letter and was invited for a meeting. I write about it in my book *Ulica Żółwiego Strumienia*.

22. Separately, that is, not in his last will, the writer left a bequest for me to run the publication of the series of his selected works, issued by Wydawnictwo Literackie in Kraków and IwPAX in Warsaw. The monthly salary, according to the bequest, was to be paid from the writer's author's fees.

23. That is not true. My relations with Marta Erdman were very good.

24. Wańkowicz's car, Fiat 126p, that I drove for a year, was really bequeathed to me by the writer, and served me well in the following years.

25. That is a mistake, as the writer returned to Poland in 1958.

26. I repeat—Wańkowicz did not keep a journal.

27. The Polish 1968 political crisis, also called March 1968—major student and intellectual protest action against the government of the People's Republic of Poland. It was followed by a wave of repressions (translator's note).

28. In my opinion, A. K. was Aleksander Kotecki-Horodyski (whom I'd never met but I have heard much about him from Wańkowicz).

29. Zbigniew Edward Racięski (1906–1997)—lawyer, soldier of the September Campaign, prisoner of the Stalinist system, soldier and war correspondent of Anders's Army, for many years a London correspondent of Radio Free Europe and New York *Nowy Dziennik* (*New Daily*), honorary member of the Foreign Press Association in London, and co-founder and for many years president of the Anglo-Polish Conservative Society.

30. Marta never spoke of taking her father's materials to the U.S. Embassy. It was invented by TW "Mieczysław."

31. Another invention of TW "Mieczysław": Wańkowicz had no materials about the Katyń massacre, or "attack on the People's Republic and the USSR" in his archive.

32. The truthfulness of the version given by "Mieczysław," of all his above-quoted "statements," seems to have been questioned.

33. IPN 0192/72 vol. 7. Attachment No. 1, "O cenzurze" ("On Censorship") M. Wańkowicz. Fragment of the book *Karafka La Fontaine'a* submitted to Wydawnictwo Literackie in Kraków, pp. 1023–12.

34. IPN 0192/72 vol. IX, Attachment No. 3, *Posłannictwo i obcość* by M. Wańkowicz.

35. Central Committee of the Communist Party (translator's note).

36. Aleksander Małachowski was a regular guest when Wańkowicz was alive—he wrote about it many times himself—and he also visited after the writer's death. He advised Marta Erdman and me, and we remained close friends for many years.

37. In Polish, Biuro Dowodów Osobistych (BDO).

38. Oleńka—nickname for Aleksandra.

39. Tomek—nickname for Tomasz.

Chapter Ten

"Work, Donkey, Work"

One day Wańkowicz deposited on my desk a postcard showing a small donkey hitched up to a two-wheel trolley overpacked "to the hilt" with crates. The poor donkey wore a truly pained expression. Shortly after employing me, my dear boss brought me that encouraging picture and wrote on it, "Work, donkey, work! Your Boss." The postcard had traveled from the Nadliwie village to Puławska Street, from Puławska Street, to Studencka Street, and was pinned to the wall, and—next to "patron saints" (my boss's term, of course), which were my employer's pictures—constituted the decor of the workplace of the "Master Bard's" secretary.

So what was it that I pulled in my trolley?

Barely moving on those two wheels as depicted in the postcard, things very often overwhelmed me, a fresh graduate, obviously needing more experience.

"You have remarkably good intentions, but you need to learn one thing at least: communications from intrusive people must be dismissed in few words. And, if necessary, strictly and firmly." I treated every letter to my boss with care; however, I found it hard to treat "strictly and firmly" (for instance) someone who "without previous appointment" came a long way from some distant part of Poland. That was why I had to strictly and firmly instruct myself to be strict and firm with such intruders at times, but generally our unique little "business" went well and to our mutual satisfaction.

So what was it that I did in that "business"? What did I do as Melchior Wańkowicz's secretary?

The work ethic said about Melchior Wańkowicz was that he worked extremely hard and very truthfully. I have never met a person who would use his time so well, who would be so demanding toward himself, and would control himself so incessantly.

He arose at seven, washed himself, dressed, had breakfast, and began skimming through the daily press. At about nine, he sat down to his desk and—as he used to say—"the aura of work" engulfed him. At such a time, he demanded absolute peace and quiet. He didn't mind me staying in his study, typing, working, or even bustling about the room. He considered it "the atmosphere of work." Yet he couldn't bear any other sounds: conversations, music. When the dog was whimpering, he told me to lock it in the most distant room.

Once he'd written a text, he gave it to me to read, and waited impatiently for my opinion. Wańkowicz did not seek words of admiration or enthusiasm, then suspecting that I wanted to weasel out of being critical with some easy compliment. Greatly valuing every single critical remark, the writer once said that only scribblers or beginning writers trembled over every single word, or were afraid of changes or deletions, as that was their "punch line."

After such joint text analysis, usually he immediately made the corrections and additions to it, and then recycled it to me again. After editing—preparing the text for print as regards spelling, punctuation, style, and layout—I typed a clean copy.

He never returned to me any completed material. Only when he had finished a bigger series, some inter-related documentation, would he then re-read everything and make some small changes.

With every reading of the text, he always made some corrections, be they minor.

As a result, the book I helped with, *Karafka La Fontaine'a* could have grown for years.

Written and edited, the author usually had a fragment of his text published in some paper. The choice of the paper depended on its circulation, its popularity and importance. Only a writer with such a name as his could allow himself to have his works published in all papers at once. Many found his strategy annoying. Wańkowicz believed that if he published something in a popular magazine, more people would read it, and that was the idea.

I had my own study next to Wańkowicz; at about eleven o'clock I came to his study with the mail. The writer was impatient for it. He received about ten letters daily. I was the one who opened the envelopes. I started with official letters—from publishing houses, editors, and so forth.

Letters from his readers were read at the end. Those were probably the most anticipated correspondence and the most pleasant to read, though they could annoy him at times, like the grand exalted words full of admiration for the "Master Bard." But on days when he received fewer such letters, he was anxious, worried, even upset. He feared losing his popularity, as it was exactly what they proved.

I read the letters out loud. Sometimes I couldn't handle some undecipherable handwriting, very often several pages long, and then I slowly faltered, as I fought my way through the text. The writer would get irritated, interrupt me, and tell me to read it by myself and "if you find anything interesting, you'll tell me at dinner."

Some letters were answered with a standard text printed on a card: "Thank you very much for your kind words. I am sending my best regards."

As I said above, letters to Melchior Wańkowicz came every day. Some of them were intrusive or irritating; the writer complained that they took his time away from productive work. And yet he was waiting for the letters every day, and they pleased him immensely. None of them was left unanswered, if only a return address was available. There were also a few anonymous letters, most of them very nice, signed "one of your many readers," "an admirer," and so forth.

People addressed the letters in various manners. For instance, someone who didn't know the exact address, wrote a short note to the mailman on the envelope.

Polish Writer
Mr. Melchior Wańkowicz Warsaw

I am hopeful that the Warsaw mail will manage to find the addressee.

or

I don't know the exact address. The post can handle it. Please deliver it.

or

Please deliver the letter. I believe in the talent of Polish mailmen. Thank you.

or

I don't have the private address of the Addressee, and so I kindly ask to send the letter there as soon as possible. Thank you!

There was always some patient hand in the post office to write the correct address. I raise a toast to all those anonymous postal employees who had the patience and goodwill to do that.

Letters of the most varied content were answered. Not only the specific, serious ones, not only those asking if Mr. Wańkowicz knew someone or someone else's uncle in Chicago, or why he'd grown a beard. He did like such letters; he told his friends of them. Some enjoyed them immensely. For example:

Dear Mr. Melchior (though I feel like writing—"Dear Mel"),

I met you ages ago as a young Mel. It all took place at Doctor Rutecka's house (Hortensia Streer 5 flat 5) where I boarded as a seventeen-year-old student. Wandzia told me you had lived there in the previous year together with a Pelagiusz, so they had "Pel-Mel" at home. And as you came, Wandzia called me: "Halinka, come here. I will introduce to you that Mel I was talking about!" In the drawing room I saw a young, handsome boy. We started a lively, animated conversation (that directness of yours!), but then you paid me a compliment which made me lose my poise completely. I was confused and embarrassed. You had said, "You have a nicely shaped bust." I considered it to be impertinent, and moreover, I was a little hurt with the fact that even though I was considered handsome, you noticed nothing else in me but that . . . bust. You must have noticed that you'd hurt my feelings, as you gave me a chance for a rebuttal by asking: "What do you like best in me?" In revenge—although I found you handsome and interesting—I said, "You've got shapely ears!" Interestingly, when I saw your photo in *Karafka*, I immediately noticed the "shapely ears" and was reminded of the story I have written about.

The nice elderly lady received the following answer from the author of *Karafka La Fontaine'a*:

Dear Madam,

I would like to thank you for so many kind words. I am glad that you have remembered me and that my ears are still beautiful. And you . . . ?

The wave of letters grew significantly after each new publication. Readers sent their own corrections, additions (which we carefully kept to use in reissues). They expressed their opinions, sometimes protested, annoyed, for instance, with the writer's appearance.

Dear Master, In today's issue of *Przekrój* I have noticed some pictures of you with a beard. It's atrocious. How can you look like that? The older a man is, the more care he should take in caring for his appearance. You must definitely shave off that awful beard.

Wańkowicz was a funster; he loved jokes. I'd like to share two anecdotes here.

One summer, Wańkowicz rented a house in Nadliwie, near Wyszków, a small town near Warsaw. He spent all his time working on a book. Joining him at the house were the housekeeper, Marta, her daughter Anna, and I. One day, we all went to a church fair in Wyszków. There were a lot of local attractions and booths with various trinkets and such. We bought a pocket mirror with a heart and the words "I love you" on it, and in it a place for a picture. Then, for quite a while, we watched some people playing dice. An elderly man, standing right next to us, looked at the tall, grey-haired Melchior and spoke: "Ain't for you anymore, Grandpa."

I quailed.

"F_ _k off, sonny," came the immediate answer.

Our four-month stay in Nadliwie was coming to an end. Cold September days started. We all wore warm clothes and put on sweaters. Over his every-day outfit, that he called "pajamas," Wańkowicz wore a long, violet velvet bathrobe. After those four months, Wańkowicz's hair was much longer, and he'd grown an impressive grey beard.

Considering the fact that writing a book was utterly absorbing for him, from time to time the writer would require you to do something different (for a change of atmosphere). Melchior asked me to go with him for a ride, as he wanted to check and practice his driving skills (he did not drive himself anymore).

We drove over the sands in the village of Strachów. Wańkowicz didn't fail to mention being the owner of eleven cars so far. The driving went really well. Encouraged by that, the Master decided to test his skills on the main road.

He drove very well, changed gears, overtook other cars, but soon he decided to turn back. He turned the car into some forest track that meandered picturesquely among the trees. Soon we saw the first cottages.

Wańkowicz stopped the car and opened the window. "Where are we?" he asked some man standing in front of a homestead.

"In Świniotop (pig's drowning place)" was the answer.

"Where?" The Master was amazed.

"In Świniotop. We've got such sands here that pigs have drowned in them."

Not wishing to check for himself just how adequate the name was, Wańkowicz decided to turn back. He turned on the engine, shifted into gear, stepped on the accelerator, and started to make a small circle. The circle grew bigger and bigger, slower and slower, and we shared the fate of the said pigs: the car was stuck in the sand!

Our driver tried to get out of the predicament, but to no avail. The back wheels were only sinking deeper. I disembarked from the auto and started digging. Since I couldn't accomplish much with my bare hands, I approached a growing group of young and old people—everyone was looking at the car with Warsaw plates to see what would happen next. I asked them for some boards.

"We don't have any," they said, and added, "You won't get out of there."

I decided to look for boards myself, and I found a pile of boards quite nearby. I took two and struggled on. It didn't help. I turned back and came over to another group of onlookers. I asked them for help, promising to pay, and some men took their shovels to help me. I decided to take the wheel.

Melchior got out of the car. Amazed, people saw a large person in a long purple robe.

The car finally moved, and I reached solid ground. The large, grey-bearded figure approached the people and addressed them.

"I am a Capuchin from Philadelphia. I came to Poland on a mission. I am going to say to all I encounter how unkind the people here are, that they don't want to help others."

Finally he told me in English to pay the helpers.

People gaped, dumbstruck, at the long purple robe, at his grey head and beard. They watched the strange figure get into the elegant, red station wagon and observed it departing, accelerating and leaving a cloud of dust.

"It's a pity," said the Master, quite pleased with himself, "that instead of paying them I didn't bless them on leaving. They would have been just as happy, or maybe more so."

My extremely hardworking boss expected his secretary to work just as hard. I didn't have regular working hours, he didn't supervise me or check me, but he knew full well that everything would be done on time, that I would remind him about any deadlines, or make the necessary calls.

Yet before it came to that, he intently observed and checked each case. Once, after a few weeks of work, back in Nadliwie, where I had to prepare the new texts, type them, answer piles of letters, and add to that driving a car and arranging all things, I mutinied. I said to myself, Sunday is for resting. I changed into a swimsuit, took a blanket, found a sunny location in the garden outside, and decided to have my "rest" with some interesting reading.

I was lying there for some fifteen minutes or so, and then I heard a typing machine's click and clatter from the open window of the boss's study. I put the book aside and settled down more comfortably to enjoy the sun . . . the machine clattered on . . . I felt awful and blushed with shame. I felt like a deserter. "Here I am lazing, knowing there is little time left for completing the writing of the book, and he is working till late at night." With a quiet groan of regret, I said good-bye to the sun, arose, and went to my room. On my way there I met my boss, who on seeing my return smiled at me and said, "I'm glad you've returned, 'cause I need you to check one thing for me here."

When I later told him about my attempt at rebellion, about the pangs of conscience as I heard the diligent typing, Wańkowicz laughed and told me that right then he was going to reproach me for not working, but when he saw me return with a repentant face, decided to say nothing.

Wańkowicz liked to talk of his remarkably organized archives. Two huge cabinets jammed full of files, all of them precisely labeled, numbered, and so forth, showed not only the secretary to be diligent and conscientious, but mainly the boss's system of work, and his meticulous character.

Every clipping, every article, either about him or by him, had a strictly defined place. Thus, there were files with translations, with manuscripts (meaning typewritten draft scripts, as the writer barely even wrote by hand), with carefully segregated correspondence. The latter correspondence consisted of letters from the exile years, private ones, political ones, correspondence with other writers (Stanisław "Cat" Mackiewicz, Maria Dąbrowska, Zofia Kossak-Szczucka, Czesław Miłosz, etc.), with journalists, publishers, and so forth. Thick files contained letters titled simply "From readers." Each of the writer's books had its own collection of reviews and letters concerning it. Each of his articles published in the press "resided" in a relevant division: *Polityka, Kultura, Literatura, Miesięcznik Literacki* (*Literary Monthly*), *Odra*, and so forth.

Contracts with publishers were kept separately, and so were "general reviews." What Wańkowicz valued most were four files titled "Attacks and Fights," that contained anonymous letters, articles attacking him, collected both in exile and later on in Poland.

Another, separate shelf contained "Powązki" (name of the Warsaw cemetery), that is, things not published. He wrote in a humorous way about one of those books in the essay: "Inżynier dusz—petentem" ("From Engineer of Human Souls to Supplicant").[1] As often as possible, he included many of these "cemetery" fragments in the books that were published.

Working together made us better friends. He liked my genuine devotion to work. He joked that I often did many things better than he. I think that my enthusiasm resulted also from the fact that all the issues that were close to him became close to me, like the house we lived in—beautiful, created fully for its host, who filled it for the whole day, never boring, always emanating with his rich, fascinating personality.

Does it not tell much about that man, old, difficult, filled with complexes, that I, a young impatient girl from an utterly different world, could live his life, be happy with each success of his, each sign of people's kindness, and at the same time be concerned with his difficult matters as if they were my own?

That never a day was similar to the previous one, never empty, boring, never pressuring?

He seemed to always be among people, and yet he was exceedingly lonely. The eighty-year-old, sensitive man felt his loneliness very acutely. He felt uneasy, anxious about the future. "I miss you so much. I feel it acutely especially today, as I think that tomorrow I am going to start another series of lonely, empty, gloomy evenings on Puławska Street. If you were just next to me, just in the next room," he wrote in one of his letters, filled—like all of them—with sorrow, anxiety, fear of the future. His housekeeper Marta lived in Bielany (Warsaw district in the northwestern part of the city). She was married, with a daughter, and with all her devotion to her job and her employer, she couldn't possibly stay at Puławska Street in the Mokotów district all the time. Overall, she'd been working for him since she was nineteen (with years off during World War II and when he was living in the United States). Life had separated him from his daughter, not only with distance, but also by their hugely different worlds. There were days when he was anxious, scared of everything; he frequently felt anxious in the mornings. When I came in the morning, he had been awake for a long time, immersed in grim contemplation. He used to say that when I came, a new day began, that life returned. When I asked what was troubling him, he would tell stories often from many years ago, recall hurts from throughout his life. All the things he said were sad, depressing, sometimes amazing. "You know, I killed a female moose once. I shouldn't have. I'm so sorry now. I know it sounds ridiculous, especially after all these years."

He had a pressing need to get some hard unhappy things off his chest. He told me of them to relieve himself, in all confidence, and, as he said, so that I "would know life." Then he was horrified that he'd shift some complexes onto me, and explained many things.

When I appeared presenting the problem of working for him, Wańkowicz very much wanted me to stay in his house. One journalist wrote that Wańkowicz had a case of Pygmalionism. I think he was right. Melchior loved creating, molding, not only situations or conversations. Before, he had invested a lot in his daughters, to some extent in his granddaughters, in Zofia Romanowiczowa, and now, at the end of his life, he seemed to have transferred that creative desire to me.

A FEW MORE WORDS

What many different features that man had! He was egoistic and altruistic all at the same time. A great liar, egocentric and callous, and yet a man sensitive to human suffering, afraid to view himself as a great writer, and a delicate, sensitive, tender man.

He was full of contradictions. I couldn't tell which of his features dominated. Was it those that depended on people, relations, or situations? For me, he was the best, most faithful friend, ready for compromise, delicate and caring. He really wanted me to see him in a better light, which was exactly how I did see him. At the same time, with other people, strangers, he could be chilly, harsh, and most often indifferent. He cared for people like actors care for their audience, as that audience conditioned success.

He also had a remarkable feature: he could make the impression of being extremely interested in his interlocutor. He asked questions, and listened with much attention. He listened carefully and asked questions if it was necessary. And at the given point it was true, but later he had no more use of his interlocutor. Wańkowicz didn't really believe in selfless friendship. He loved the admiration of him as a person. But there were many people he really genuinely liked, called them, showed interest in their matters.

He didn't have really close friends. The closest friend of many years he would be able to sacrifice immediately when a split appeared, when the friend didn't quite yield to him, when he or she had a different opinion, be it right or wrong.

Wańkowicz was incredibly interested in people of distinctive personality, stemming from a different cultural background, connected with different trends. He found them interesting, didn't avoid contact, and sometimes even encouraged some closer relationship. He treated them with the same whole reality, faithful to his rule of "La Fontaine's carafe"; he saw people and events like an element, without differentiating.

Holding his life with a heavy hand, if it slipped out of his grasp, he'd rebuild it like he wanted it to be—then would pass that version to others and believe it himself. Everything was explained so as to make it good for him. He believed that even the most tragic, hardest moments in our lives could be transformed into an advantage for us. He was a fantasist. He had created the kind of family he wanted it to be. He presented himself in a way he wanted others to see him. Had he had a close, devoted person next to him, loved him or her, and had that someone left him, it would have been the greatest suffering to him, but he would have hidden it from others. To himself, he would have explained it was good after all, as there were also bad sides, and he would have tried to remember those bad things. That was the easier way to act—for himself and in front of others. That was his defense, and his shield.

A lot of people visited him; nearly the whole of intellectual Warsaw passed through his house. To each guest he was different, which was great diplomacy on one hand, a great game, a fine thread hanging between the two Poles, and on the other hand, a normal reaction. After all, we all desire different things from different people. There are certain topics which we don't discuss with our best friend, but rather share them with someone less close, for a variety of reasons.

Everyone who knew Wańkowicz closer, often considered him to have similar views as himself. Hence after his death, there was an amazingly self-contradictory collection of names of people who believed him to be "their" man. He knew how to release people's hopes and subconscious desires.

He was curious about new people, and found something interesting in everyone, but there were a few whom he did wish to see again. For that reason, more frequent guests in his "Dear Home" were considered friends, and Wańkowicz liked them unconditionally.

Krzysztof Kąkolewski belonged to a different group of people than Mieczysław Kurzyna, Kurzyna to a different one than Aleksander Małachowski, Jan Józef Lipski, Marta Miklaszewska, or Jan Olszewski.

All the ladies-in-waiting ought to be listed separately—Barbara Wachowicz, Zenona Macużanka, Swietłana Załuska, Krystyna Goldbergowa, Alicja Tejchmowa, Barbara Seidler—women truly devoted to him, and much liked by him. But it would be difficult to call it "friendship." His was longing for a woman, or more precisely for femininity, for warmth, for home atmosphere.

Toward women he was full of admiration and compliments. He could always say something that would bring out the princess in each of them. Each felt like the only one, wholesome. That was not an easy thing to do. He wanted to be seen as a great ladies' man; he wanted to have that sort of reputation.

The house was always full of flowers. In the garden, Marta, the housekeeper, grew beautiful marguerites, asters, or geraniums. When Wańkowicz returned from the hospital, he told me to place the beautiful orchids he was given by Barbara Wachowicz at his bedside. In the last few weeks, many sword lilies were sent to his house; he delighted in their elegance and color.

Women liked him, phoned him, and visited. A frequent guest was Krzysztof Kąkolewski with his charming wife Joanna. For them Wańkowicz always had much warmth and time.

On Tuesdays, the delicious dinners by Marta the housekeeper attracted Andrzej Kurz, a publisher from Kraków. I joked that he treated our house like a restaurant during his trips from Kraków, which took place almost every week. Wańkowicz invited him with pleasure, saying over the phone, Mister Andrzej, "on the old route of our fathers"[2] come over today. There might be something in the pot for you. I know you like shish kebab!"

When it happened that Mister Andrzej did not visit Studencka Street, Wańkowicz kept fussing and reminding him of that during his next visit. Wańkowicz admired and appreciated his visitor's diplomacy, and always wanted to get all the news from him.

Other visitors were Mieczysław Kurzyna, a longtime friend of his, Zdzisław Borówka, as well as Zbigniew K. Rogowski. He was a nice man and a welcome guest, called an "advertising agency" for his popular column in the Kraków weekly *Przekrój*.

His contacts with relatives were rather poor. He wrote to his daughter, phoned Marieta (Maria), his sister-in-law, talked of business with Jan Sawa, the husband of his brother's granddaughter.

When a visitor stayed for too long (now please forgive us, everyone, if it ever happened to you) or was simply boring, we usually said: "Wait a minute, isn't Małachowski coming over today?" Sometimes it worked at once, and the visitor said his goodbyes. But what were we to do when we kept repeating that and looking at our watches, and there was no reaction? In such cases, Marta entered the scene. It was enough to mention it to her, as she already knew what to do. She came in to say: "Sir, Mr. Małachowski has just come. He is waiting in the salon."

Fortunately, the house was big, and on the way out the guests did not go through the salon.

He liked hosting guests; he liked serving them some exquisite food. He often treated them to different delicacies, goodies, or some sophisticated dishes, like octopus, snails, frogs, and so forth.

When a journalist, Bohdan Czeszko, wrote in *Nowe Książki* (*New Books*) that since eating Lithuanian dumplings (called *kołduny*) at Wańkowicz's house he didn't want to eat them anywhere else, Wańkowicz was extremely pleased and repeatedly said it to others.

He was also greatly pleased when Izabella and Janusz Odrowąż-Pieniążek told him that French frogs weren't that tasty as his.

He was a true gourmet. Once Janina Lewandowska, an editor, was to come from Kraków. The first talks concerning *Dzieła wybrane* (*Selected Works*) took place. We were then staying in Nadliwie, but for that day we made a special trip to Warsaw. Wańkowicz wanted to treat her to a great dinner. Marta wasn't there, so he decided to eat out. Rumor had it that the restaurant Pod Dębami in Wilanów served great food.

We took our guest there. Elegant cars waited in the parking lot. We went in; the entrance was downstairs and to the left. We were a bit surprised. Where were all those dignified guests?

Instead, there were some tourists; a few men were drinking beer. It looked like a diner. Well, from a menu that offered little choice, we ordered a meal. Wańkowicz was cross. The waitress forgot to bring the forks; the soup was cold. Though disappointed, we ate and left. Some hospitality!

As we were walking out, I was surprised to see a notice: "To the restaurant" and an arrow pointing upstairs. I showed it to Wańkowicz and our guest. "Ladies, do you possibly have space left for a meal?" asked my dear boss desperately.

As it were, we had no space, and thus Wańkowicz was confirmed in his belief that there was no place like home.

I think he taught me to be open to everything, to be sensitive, and also, despite my age, to be happy with the here and now, with small things.

He bought a watch in August. He chose one that was self-winding and showed the date. My goodness, how happy he was with it! As the watch needed motion and movement to stay wound, he switched it from the left wrist to the right one as lately he had been typing with one hand only. While sleeping he wore the watch. Every day he checked if the date had changed, if it really happened at midnight, or what would happen when there were thirty days in the month and not thirty-one.

When he had a visitor, Wańkowicz would ostentatiously look at the watch and say, "Now, what date is today? 'Cause, you know, I've got this watch."

Being very funny for me, sometimes when he had guests I asked the question myself, "What date do we have today? You know, my boss has got this fantastic watch."

Desperately loving any novelties, any new conveniences, he spared no money on them, although—as I've said before—my boss wasn't wasteful. He economized on some strange things, like paper.

Someone flipping through Wańkowicz's draft typescripts may be surprised, as the reverse sides of pages are often filled with writing. Believing it a waste to throw out paper with one clean side, the man of words turned the page and wrote on the other side.

Every day he toured the house turning off any unnecessarily burning lights, annoyed with me for wasting energy.

Generally, if wanting to please me, he wore gifts from me: ties, sweaters. And the other way around, acting the disciplinarian, he would pointedly wear a gift from someone else, say, a tie, to show I had done another thing or something wrong.

When he phoned someone he didn't know, he used to say: "Wańkowicz speaking," and then allowed the other person a moment to ooh and aah, all those "the Master!!!" things. When (seldom) there was no such reaction, he anxiously asked, "Wańkowicz speaking, do you want me to spell my name?"

Usually the answer to that was "No, there's no need. I know the name."

I noticed such exchanges often, and as he was dialing the number, I copied his voice, saying, "Wańkowicz speaking, should I spell it?"

He believed that people of uncommon mind had a duty to serve people, and for average people, diligent execution of their duties was perfection. The writer required a lot from others: he appreciated and valued people with passion, honored human effort and dedication to a cause, and hated cowardice and indecision.

Writing was his one and only passion, and all he did was subordinate himself to that one thing.

He wasn't an expert in many fields. He hated music, had problems with contemporary literature, didn't understand, didn't "get" the new convention.

He believed that others were richer than he with that very knowledge of the new.

Not thinking himself well read, the author appreciated his ability for synthesis. Each newly read book was utilized to the fullest. Always reading with a pencil in hand, some fragments were marked, and sometimes they were given to me to make extracts.

Films were received in the same way. He liked going to the cinema and did it rather frequently. The "Moskwa" cinema was his favorite one, and living just across the street for thirteen years, there were no problems getting there. Neither did he have problems with the tickets. It was enough for him to phone the cinema, and the tickets were waiting for him. During a movie, he often commented aloud and with a wicked tongue. I remember particularly a few movies I watched with Wańkowicz. *The Bear and the Doll* (*L'ours et La Poupée*) with Brigitte Bardot was one of them.

He sat comfortably, having been led into the room with all honors. He was definitely content. The movie started. He tried to watch carefully and get the plot, but it seemed to grow more difficult for him, as finally he gave up the effort and closed his eyes. The indifference lasted for quite some time, and finally the people sitting closest to us and I realized he had fallen asleep. The film went on. He woke up, took a look, yawned, and asked me if I really had to watch it. As the question assumed the answer of "no, I do not really have to," we stood up and quietly (quietly, my foot!—pushing toward the exit in the middle of the movie) left the theater. I never found out if Wańkowicz's boredom with the film was due to acting or his real feelings.

Still, he avidly sought good films, and so we went to see another one: *The Sicilian Clan* (*Le clan des siciliens*).

Everything was fine, but I kept glancing at him in the fear of his again falling asleep, as then I would really have to go home before the end. But no, he seemed interested, as he kept pulling my sleeve and asking questions. At one moment in the film, the handsome Alain Delon said to his lady friend, "Don't come any closer. I haven't had a woman for two years."

The writer hadn't managed—or pretended that he did not—to read the caption in time, and asked me in a resounding whisper, "Tell me, he hasn't had who?"

"A woman," I whispered very softly.

"Who?" he repeated, annoyed, as if he didn't catch it.

"A woman," I hissed in his ear, arousing some laughs and some heads turning in the amused audience.

Accustomed to traditional cinema, modern film editing eluded him. He also had exceptional trouble remembering faces; hence it was difficult for him to follow some plots.

"Why is this train on the move? Where did it come from?"

"Because he's traveling on it," I replied.

"What he?"

"Well . . ."

"Tell me, who is he?"

And then, "Oh, all right, but you see, he looks somehow different. I didn't recognize him."

Not seeming to understand anything was sometimes my impression, yet for instance after watching *Vanishing Point,* he amazed me with his mature, wise reception of it. He'd caught everything, every single motif that had been carefully hinted at.

He was irritated with the long-drawn-out bits in *W pustyni i w puszczy* (*In Desert and Wilderness*),[3] but a few scenes he found delightful. A few weeks later, Krzysztof Fus, a photographer, visited him with the journalist Bożena Sawa, who wanted to prepare an interview with him for *Panorama Śląska* (*Silesian Panorama*) (one of the writer's last interviews). When hearing that it was Krzysztof who played the lion in the movie recently seen, the one based on Sienkiewicz's novel, the author was curious about the details, and asked him many questions which he remembered having after the movie.

Meeting the movie's set designer, Wiesław Śniadecki, Wańkowicz returned to the topic of the film and looking through the drawings of the character's outfits. A long and extremely interesting conversation transpired, just five days before his death. I was stunned with his knowledge of the history of Sudan and Egypt, of the customs and situation there.

In May, two months after the surgery, we saw *The Godfather*, and it didn't really make an impression on him. He was tired and had a very bad cough, only temporarily quieted, which could burst out at any time. Wanting to please me with the movie, he did not complain, and watched it until the end.

The news on TV was never watched. Claiming it was boring, our author preferred working instead. Neither did he like films, unless I picked out a title that interested him for some reasons, but those were few and far between.

My watching TV was annoying to him. He thought it to be a waste of time, and didn't like the way of spending leisure time to be thus forced on him.

What he always did like watching, and told me to look for them, were all sorts of documentaries about animals and nature. He also bought many books about animals, and often took his comparisons from that area. I remember how delighted he was after watching a German film about dolphins.

At the beginning of July, two months before his death, the writer watched the Football World Cup. Overjoyed when Poland won, at the same time he found the highly enthusiastic reaction of the crowd rather annoying.

Wańkowicz wanted to write an article to bridle the crowd enthusiasm. He said that Uruguay had won the World Cup before World War II, and that it meant absolutely nothing. Smaller countries had complexes. For instance, San Marino printed the most beautiful stamps. So did Poland.

Shocking me with stories or jokes taken from who knows where and who knows how amused him. All was fine as long as these annoyed me, as long as I told him I didn't like "filthy" jokes. I knew that all was fine as long as I reacted just like that. I would have hurt him if I had laughed at the jokes, if I'd been truly amused with them. Then he would have stopped it. He loved scandalizing and shocking, but hated actual depravation and corruption. In fact, he missed affection, tenderness, real warmth.

Keeping life under his control and directing it almost just as he wanted, he helped himself with myths, great myths. In the last months of his life, very ill, he analyzed and summarized his life, speaking of its negative side. From all his life, he remembered mainly the tough, difficult, bitter, painful things.

He wanted his old age to be calm, and wished for a great, traditional death. He claimed that the times of dying greatly, with family at the bedside, with the last instructions, were gone.

Wańkowicz was pleased that with the big house and devoted people, he could afford the luxury of such a death. In the case of being in the hospital and should his condition worsen, he asked to be brought back home for those last few days, even the last hours. Wishing for a dignified death, he prepared for it. For him, death was something as great as birth, a mystery, the last great experience in human life. He was curious about death.

When, three hours after the writer was admitted to the hospital and after our last conversation, I phoned the hospital, the first thing I felt was astonishment. "What do you mean, he's dead?"

He didn't want it that way. He didn't know. He had told me to come, instructed me on what to bring. He lost consciousness not knowing it was the end. The life, which had always listened to him, had to listen to him, didn't bow to him now. The great combat with death, which he'd been preparing for over months, didn't happen. He would have accepted it with dignity; he had that courage. I was amazed and overcome by life's inconsideration, with the surprise destiny had in store for him.

Slowly, with time, other thoughts came.

He fought all his life: against people—friends or strangers—against situations which he knew he had to win.

He was afraid of suffering, of being crippled, of slow decay. He envied others their quick, sudden deaths.

He wasn't religious, so nothing could help him. He was alone with his mind, with his clear, cruel, truthful thoughts. He was afraid of death.

Maybe it was then, at the very end, that he was spared one more combat: one against his own body that could play a trick on him—and could defend itself at his expense.

He was a contradiction: at the same time he desired and detested public awards, medals, an official funeral, or great death.

Life makes its own choices.

Figure 10.1. Wańkowicz taking "advice" from author a after lecture

NOTES

1. See M. Wańkowicz, *Przez cztery klimaty* (*Through Four Climates*) (Warsaw, 1972).
2. Quote from a Polish soldiers' song of 1915 (translator's note).
3. *In Desert and Wilderness*, a film based on a popular novel for young people, written by Polish Nobel Prize–winning novelist Henryk Sienkiewicz in 1912.

Chapter Eleven

Polish Literature's Eager Beaver Student

Readers often ask me: "How did it happen that you met the writer and started working with him?" I wrote about it in my book *Ulica Żółwiego Strumienia*, and I want to repeat it also in a book about Wańkowicz.

In my fourth year of studies, I chose the documentary work of Melchior Wańkowicz for the topic of my master's thesis. My adviser, Professor Zdzisław Skwarczyński, grimaced with reluctance on hearing my choice of the topic. He tried to discourage me: "You will have no access to the writer's work published outside of Poland. Maybe you'll consider this obstacle and decide to take a different topic?" I replied I had access to the books by the author of *Kundlizm* and that I didn't want to search for another topic. Wańkowicz was a writer much respected in my family home, and his books—generally unavailable—were obtained by my father, Henryk Ziółkowski, a devoted literature lover. He had many of them in his collection. He highly valued the three-volume Rome edition of *Bitwa o Monte Cassino* and *Drogą do Urzędowa* issued in New York. My father's respect and appreciation for the writer grew particularly after the latter's political trial in 1964. I was also hoping to gain access to some books through the help of the then director of the University Library in Łódź, Michał Kuna, a generous and helpful person. He often enabled one to gain access to books listed separately as not available to everyone due to their political message or their anti-Communist authors.

I prepared to engage my topic carefully and systematically. I started with reading the pre-war books by Wańkowicz, such as *Strzępy epopei, W kościołach Meksyku, Szpital w Cichiniczach, Opierzona rewolucja, Sztafeta*. After the war, only *Szczenięce lata* and *Na tropach Smętka* were re-issued. I read of the critics' reaction to the books and their reviews published both in pre-war and post-war papers. I wrote a separate essay on *Strzępy epopei* and the book *Moje wspomnienia* (*My Memoirs*) by General Józef Dowbor-Muśnicki. Then I read the books *Wrzesień żagwiący, Dzieje rodziny Korzeniewskich, Kundlizm, Drogą do Urzędowa, Tworzywo,* and *Ziele na kraterze.* I had trouble accessing *De profundis* issued in Tel Aviv, and *Polacy i Ameryka* (*Poles and America*) issued in New York.

Finally, I wrote a letter to the writer, in which I carefully outlined my problems. The address wasn't difficult to find. Soon I received an answer inviting me to Warsaw for a short afternoon meeting. He set the day and time: 20 May 1972, 5 p.m.

I was excited and was looking forward to the meeting awaiting me. I came to Warsaw early in the afternoon, took a streetcar, disembarked earlier, and walked slowly down Marszałkowska Street. The last half-hour I spent drinking tea in a café, just opposite Wańkowicz's home, at the corner of Puławska and Rakowiecka streets. The café was adjacent to the "Moskwa" cinema, that was torn down after 1989, and now where stands a trade and banking center.

To reach the flat No. 35 at 10 Puławska Street, you took the elevator to the six floor; then you had to take the stairs to go up one floor. When I rang the doorbell, the door was opened by Wańkowicz himself. He invited me to the sitting room, beautifully furnished with period furniture including a period couch, armchairs, a writing desk, a secretary, on which stood a Philips box radio, a small table with a TV, a divan with a hand-painted *toile de Geneve* canvas hanging above it, an antique table with a chair, and a small folding Chippendale table. Above the couch, two historic sashes were hung (richly embroidered garments once worn by nobility), a copy of Walenty Wańkowicz's[1] painting *Mickiewicz na Judahu skale,*[2] and a framed inscription and signatures of people gathered at the fiftieth wedding anniversary of Zofia and Melchior Wańkowicz. Almost the whole floor was covered with a carpet. Many family pictures in decorative frames stood on the shelves and tables.

I was offered coffee and a chocolate cake from Wedel[3] served by the housekeeper on a small silver tray in the shape of a leaf, and observed everything curiously, mainly Wańkowicz himself. Having a broad face, and rather long, disheveled hair, his heavy-lidded eyes were lively and sharp. He seemed large and obese to me, but his moves were light-footed, and thus he avoided the impression of being heavy. There was something dignified, something of a nobleman, in the moves of the large-framed man. An aura of coldness, impatience, and weariness seemed to envelope the writer.

"Which of my books have you read?" he asked me. "Tell me directly with what problems you have come to me. I have no more than forty-five minutes. This is how much time I usually give journalists visiting me."

"I know almost all your books," I replied. "I also know the critics' reactions to some of them. I have many questions, all of them written down." I opened a large, academic notebook.

He looked at my notes.

"Have you read them? Even the pre-war ones, not re-issued after the war? Do you know *Opierzona rewolucja* and *Strzępy epopei*? Do you know my books published outside of Poland?" He asked questions one after the other.

"My father has in his collection, for example, *Drogą do Urzędowa*. . . . I have brought a few of my essays prepared for university classes, concerning your books, for instance on *Strzępy epopei*. . . ."

"Could you show them to me?" He interrupted our conversation, took my typescripts, and started to read. The first ten minutes passed. I drank the coffee, ate the cakes, and glanced at him. He seemed completely engrossed in the reading, and paid me no attention. "I hope I can reasonably use the time left," I thought.

"You are capable of critical thinking," he said, interrupting his reading and giving me a close look. "You have prepared yourself carefully and read my books and their reviews. I've forgotten about some matters, and thanks to you, I'm recalling them now."

Wańkowicz grew gentler, his voice became warmer, and the whole atmosphere changed from tense and impatient to warm and pleasant. He asked questions, one after another, and seemed pleased with my answers and maybe somewhat surprised by them.

"You know, I am approached by students who write their master's theses on my work, and then it turns out that they have come to me with scanty knowledge. They know just a few books, as if they'd come across them by chance, and give all sorts of explanations. And I feel as if they want to see me like some monkey in a zoo. As if my time didn't matter to them. And my time is very dear to me."

He started to talk about himself, about a new book, which he hadn't titled yet. He planned to share in it his observations from his whole life, concerning work and the very process of writing. He still needed to collect much material for it.

"At my age, when I don't travel anymore and don't collect materials for reportages, I would like to tell others how I used to do it. The old heron," he laughed, "cannot fish anymore, but it wants to tell of it and it may teach others something. I need many examples of how others did it and still do it, both writers and artists, creative people. What the creativity process itself consists of, if there is inspiration or not, what the greatest obstacle on the outside is, what dangers reside within us. What conditions are needed to write, if we impose them ourselves, or submit ourselves to them. For instance, Hemingway wrote while standing at a writing desk and liked the smell of apples being dried."

An hour passed, then another one. Wańkowicz suggested that we have supper together. It had been prepared by the housekeeper in the kitchen. The kitchen itself was spacious. It consisted of two sections: a dining part with a large table and a glassed cabinet, and a section for preparing and cooking the meals. Supper consisted of cold meat and salad. Wańkowicz kept asking new questions, also about me and my family. After supper we went to a long, narrow study. By the window stood a desk, and at the desk stood a huge, comfortable armchair on wheels. From the window and the door leading out onto a small balcony, Puławska Street could be viewed. Next to the desk, a glassed bookcase stood, a table, and another, smaller one. There were many pictures, including four portraits—of the writer, his wife, and daughters: Krystyna and Marta. A beautiful Mexican saddlecloth, embroidered mainly in red and golden threads, drew my eyes. Both the longer walls were covered by shelves that reached the ceiling with each shelf tightly packed with books. Wańkowicz was clearly pleased to show me his—as he put it—aids: two tape recorders, and cameras including his famous Leica. He liked technological novelties. I can imagine how he would have appreciated the computer and the Internet.

We sat on small sofas opposite each other. The study seemed cramped, but also carefully furnished and cozy. Wańkowicz talked much and while talking, looked at me closely. I discovered features in him that were new for me: patience, softness, and some authentic openness.

He told me then of his unpleasant experience with a researcher, Aleksander Horodyski-Kotecki, who helped him gather materials for the book *Wojna i pióro* (*War and Pen*) and later wanted to be considered as co-author.

"I now suggest that you gather for me the materials I need for my newest book," he said.

He showed me a precise plan he'd prepared of chapters with working titles, with subheadings and additional notes. He gave me copies of the plan and explained that he expected me to prepare quotations on "note sheets." The note sheets were to be of a particular size about one-half of a standard page, and have the number of the main plan, subheading, and chapter written in the corner. The quoted fragment was to have a full bibliography of the quoted source. I was to use mainly books that were monographs and biographies. The writer offered me an advance payment of 500 zlotys, quite a sum for my student pocket. I was to define independently the hours I worked. If the cooperation went well, I was to come to Warsaw twice a month with new material.

I was honored and pleased with the proposal. The whole meeting surpassed all my wildest dreams or expectations. Wańkowicz asked me to come the next day, Sunday, at 10 a.m., to accompany him to the book fair, during which he had two hours to sign his books. In front of the Palace of Culture, bookstalls of renowned publishing houses stood presenting novelties and titles published within the last year. Usually whole crowds of people gathered there who wanted to buy books and use the occasion to obtain an autograph from their favorite writer. That day, in front of the PIW[4] publishing house bookstall, who had organized the meeting with Wańkowicz, a long queue had been standing for the last hour. Each of the people in the queue had brought from home several copies of the writer's books, planning to also buy some re-issued titles at the fair and acquire a signature on each book. The PIW institute had issued a collection of the writer's articles, *Przez cztery klimaty, 1912–1972* (*Through Four Climates, 1912–1972*). This was a new title, and everyone wanted to buy it. When Wańkowicz's characteristic figure appeared, he was immediately surrounded with a crowd of people. He was clearly pleased with that. He talked to some people, showed interest in their affairs. He sat down in the chair and, not raising his eyes from the books, he silently signed his name on the copy put before him. I was sitting next to him; he asked me to write the date.

He became tired. After an hour, his pen moved slower and slower with each signature. The queue was moving slowly, and it wasn't certain if Wańkowicz would be able to sign the books for all the interested people on that day. At some point a woman holding a boy in her arms said: "Start reciting, Piotruś." The little Piotruś began to recite fragments of *Ziele na kraterze*. Wańkowicz stopped signing the books for a few minutes, but then he noticed people were getting impatient, and came back to signing, paying no more attention to the reciting boy. The mother, clearly offended with his indifference, took the boy away, mumbling something to herself.

I was dazed by it all, also with the sad event. I felt sorry both for the boy and for his ambitious mother. I understood it was difficult for Wańkowicz to find a way out of the situation without hurting someone's feelings, but I expected him to show perhaps some more understanding. When I returned to the subject later, the writer told me how people tired him more and more, and how difficult it was to meet the often importunate and unpleasant requirements and expectations. He was glad to meet people, he needed them, but at the same time they often tired and annoyed him.

After the book fair, we had dinner in the Palace of Culture, in a Russian restaurant Trojka. Following our dinner together, Wańkowicz took me to the train station. We agreed that I was to come in two weeks with the first portion of the materials that I had gathered. I was taking a true treasure with me to Łódź, a few books with his inscription, and also I was taking one of the files from the writer's archives. So that I could read its contents at home, he lent it to me with the admonition, "You've come to gather materials for your master's thesis—seek them in my archives yourself."

It was only after some time that I was able to fully appreciate the gesture and the trust placed in me by the writer. I saw how reluctantly, distrustfully he allowed others even a peek in his archive materials on-site, and he allowed me to take them to Łódź!

Now, after years, I think that after his unpleasant experience with the researcher Aleksander Horodyski-Kotecki who judged himself a co-author of their book, when Wańkowicz saw in me such an "eager beaver from Polish philology," he thought he might obtain material for a new book not fearing that the student researcher he employed would come up with a similar idea.

I returned home with lots of enthusiasm as to my plans for the near future. At once, I borrowed some biographical books about writers and artists and started reading them with regard to the book that Wańkowicz was preparing. I didn't have to spend time in the library searching for materials for my thesis. With the materials I'd brought from Warsaw, I could work with them at home.

After the two weeks had passed, I came to Warsaw and brought the materials I'd collected on cards. Wańkowicz read them and decided that he was "employing me as his researcher." I returned the file from his archive, and took another one to Łódź. My master's thesis was developing well; I read many books and wrote the quotations onto the note sheets.

Regularly, every two weeks, I came to Warsaw by train on Saturday. Nearly every week there came a letter, sometimes two, informing me what my employer-boss was expecting of me. Work on the book went smoothly. The writer decided to prepare two volumes. He also gave the book a final title: *Karafka La Fontaine'a—La Fontaine's Carafe*. He chose it to emphasize the diversity and objectivism of his view and opinion. At that time—as well as later—he very much stressed the feature, which he'd come to value particularly. The title came from an anecdote. La Fontaine was once asked to settle a dispute arisen among the revelers gathered in the inn. In the middle of the table there stood a crystal decanter with wine. Sun rays were coming through the window and reflecting off the carafe. One of the revelers said they were reflected red. Another denied, saying they were blue. The third one said they were pink. When asked, La Fontaine went around the table and said that each of the men was right: depending on the side you were looking from, as the sun refracted in the carafe it showed different colors. What was most important, as he said, was to see all the colors together, to understand there wasn't just one.

The second volume of *Karafka La Fontaine'a* is dedicated to me: "To my secretary, Aleksandra Ziółkowska, without whose committed cooperation this book would most likely have been worse than it is."

This dedication to me was an extraordinary gift, just like bequeathing his archive to me in his last will had been one. I believed then—and I still do— that I owed a debt of gratitude toward the hope pinned on me, toward the confidence the writer had placed in me, and that I ought to pay that debt in any way I can. I have always endeavored to do so, and I always will do so.

For the first money I'd earned and saved, I bought a winter sheepskin coat, which I was very pleased with. Spring passed, summer came, and vacation was slowly coming on. Wańkowicz sent a letter to my parents. Asking that I stay for two weeks in the Artists' Retreat in Obory near Warsaw, he wrote,

> In closing, in the foremost I should like to express my remorse toward the Mother. I am somewhat more certain of the Father due to his interests. We would find much in common: I knew personally Dmowski, Balicki, Zygmunt Wasilewski, was a correspondent of the *Warsaw Gazette* (*Gazeta Warszaws-ka*), etc. I would be extremely pleased if, visiting Warsaw, you would be so kind as to accept a dinner invitation, and by that occasion I could show you my archives and my (truly modest) library, in the case of which I would like to ask your advice. I shake your hand, Sir, and kiss the Lady's hands—Melchior Wańkowicz. 9th August 1972.

I spent two weeks in the Artists' Retreat in Obory near Warsaw, working on the book. Before I even completed studies and defended my thesis, Wańkowicz had offered me a permanent job as his secretary and assistant. Knowing I wanted to write a doctoral thesis, he himself phoned Professor Julian Krzyżanowski asking him to be my guidance counselor.[5] Altogether, from that day we'd met, when I was completing studies and coming regularly to Warsaw for a year, then as I moved to Warsaw and worked permanently— until the writer's death in September 1974—two years and four months had passed. Such a short time, and so important. So vitally important.

For long days, Wańkowicz was working on the book, which fully engrossed him and which was the most important matter to him. He required much of me, and I think I submitted to his authority. To watch and to some extent participate in the book's creation was for me a truly fascinating experience. I felt tremendous awe, respect, and almost girlish admiration for the writer. He had a fascinating personality. He always had a great sense of humor. Life lived next to him was nearly a run of interesting events, conversations, often surprises. He gave much of his attention and time to me. Noting that I was very anxious to absorb all and very grateful, time was taken to explain to me things I didn't know or hadn't done before. Having much patience for me, almost as if he was placing much hope in me, the eminent writer spoke of the need to learn, to gain as many "skills" in life as possible.

"You never know when you may need them. And it's also worth knowing well something that is very practical. Each person," he said, "should have their own selected discipline about which they know a lot, about which they want to learn something new all the time. Have a passion. You cannot know the whole literature. Choose one writer, but get to know his works thoroughly" (Years later, one of my friends added to it: "You may choose one title, one book, but learn everything about it. I would choose *The Magic Mountain* by Thomas Mann.")

Wańkowicz told me about himself, his life. Sometimes it seemed to me that he did it to make me think in new categories. I think he wanted to show me that life wasn't grey or rosy, that it often had the color and sense that we gave to it ourselves. "Aim high." I remembered a Japanese proverb: "When you fall, never get up empty-handed." Wańkowicz added a Polish one: "If you're going to fall, let it be from a high horse. The heavier you fall, the stronger you will bounce back."

Years later I learned one more saying: "If you aim high, you'll get high. Even halfway up it is already high. If you aim at an average level, you'll attain less. If you aim low, you'll attain nothing."

He told me much about the hardships in his life and how he overcame them later. He spoke of the significance of hardships, difficulties, and challenging situations in human life.

"After years, some good may come out of them for you," he said. "You might not understand that yet, but remember this. It is important how you treat them. Whether you yield to them and surrender, or struggle up and make them a value."

There is often in our lives one event that everything begins from and everything comes back to. One experience which gives this special psychological hue. One day which makes you see the world and yourself in a different light. It may be an illness you or someone close to you suffers, death, love, childbirth, an artistic experience, a journey, a meeting. Later, although some greater and more important things came, events are divided into "before" and "after."

For a long time I used to say that something happened "before I'd met Wańkowicz."

For a long time now, I haven't said that. So many years have passed that almost everything qualifies under "after meeting Wańkowicz."

The work with Wańkowicz opened areas to me of which I had only known from obscure accounts of others. Wańkowicz and his work, his surroundings, everything fascinated me. A two-and-a-half-year period began in my life when I was staying in the immediate proximity of the writer. There are board games for children where a pawn standing on a specific field moves several places ahead. Something like that happened in my life as a humble student of the Łódź University at the moment I met the author of *Karafka La Fontaine'a*. When I started working for him, my life gained pace and excitement. My observations began to concern issues that were important, serious, that required manifold sensitivity. I was also aware of myself being a subject of processing, creating, molding by another, powerful personality.

I didn't mind that—on the contrary, it impressed and pleased me. I was at an age where it might be the easiest to accept and soak up learning and criticism. I submitted myself to the atmosphere, the requirements, the discipline of work, the rhythm of the day imposed by the writer. As he said himself, he had less and less time left, and he very much wanted to do something sensible with it. Writing was his job, life choice, passion, and love. In me, he saw a person committed to him, one who knew his books and their topics well, and who had much respect, esteem, sometimes admiration for them. Yet the said admiration was not as childish or irritating as to disturb his work, but rather allowed him to push the work forward. I was committed to him and didn't protest when he imposed sometimes difficult working conditions, particularly as concerned the number of hours we worked. Maybe if I had been older and had a more settled private life, it would have been more difficult for me to reconcile my work for Wańkowicz with my personal life. When we grow up, we often start—be it right or wrong—to value ourselves in some stubborn way. We often refuse to devote ourselves fully and with dedication to anything. We either have no time for that, or life itself tempts us too much and distracts us in the possible choices. Wańkowicz taught me to work, focus, pay attention, concentrate, use the time well.

> Don't waste time; don't waste the days. If you work, commit yourself to it. When you feel tired, rest, but plan your leisure. Be aware of the passing of time. Have no empty days. Fill them—with work, reading, play, or sport. But try to watch what is happening with you. Don't spend days doing nothing. Learn life, and get to know people. When Adam and Eve, expelled from Paradise, caught their first breath of earthly air, they were able to know love, jealousy, deceit, meanness, envy, desire, and weakness. And such are whole generations of people. Look at them, and that knowledge will support you and add to your own strength.

He said: "Get tight and tough. Watch, and try things yourself. But whatever you see or do, do it for future topics. Don't let anything pull or suck you in. Someone changed into a tree cannot paint it. To paint a tree well, you have to take a good look from up close, then turn away and look from afar."

Karafka La Fontaine'a is thus a book very close to me. As is the lesson that light often refracts producing a different color for each person, and that a writer tries to see them all. I also came to understand the great difficulty of grasping and naming what the creative process actually is.

After the first volume of *Karafka* was issued, I wrote a review[6] in which I stressed that readers may interpret Wańkowicz's books in various ways. When they come to a place where the writer renders dark colors (*Kundlizm,*

Klub trzeciego miejsca [*Third Party Club*]) they believe him to be a pessimist. Others will ridicule the author's optimism for the rosy colors he shows (*Sztafeta, Tworzywo*). And all those books are actually one and the same carafe, which the writer was criticized for at various times and in various moods of his life.

Karafka La Fontaine'a prompted interesting general comments among critics. Krzysztof Teodor Toeplitz wrote about Wańkowicz in *Życie Warszawy*[7] as an "exceptional phenomenon of our literature. In *Karafka La Fontaine'a*," Toeplitz continued, "we distinctly see a writing technique composed of an amazing amount of annotations, sources, cards, notes, which—however—do not give birth to a scientific study, but to a work of art."

In *Nowe Książki*,[8] Anna Bojarska wrote: "Books on the art of writing and on writing as a job are emerging like wildfire in countries of protestant tradition and the protestant cult of work."

In *Karafka La Fontaine'a*, Wańkowicz shows his great passion of all his life—writing. It is a methodology book, in which the writer shares his observations and experience of many years of creative work. For a long time now, *Karafka* has also been a textbook for students of journalism—it is recommended to anyone interested in the creative process.

In his last work, Melchior Wańkowicz considers what talent or a creator's individuality is, and stresses the significance of curiosity, commitment, various writing skills, just the ability to tell an anecdote well. But foremost he stresses the significance of work. He puts work before anything else.

He bequeathed his archives to me. He placed his trust in a then twenty-three-year-old girl, whom he knew was writing first a master's and then a doctoral thesis on him. This trust has obligated me since the very beginning. I try to fulfill what I see as duties resulting from the trust placed in me. I refer to the writer's archives in my essays and books. Right after the writer's death, I wrote *Blisko Wańkowicza* (*Near Wańkowicz*).[9] The book had three issues and over one hundred thousand copies were sold. That first book of mine on Melchior Wańkowicz I wrote spontaneously, right after his death, still affected by his leaving, aiming to record moments which quickly dim away in one's memory. I didn't consider whether or not I was impoverishing any myth or maybe creating a new one. I did not want to synthesize one life, but rather to show many common days from the last years of life of a great writer. The book was popular and, despite the high number of copies, difficult to obtain. That fact was noted in a funny commentary by the valued Kraków weekly *Tygodnik Powszechny*:[10]

> The first reply to the mini-competition of our column (topic): "How I obtained a best-seller." Thanks to a friend I work with, *Blisko Wańkowicza* by Aleksandra Ziółkowska became mine. His friend—employed in the Book House book-

store—through his friend, working with the book division, left one copy from under the counter, in turn, with a bookseller friend of his. And all that worked because this year my friend is getting the successive issues of *Tygodnik Powszechny* from me once I read them—and feeling indebted, he activated that chain of contacts. [11]

Then I wrote *Proces 1964 roku Melchiora Wańkowicza* (*The Trial of 1964 of Melchior Wańkowicz*), [12] and later *Na tropach Wańkowicza* (*On the Trail of Wańkowicz*). [13] The latter had three supplemented and enlarged editions. I published several volumes of the writer's correspondence, where I wrote the footnotes and introductions. I was the editor of and author of comments in the sixteen-volume series of Wańkowicz's *All Works* (*Dzieła wszystkie*). [14]

Years went by. I am writing other books, on various topics.

To some extent I think I owe Wańkowicz my interest in the world and human lives. I learned a lot and gained extraordinary experience. Thanks largely to him I have become a writer. In writing this book on Wańkowicz, I am paying a certain debt I sincerely believe I owe him.

NOTES

1. 1799–1842, a painter, family to Melchior Wańkowicz, and friend to the great poet Adam Mickiewicz (translator's note).

2. *Mickiewicz on the Rock of Judah* (translator's note).

3. Famous Polish confectionery company, founded 1851 (translator's note).

4. Państwowy Instytut Wydawniczy—State Publishing Institute, a Polish state publishing house founded in Warsaw in 1946. PIW specializes in literature, history, philosophy, and social sciences (translator's note).

5. When Professor Julian Krzyżanowski died, the eminent specialist in literature Professor Janina Kulczycka-Saloni became the guidance counselor of my thesis.

6. Aleksandra Ziółkowska, "Z Wańkowiczem przy Karafce" ("With Wańkowicz and the Carafe"), *Głos Robotniczy* (daily issued in Łódź 1945–1990—translator's note), nos. 10–11, 1973.

7. *Życie Warszawy* (*Life of Warsaw*); Warsaw daily [1944–2011], *Perfidia* [*Perfidy*]), 7 February 1973.

8. "Przeciw szklaneczce Musseta" ("Against a Glass of Musset"), *Nowe Książki* (*New Books*), no. 12, 1981.

9. *Blisko Wańkowicza* (*Near Wańkowicz*) (Kraków: Wydawnictwo Literackie, 1975, 1978, 1988).

10. Polish Roman Catholic weekly magazine, focusing on social and cultural issues, established 1945 (translator's note).

11. *Tygodnik Powszechny*, Kraków, 20 June 1976, no. 25 (1430).

12. *Proces Melchiora Wańkowicza w 1964 roku* (*The Trial of 1964 of Melchior Wańkowicz*) (Warsaw, 1990).

13. *Na tropach Wańkowicza* (*On the Trail of Wańkowicz*) (Warsaw, 1989, 1999); *Na tropach Wańkowicza po latach* (*On the Trail of Wańkowicz after Many Years*) (Warsaw, 2009).

14. *Dzieła Wszystkie* (*Total Works of Wańkowicz*), 16 volumes, Aleksandra Ziółkowska-Boehm (ed.) (Warsaw: Prószyński i S-ka, 2009–2012).

Select Bibliography

Dąbrowska, Maria. *Dzienniki.* Edited by Tadeusz Drewnowski. London and Warsaw, 1988.

Franaszek, Andrzej. *Miłosz: biografia.* Kraków, 2011.

Friszke, Andrzej. *Jan Józef Lipski "KOR."* Warsaw, 2006.

Giedroyc, Jerzy. *Autobiografia na cztery ręce.* London and Warsaw, 1994.

Giedroyc, Jerzy, and Andrzej Bobkowski. *Listy 1946–1961.* Edited by Jan Zieliński. Warsaw, 1997.

Giedroyc, Jerzy, and Konstanty A. Jeleński. *Listy 1950–1987.* Edited by Wojciech Karpinski. London and Warsaw, 1995.

Giedroyc, Jerzy, and Jan Nowak-Jeziorański. *Listy 1952–1998.* Edited by Dobrosława Platt. Wrocław, 2001.

Giedroyc, Jerzy, and Juliusz Mieroszewski. *Listy 1949–1956.* Edited by Krzysztof Pomian. London and Warsaw, 1999.

Giedroyc, Jerzy, and Czesław Miłosz. *Listy 1973–2000.* Edited by Marek Kornat. London and Warsaw, 2012.

Giedroyc, Jerzy, and Melchior Wańkowicz. *Listy 1945–1963.* Edited by Aleksandra Ziółkowska-Boehm and Jacek Krawczyk. Warsaw, 2000; [transl. fragments:] "Correspondence between Melchior Wańkowicz and Jerzy Giedroyc." *Sarmatian Review.* September 1999.

Giedroyc, Jerzy, and Jerzy Stempowski. *Listy 1946–1969.* Edited by Andrzej Stanisław Kowalczyk. London and Warsaw, 1998.

Habielski, Rafał. *Dokąd nam iść wypada? Jerzy Giedroyc od Buntu mlodych do Kultury.* London and Warsaw, 2006.

Kąkolewski, Krzysztof. *Wańkowicz krzepi-wywiad rzeka.* London and Warsaw, 1977.

Kister, Hanna. *Pegazy na Kredytowej.* London and Warsaw, 1980.

Kula, Marcin. *Narodowe i rewolucyjne.* London and Warsaw, 1991.

Kurzyna, Mieczysław. *O Melchiorze Wańkowiczu nie wszystko.* London and Warsaw, 1975.

Łubieński, Tomasz. *1939. Zaczęło się wrześniu.* London and Warsaw, 2009.

Majewska, Włada. *Z Lwowskiej Fali do Radia Wolna Europa.* Ed. Regina Wasiak-Taylor. Wrocław, 2006.

Małachowski, Aleksander. *Żyłem . . . szczęśliwie.* London and Warsaw, 1993.

Malcer-Zakrzacka, Anna. "Obrazy społeczeństwa polskiego w twórczosci emigracyjnej Melchiora Wańkowicza. Rozprawa doktorska na Wydziale Filologicznym." PhD dissertation manuscript. Faculty of Languages. University of Gdańsk.

Masłoń, Krzysztof. *Nie uciec nam od losu.* London and Warsaw, 2006.

Miłosz, Czesław. *A Year of the Hunter.* New York, 1994. [transl.] *Rok Myśliwego.* Paris, 1990.

Narutowicz Krzysztof (Alicja Grajewska). Konstelacje: Warsaw, 1980.

Nowak-Jeziorański, Jan. *Polska z oddali.* London, 1988.
Pomian, Grażyna. *Kultura i jej krąg.* Lublin, 1995.
Romanowiczowa, Zofia. *Sono felice.* London, 1977.
Siedlecka, Joanna. *Obława: losy pisarzy represjonowanych.* London and Warsaw, 2005.
———. *Kryptonim "Liryka." Bezpieka wobec literatów.* London and Warsaw, 2008.
Sokólska, Urszula. *Leksykalno-stylistyczne cechy prozy Melchiora Wańkowicza.* Białystok, 2005.
Terlecki, Tymon. *Emigracja naszego czasu.* Ed. Nina Taylor-Terlecka and Jerzy Święch. Lublin, 2003.
Thompson, Ewa M. *Imperial Knowledge. Russian Literature and Colonialism.* Westport, CT: 2000; [transl.] *Trubadurzy imperium: Literatura rosyjska i kolonializm.* Kraków, 2000.
Toruńczyk, Barbara. *Rozmowy w Maisons-Laffitt. 1981.* London and Warsaw, 2006.
Urbanowski, Maciej. *Oczyszczenie. Szkice o literaturze polskiej XX wieku.* Kraków, 2002.
Wolny, Kazimierz. *Reportaże wojenne Melchiora Wańkowicza (1939–1945).* Kielce, 1995.
———. *Sztuka reportażu wojennego Melchiora Wańkowicza.* Rzeszów, 1991.
———. *Wokół twórczości Melchiora Wańkowicza: w stronę dziennikarstwa, socjologii, polityki oraz krytyki literackiej.* Kraków, 1999.
Zajączkowski, Krzysztof. *Lekarz z Westerplatte. Major Mieczysław Słaby 1905–1948.* Rzeszów, 2008.
Ziółkowska-Boehm, Aleksandra. *Blisko Wańkowicza.* Kraków, 1988.
———. *Proces Melchiora Wańkowicza 1964 roku.* London and Warsaw, 1990.
———. *Na tropach Wańkowicza.* Warsaw, 1999.
———. *Na tropach Wańkowicza po latach.* London and Warsaw, 2009.
———. *Ulica Żółwiego Strumienia.* London and Warsaw, 2004.
Żebrowski, Marek. *Dzieje sporu: "Kultura" w emigracyjnej debacie publicznej lat 1947–1956.* London and Warsaw, 2007.

Index

About the Author

Photo by Andrzej Bernat

With an advanced education, including a PhD in humanities from Warsaw University in her native Poland, Aleksandra Ziółkowska-Boehm benefited from the early tutelage of the famous Polish writer Melchior Wankowicz while working as his assistant.

Ziółkowska-Boehm has been the recipient of several literary awards, including a literature fellowship by the Delaware Division of the Arts in 2006, a Fulbright scholarship at Warsaw University in 2006–2007, and a Fulbright award in 1985 from the Institute of International Education.

She is a member of: in Warsaw, the Society of Polish Writers (SPP), ZAIKS; in London, the Polish Writers Union Abroad (award 2007); in the USA the Polish American Historical Association, The Kosciuszko Foundation, Polish Institute of Arts and Sciences, Jozef Pilsudski Institute of America and American PEN Club, and The Fulbright Association.

Among her books are historical biographies, autobiographical stories, the current outlook of Native Americans, and about her beloved feline Suzy. She is the author of many books published in her native Poland, Canada, and also in the United States, including *Open Wounds—a Native American Heritage*, *On the Road with Suzy: From Cat to Companion*, and *Kaia, Heroine of the 1944 Warsaw Rising*. Coming soon: *The Polish Experience through World War II: A Better Day Has Not Come* and *Ingrid Bergman and Her American Relatives*.